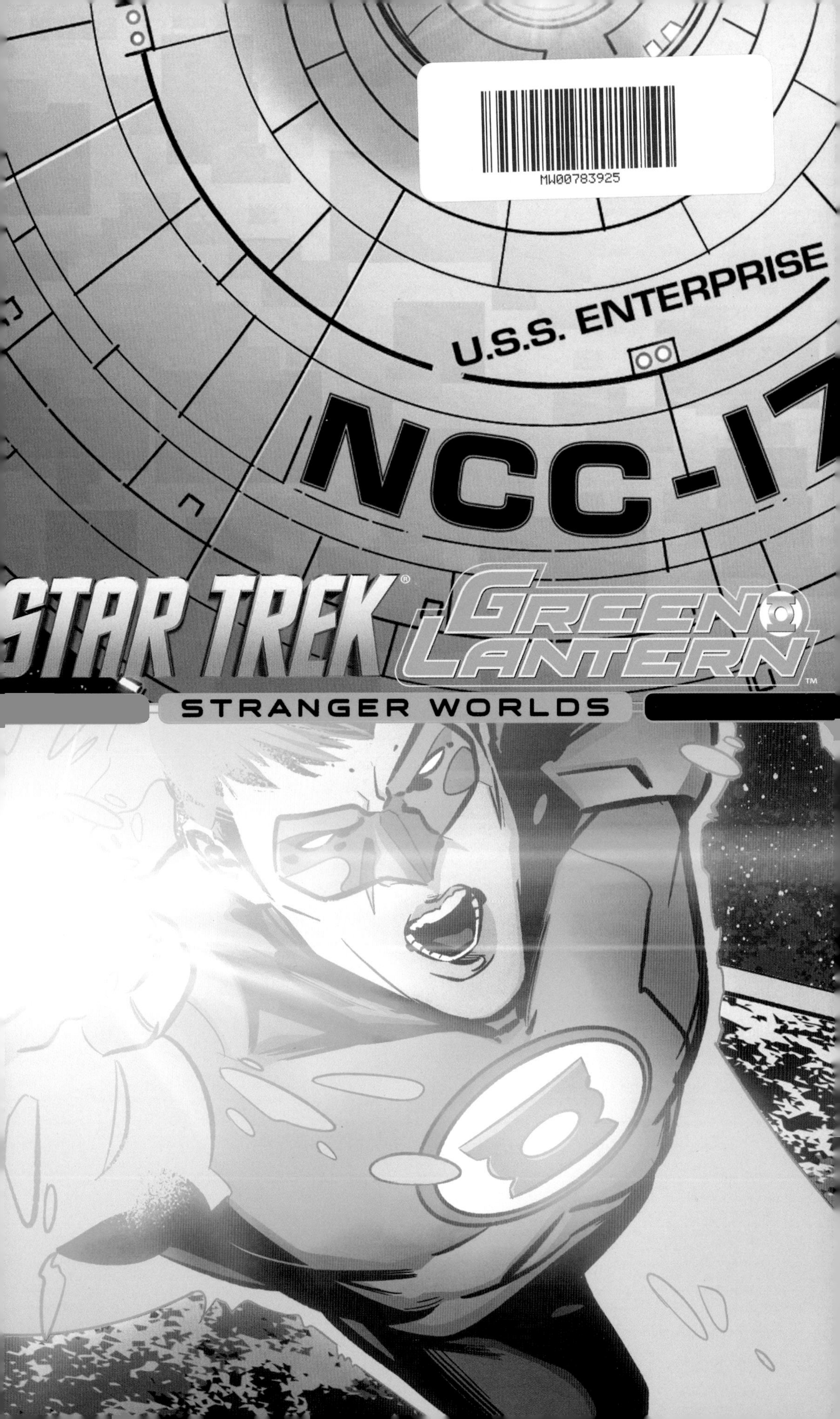
U.S.S. ENTERPRISE
NCC-17
STAR TREK®
GREEN LANTERN™
STRANGER WORLDS

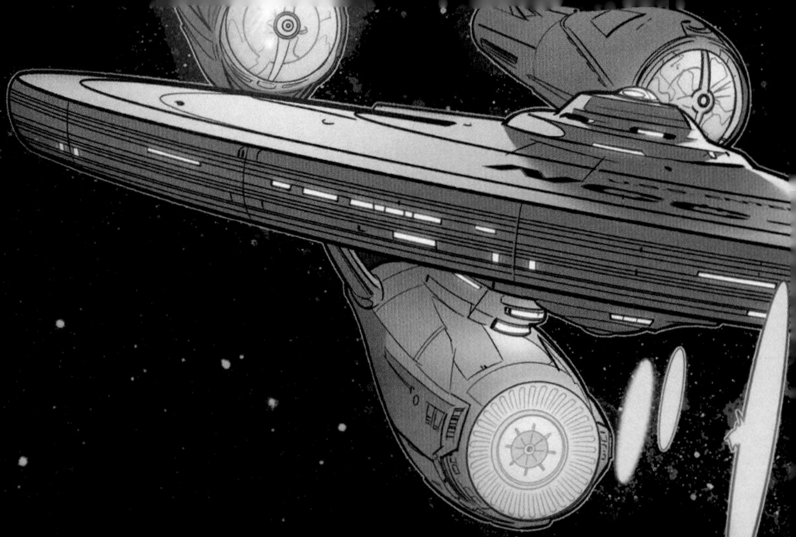

COVER BY
ANGEL HERNANDEZ

COVER COLORS BY
MARK ROBERTS

COLLECTION EDITS BY
JUSTIN EISINGER
AND ALONZO SIMON

COLLECTION DESIGN BY
ROBBIE ROBBINS

Become our fan on Facebook **facebook.com/idwpublishing**
Follow us on Twitter **@idwpublishing**
Subscribe to us on YouTube **youtube.com/idwpublishing**
See what's new on Tumblr **tumblr.idwpublishing.com**
Check us out on Instagram **instagram.com/idwpublishing**

ISBN: 978-1-63140-966-0 20 19 18 17 1 2 3 4

STAR TREK created by Gene Roddenberry.
Special thanks to Risa Kessler and John Van Citters of CBS Consumer Products for their invaluable assistance.

Originally published as STAR TREK/GREEN LANTERN, VOL. 2 issues #1–6.

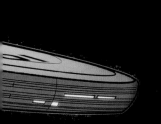

written by **Mike Johnson**

art by **Angel Hernandez**

colors by **Mark Roberts**

letters by **Andworld Design**

series edits by
IDW Publishing's
Chris Cerasi and **Sarah Gaydos**

DC Entertainment's
Jim Chadwick and **Michael McCalister**

STAR TREK® GREEN LANTERN™
STRANGER WORLDS

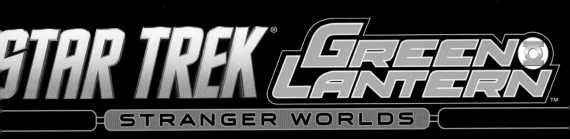

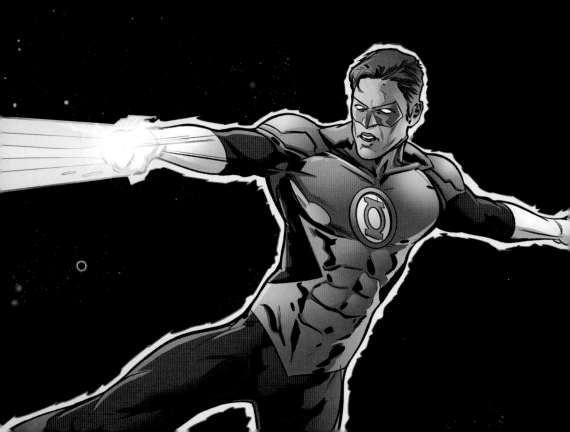

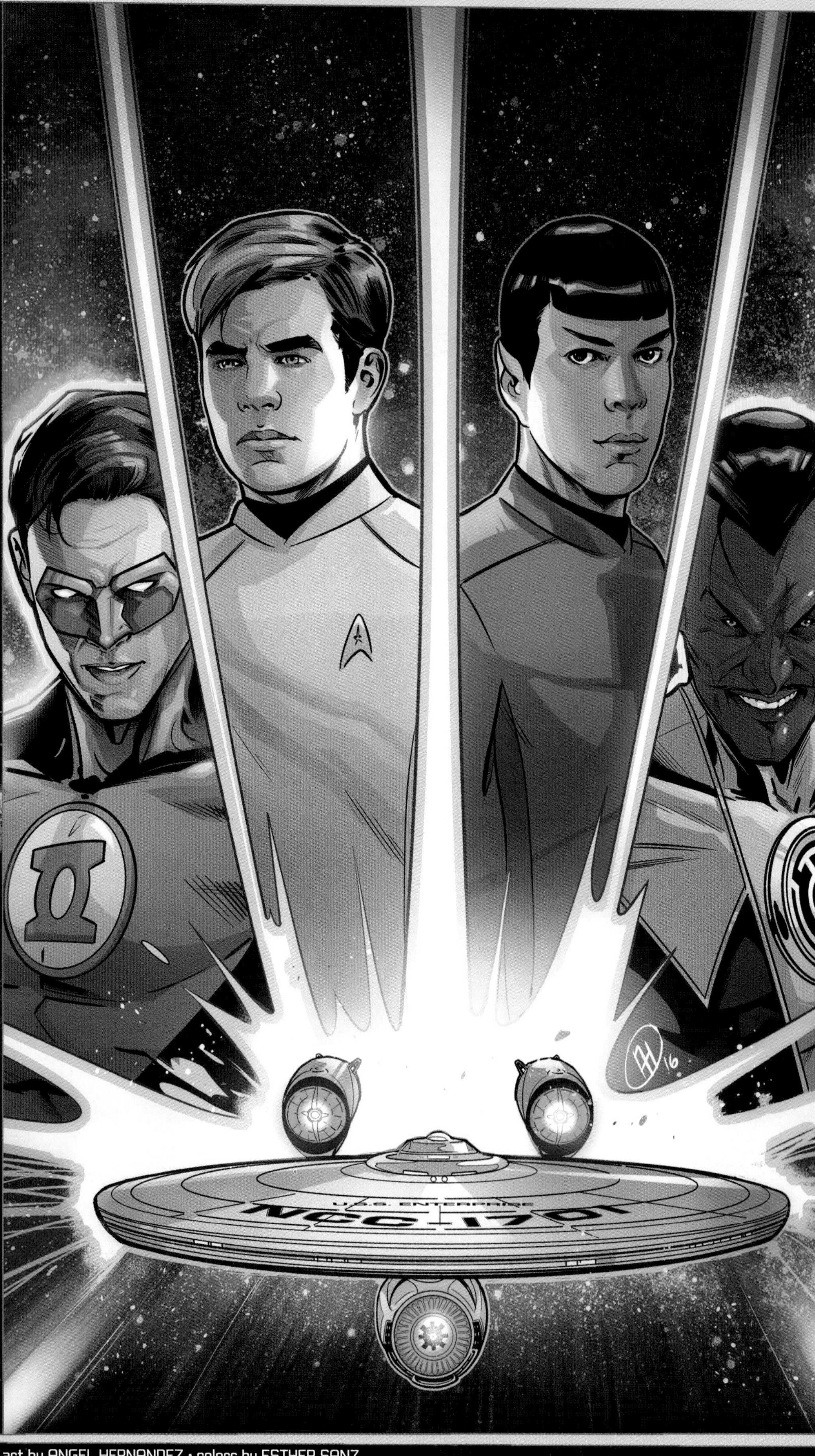
U.S.S. ENTERPRISE
NCC-1701

art by ANGEL HERNANDEZ • colors by ESTHER SANZ

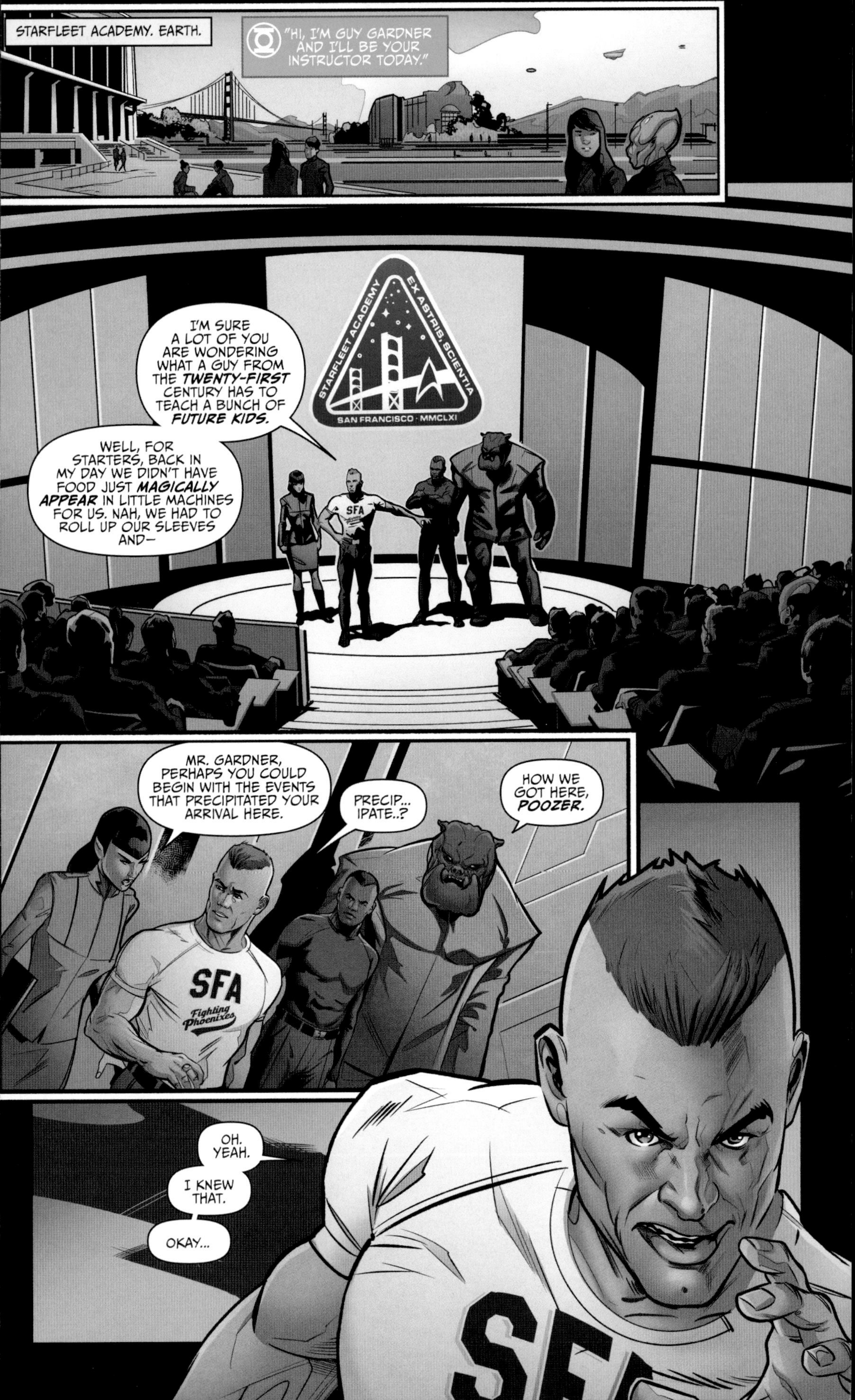
STARFLEET ACADEMY. EARTH.
"HI, I'M GUY GARDNER AND I'LL BE YOUR INSTRUCTOR TODAY."
STARFLEET ACADEMY
EX ASTRIS, SCIENTIA
SAN FRANCISCO · MMCLXI
I'M SURE A LOT OF YOU ARE WONDERING WHAT A GUY FROM THE **TWENTY-FIRST** CENTURY HAS TO TEACH A BUNCH OF **FUTURE KIDS.**
WELL, FOR STARTERS, BACK IN MY DAY WE DIDN'T HAVE FOOD JUST **MAGICALLY APPEAR** IN LITTLE MACHINES FOR US. NAH, WE HAD TO ROLL UP OUR SLEEVES AND—
MR. GARDNER, PERHAPS YOU COULD BEGIN WITH THE EVENTS THAT PRECIPITATED YOUR ARRIVAL HERE.
PRECIP... IPATE..?
HOW WE GOT HERE, **POOZER.**
SFA
Fighting Phoenixes
OH. YEAH.
I KNEW THAT.
OKAY...

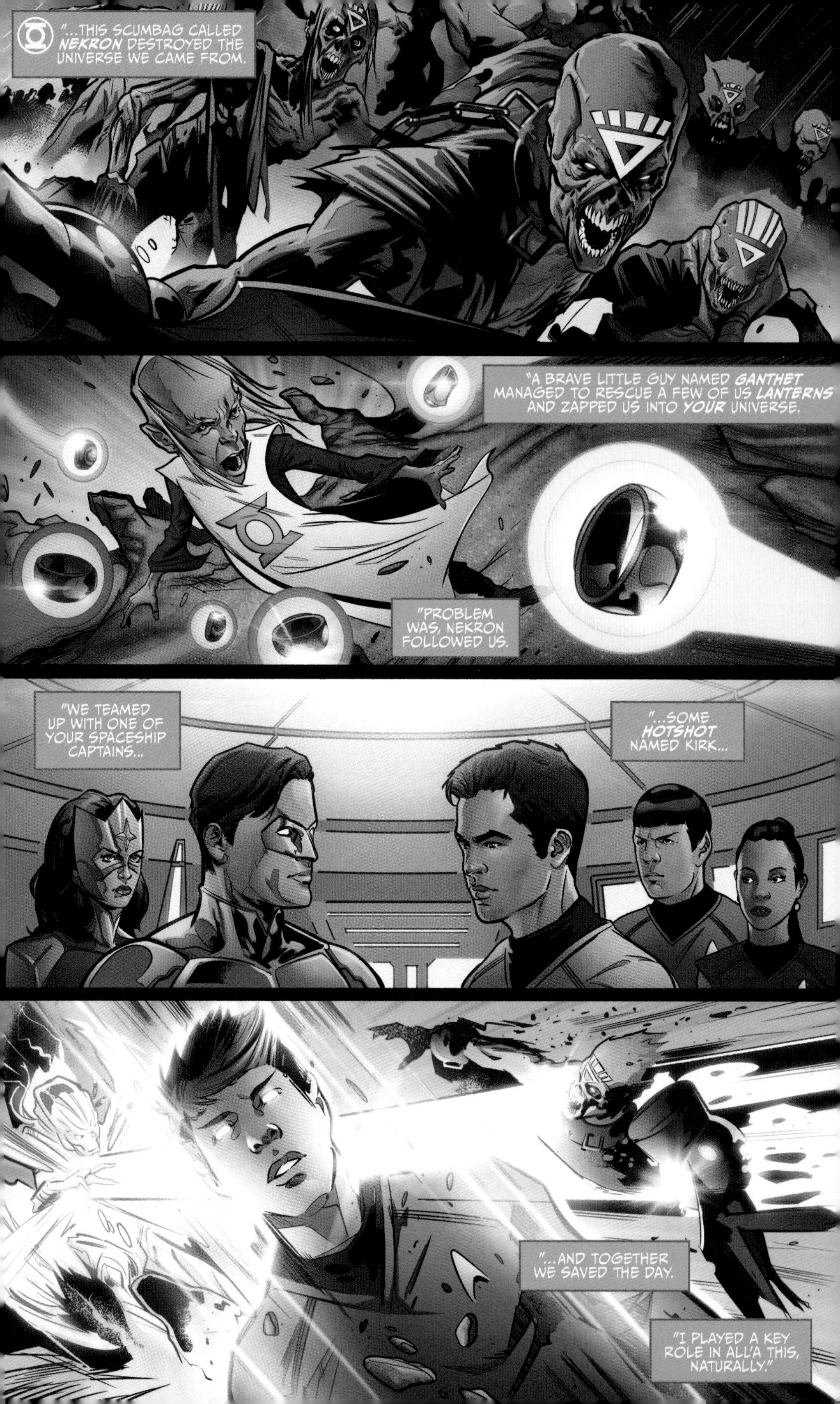
"...THIS SCUMBAG CALLED NEKRON DESTROYED THE UNIVERSE WE CAME FROM.
"A BRAVE LITTLE GUY NAMED GANTHET MANAGED TO RESCUE A FEW OF US LANTERNS AND ZAPPED US INTO YOUR UNIVERSE.
"PROBLEM WAS, NEKRON FOLLOWED US.
"WE TEAMED UP WITH ONE OF YOUR SPACESHIP CAPTAINS...
"...SOME HOTSHOT NAMED KIRK...
"...AND TOGETHER WE SAVED THE DAY.
"I PLAYED A KEY ROLE IN ALL'A THIS, NATURALLY."

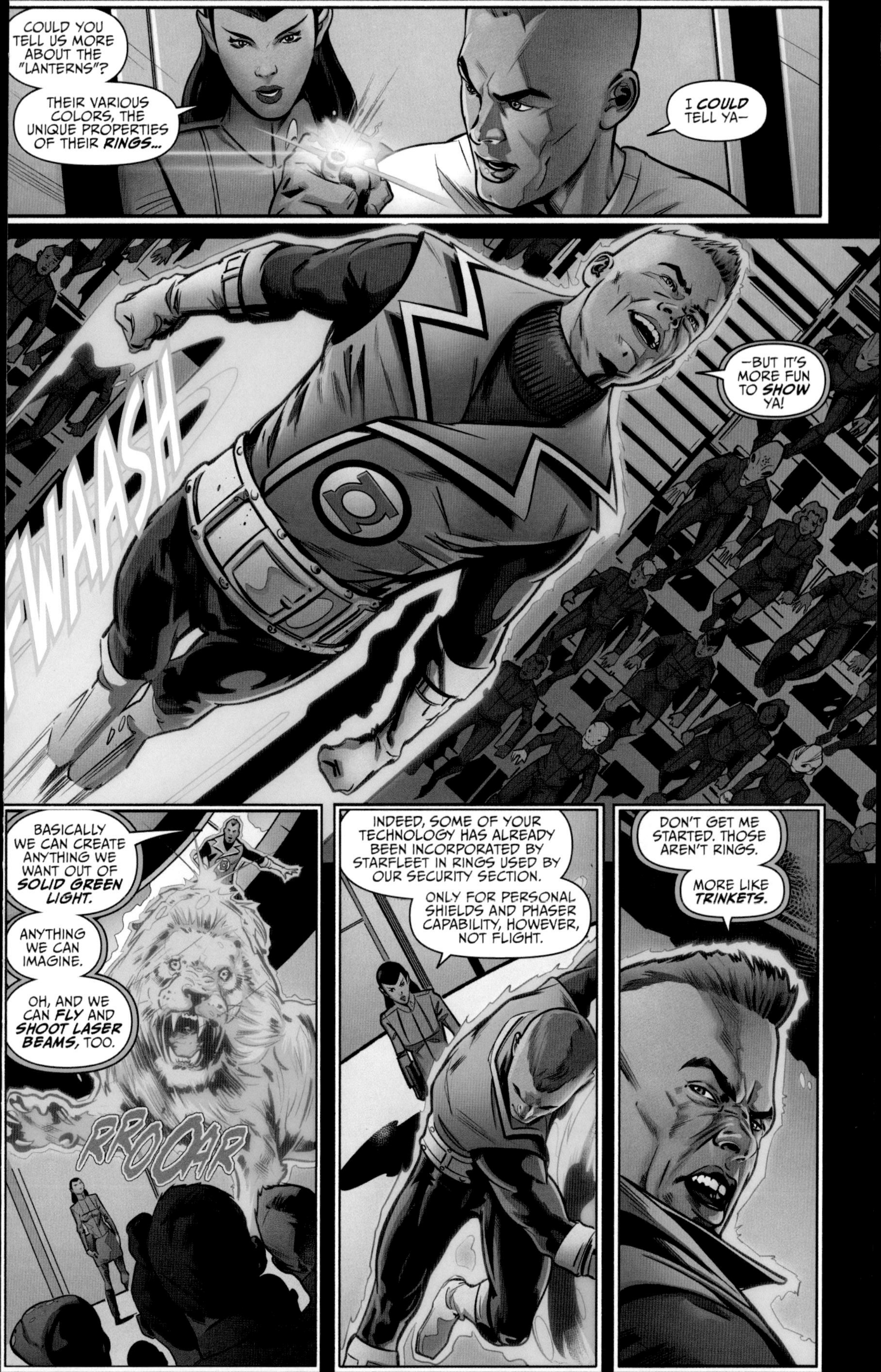

COULD YOU TELL US MORE ABOUT THE "LANTERNS"?
THEIR VARIOUS COLORS, THE UNIQUE PROPERTIES OF THEIR *RINGS...*
I *COULD* TELL YA—
FWAASH
—BUT IT'S MORE FUN TO *SHOW* YA!
BASICALLY WE CAN CREATE ANYTHING WE WANT OUT OF *SOLID GREEN LIGHT.*
ANYTHING WE CAN IMAGINE.
OH, AND WE CAN *FLY* AND *SHOOT LASER BEAMS,* TOO.
RROOAR
INDEED, SOME OF YOUR TECHNOLOGY HAS ALREADY BEEN INCORPORATED BY STARFLEET IN RINGS USED BY OUR SECURITY SECTION.
ONLY FOR PERSONAL SHIELDS AND PHASER CAPABILITY, HOWEVER, NOT FLIGHT.
DON'T GET ME STARTED. THOSE AREN'T RINGS.
MORE LIKE *TRINKETS.*

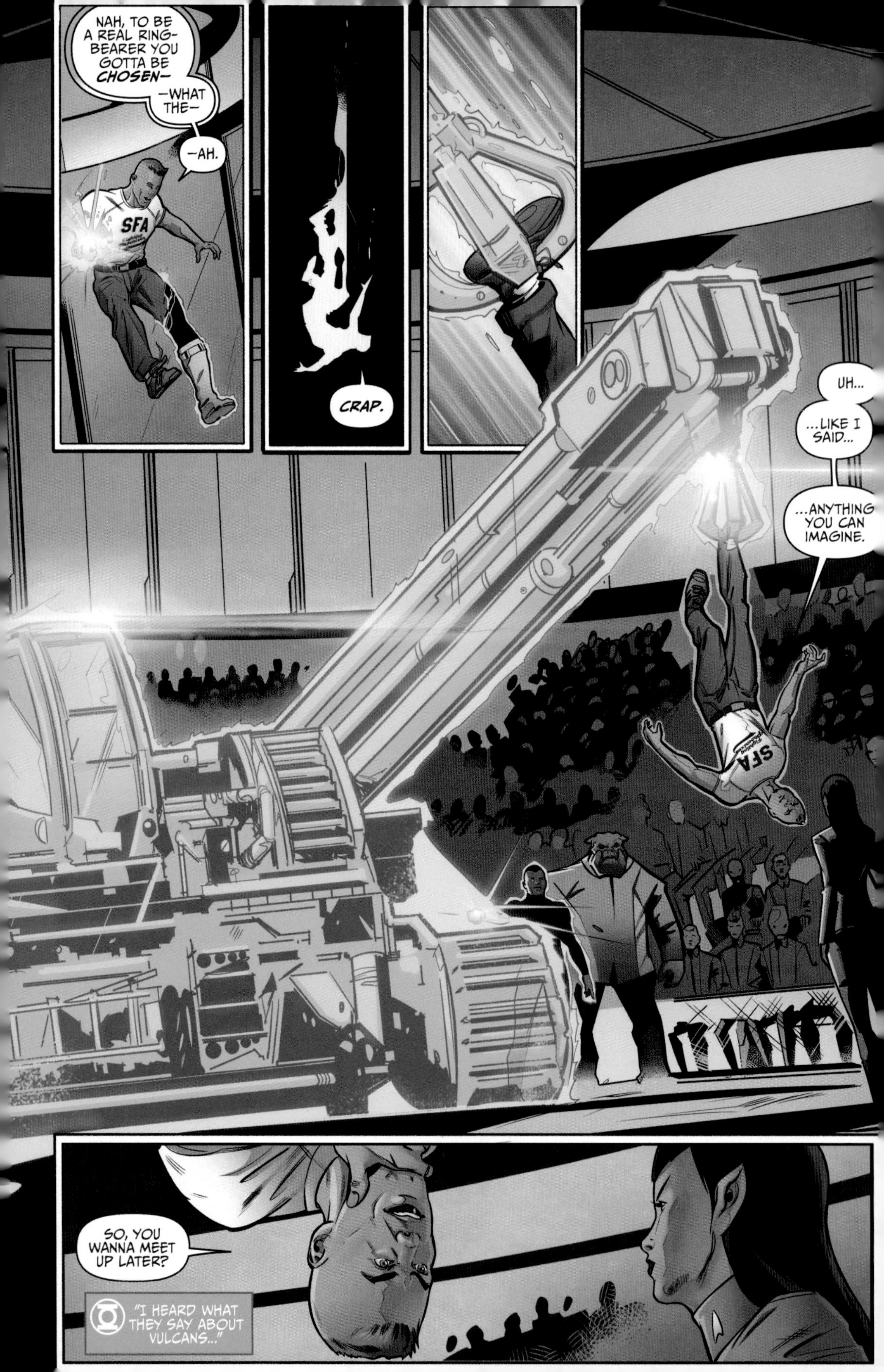
NAH, TO BE A REAL RING-BEARER YOU GOTTA BE CHOSEN—
—WHAT THE—
—AH.
CRAP.
UH...
...LIKE I SAID...
...ANYTHING YOU CAN IMAGINE.
SFA
SO, YOU WANNA MEET UP LATER?
"I HEARD WHAT THEY SAY ABOUT VULCANS..."

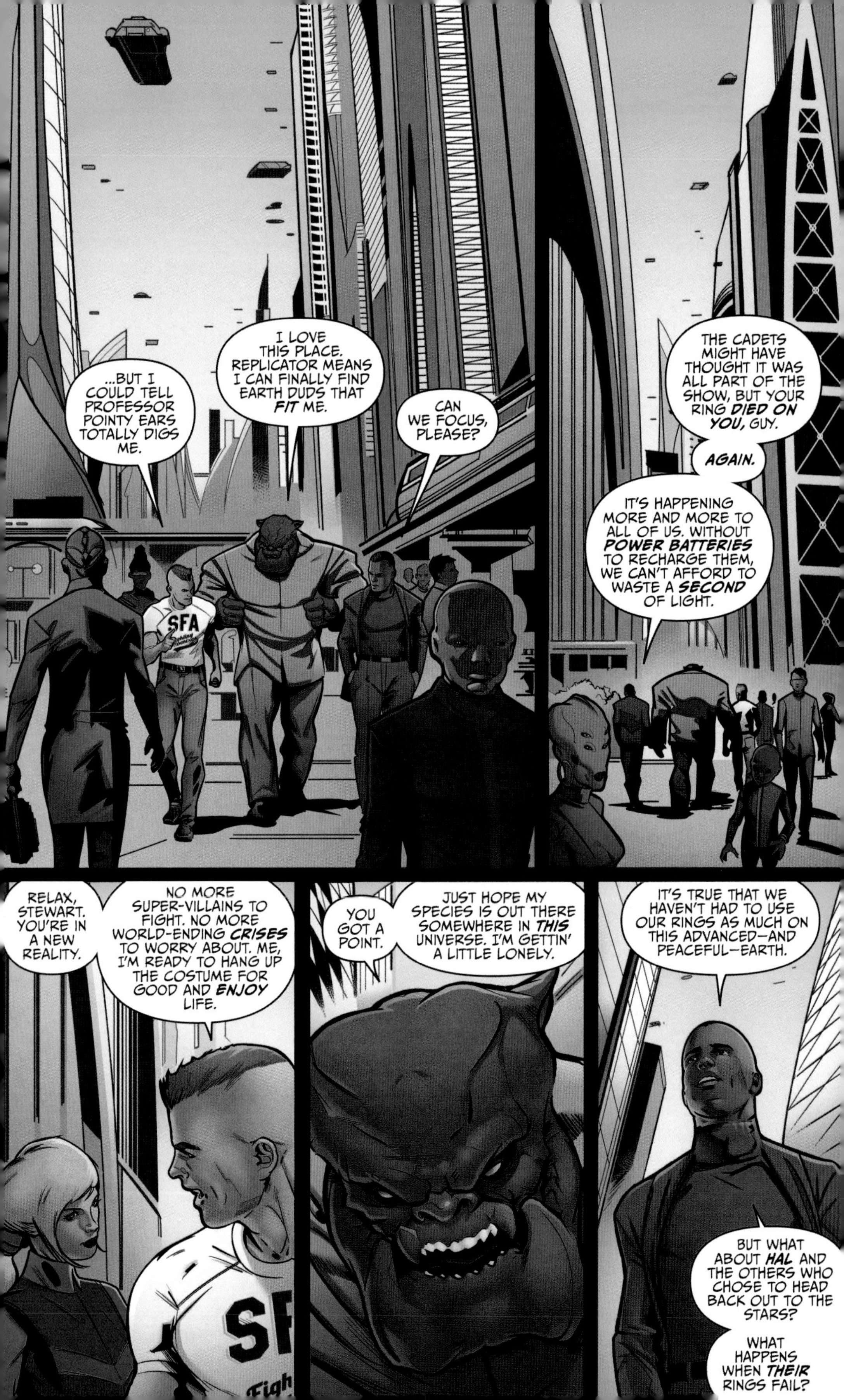
...BUT I COULD TELL PROFESSOR POINTY EARS TOTALLY DIGS ME.
I LOVE THIS PLACE. REPLICATOR MEANS I CAN FINALLY FIND EARTH DUDS THAT *FIT* ME.
CAN WE FOCUS, PLEASE?
THE CADETS MIGHT HAVE THOUGHT IT WAS ALL PART OF THE SHOW, BUT YOUR RING *DIED ON YOU,* GUY.
AGAIN.
IT'S HAPPENING MORE AND MORE TO ALL OF US. WITHOUT *POWER BATTERIES* TO RECHARGE THEM, WE CAN'T AFFORD TO WASTE A *SECOND* OF LIGHT.
RELAX, STEWART. YOU'RE IN A NEW REALITY.
NO MORE SUPER-VILLAINS TO FIGHT. NO MORE WORLD-ENDING *CRISES* TO WORRY ABOUT. ME, I'M READY TO HANG UP THE COSTUME FOR GOOD AND *ENJOY* LIFE.
YOU GOT A POINT.
JUST HOPE MY SPECIES IS OUT THERE SOMEWHERE IN *THIS* UNIVERSE. I'M GETTIN' A LITTLE LONELY.
IT'S TRUE THAT WE HAVEN'T HAD TO USE OUR RINGS AS MUCH ON THIS ADVANCED—AND PEACEFUL—EARTH.
BUT WHAT ABOUT *HAL* AND THE OTHERS WHO CHOSE TO HEAD BACK OUT TO THE STARS?
WHAT HAPPENS WHEN *THEIR* RINGS FAIL?

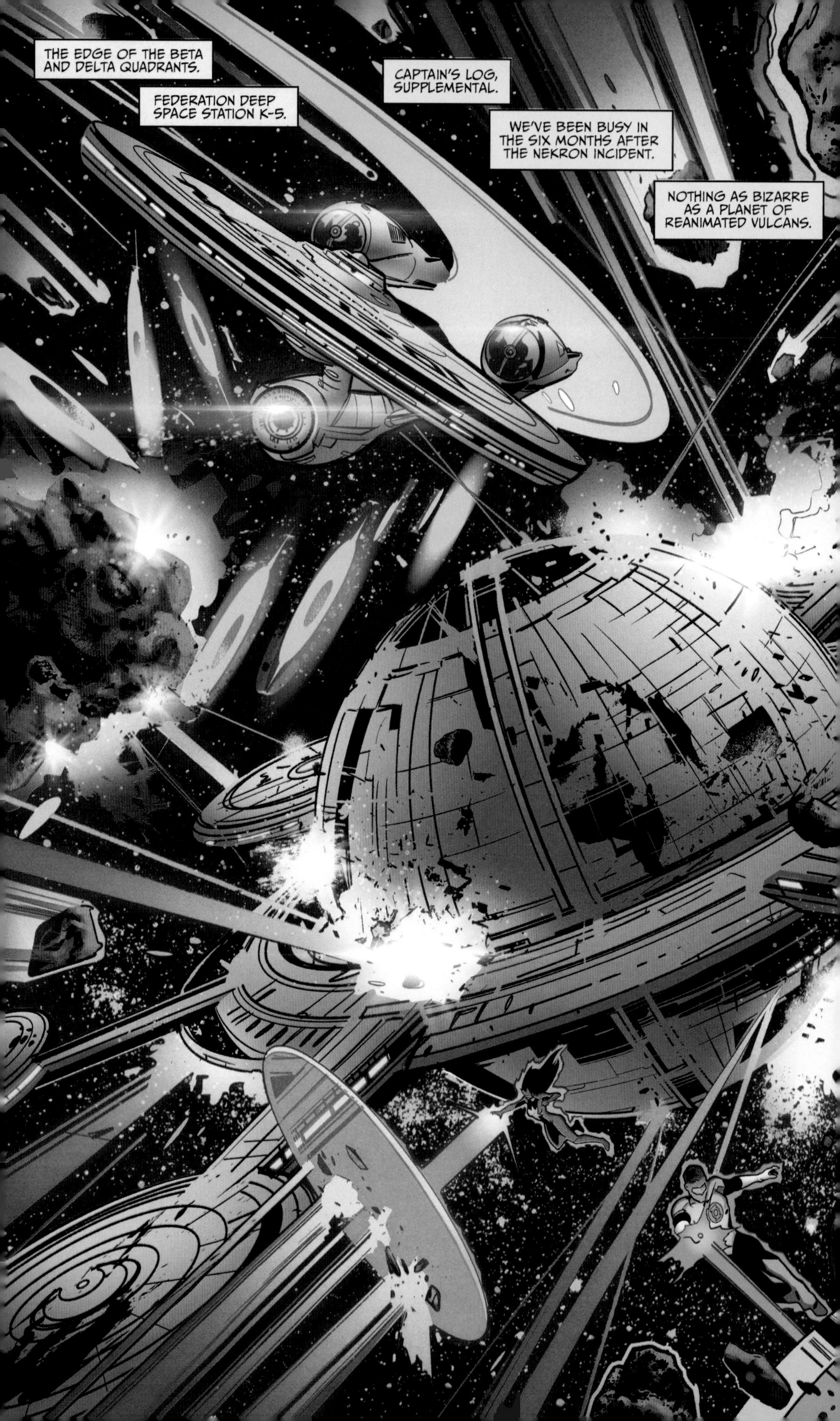
THE EDGE OF THE BETA AND DELTA QUADRANTS.
FEDERATION DEEP SPACE STATION K-5.
CAPTAIN'S LOG, SUPPLEMENTAL.
WE'VE BEEN BUSY IN THE SIX MONTHS AFTER THE NEKRON INCIDENT.
NOTHING AS BIZARRE AS A PLANET OF REANIMATED VULCANS.

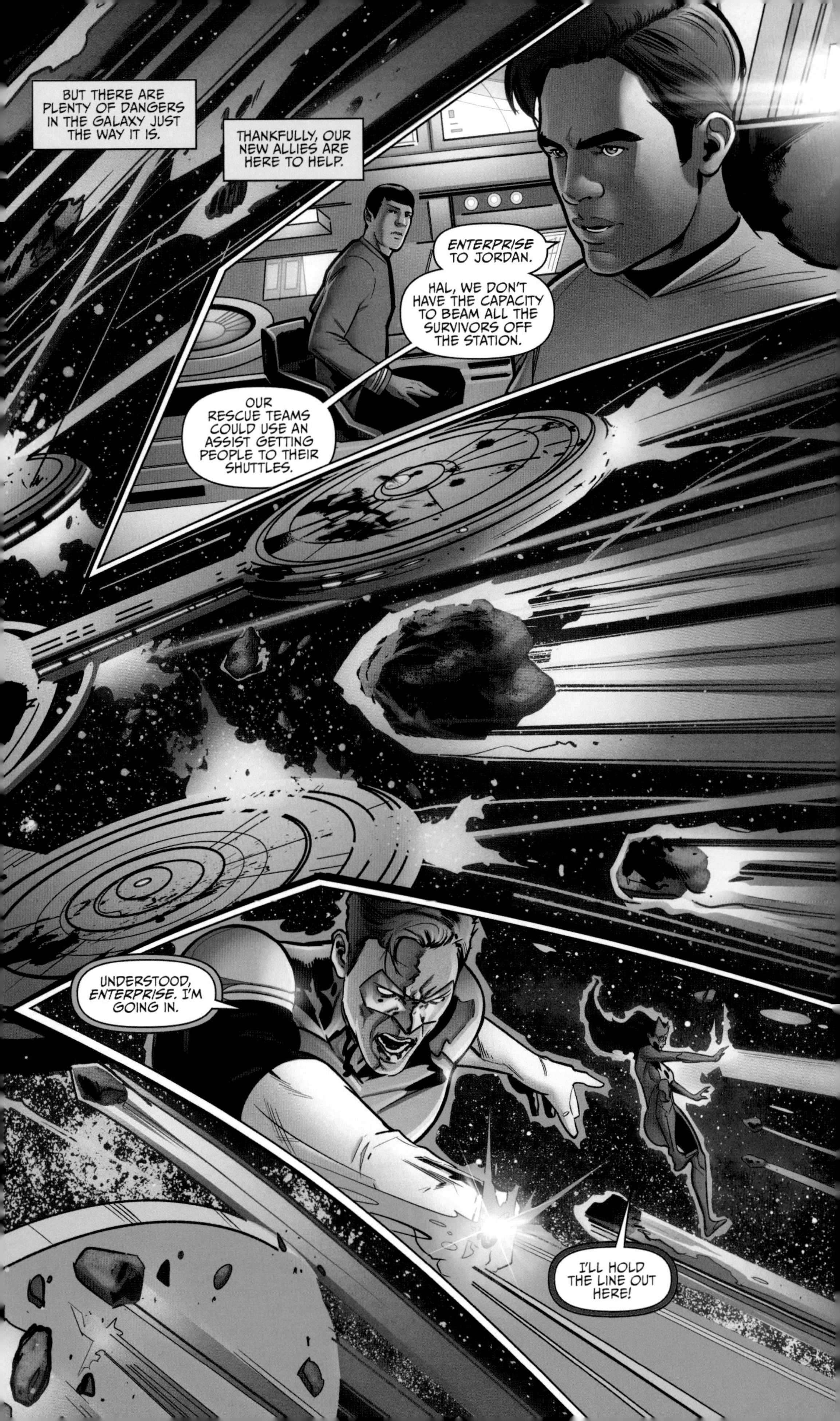

BUT THERE ARE PLENTY OF DANGERS IN THE GALAXY JUST THE WAY IT IS.
THANKFULLY, OUR NEW ALLIES ARE HERE TO HELP.
ENTERPRISE TO JORDAN.
HAL, WE DON'T HAVE THE CAPACITY TO BEAM ALL THE SURVIVORS OFF THE STATION.
OUR RESCUE TEAMS COULD USE AN ASSIST GETTING PEOPLE TO THEIR SHUTTLES.
UNDERSTOOD, ENTERPRISE. I'M GOING IN.
I'LL HOLD THE LINE OUT HERE!

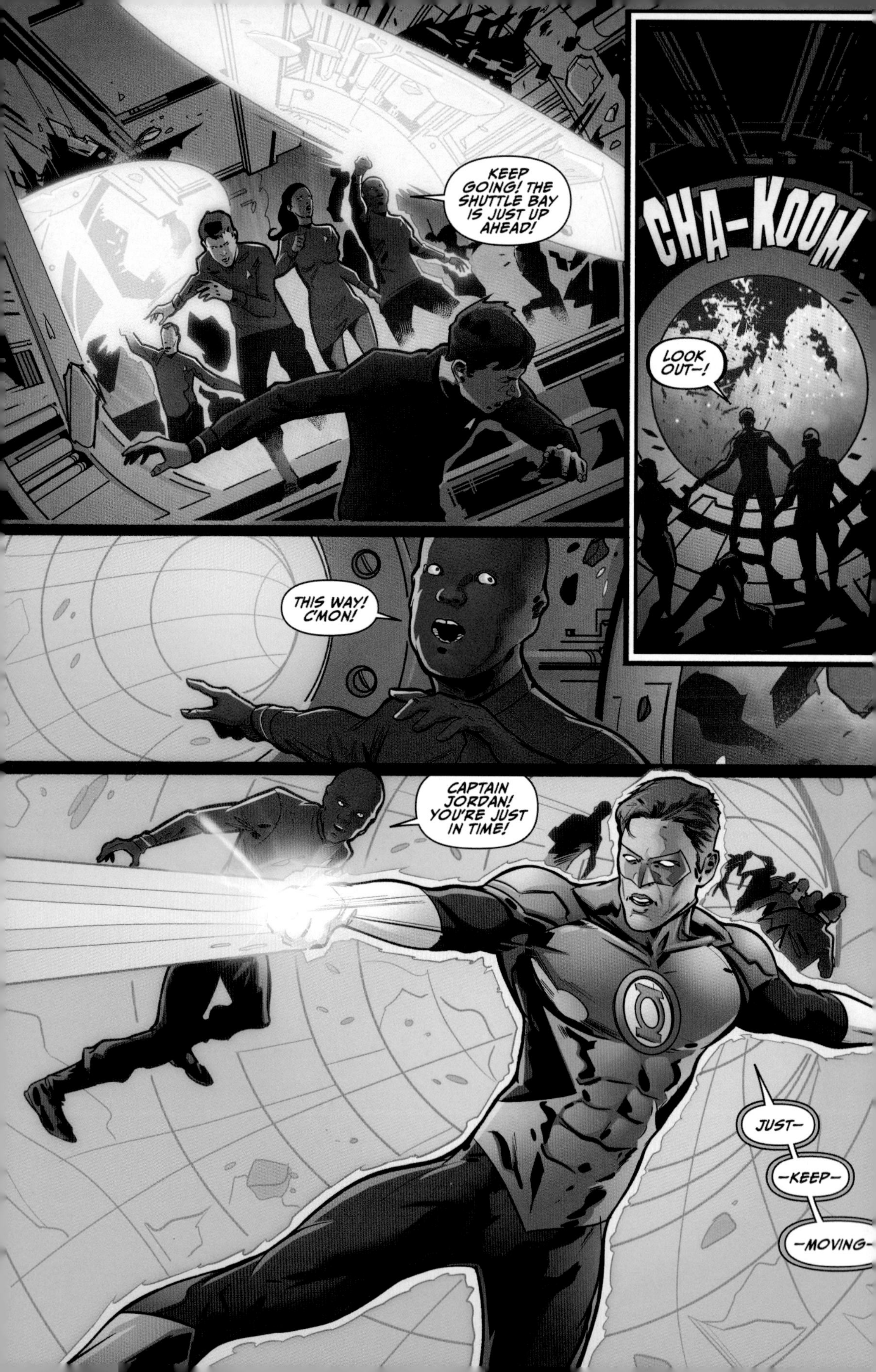
KEEP GOING! THE SHUTTLE BAY IS JUST UP AHEAD!
CHA-KOOM
LOOK OUT--!
THIS WAY! C'MON!
CAPTAIN JORDAN! YOU'RE JUST IN TIME!
JUST-
-KEEP-
-MOVING-

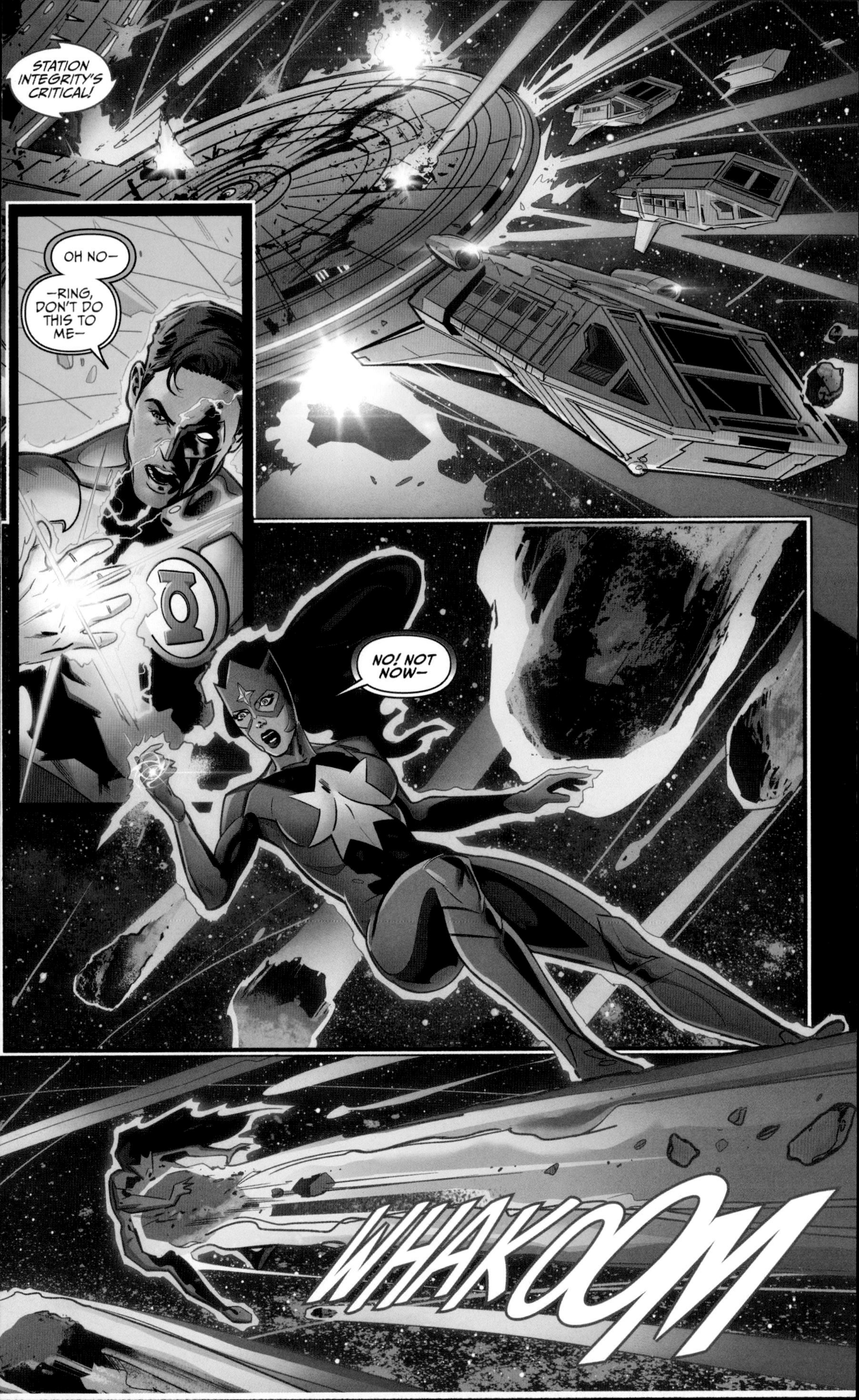
STATION INTEGRITY'S CRITICAL!
OH NO—
—RING, DON'T DO THIS TO ME—
NO! NOT NOW—
WHAKOOM

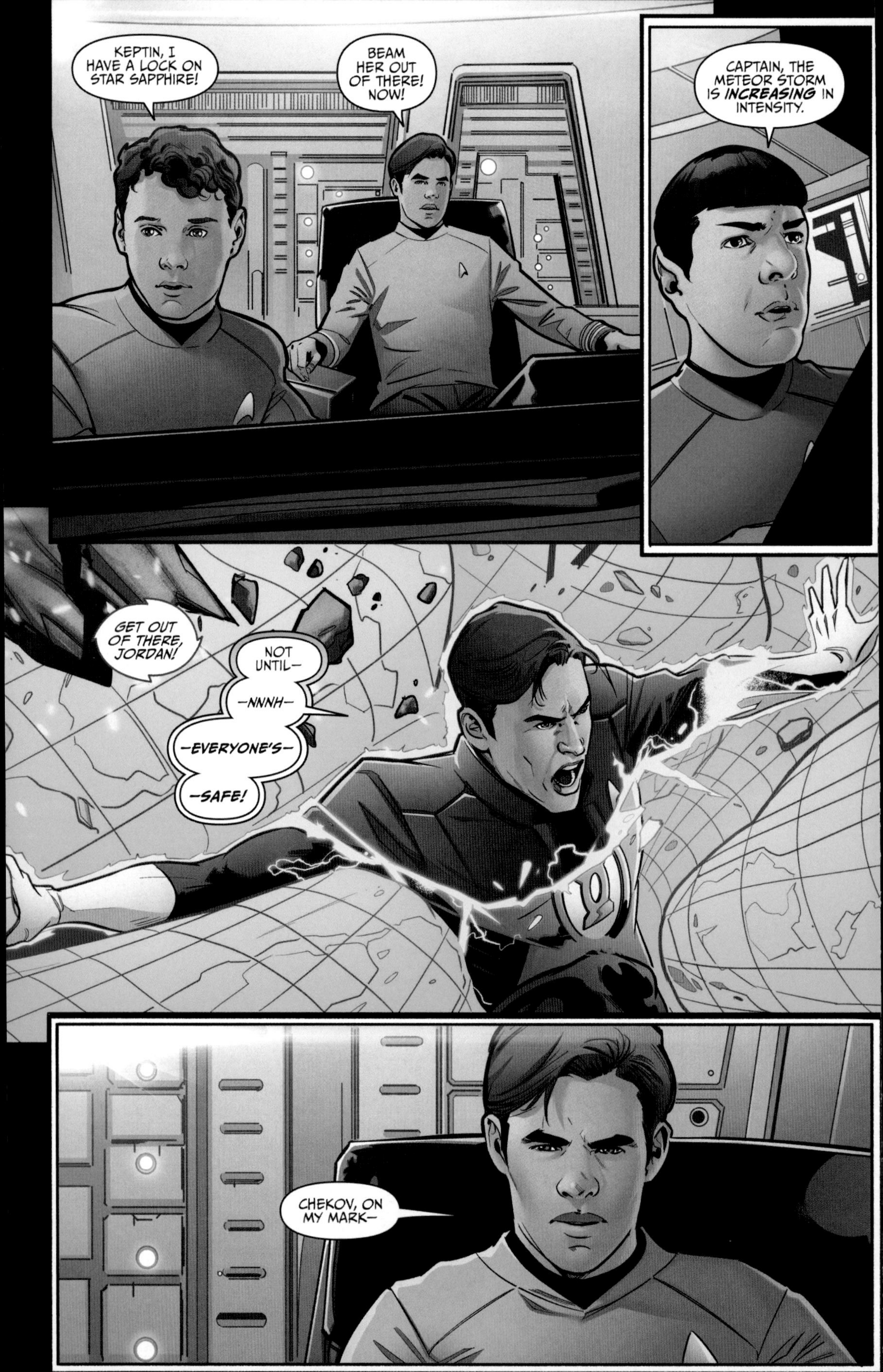
KEPTIN, I HAVE A LOCK ON STAR SAPPHIRE!
BEAM HER OUT OF THERE! NOW!
CAPTAIN, THE METEOR STORM IS *INCREASING* IN INTENSITY.
GET OUT OF THERE, JORDAN!
NOT UNTIL—
—NNNH—
—EVERYONE'S—
—SAFE!
CHEKOV, ON MY MARK—

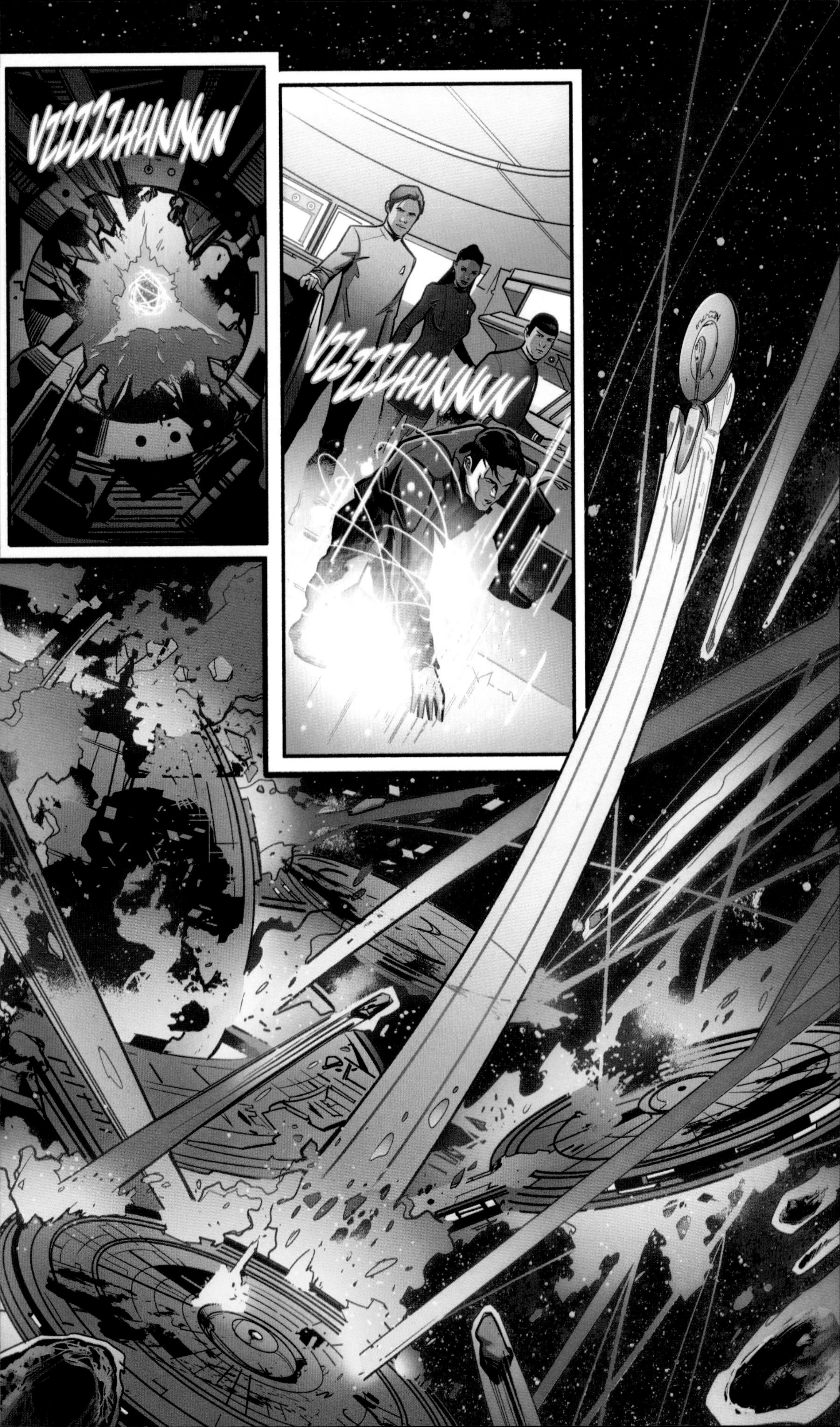
VZZZZZHHNNNN
VZZZZZHHNNNN

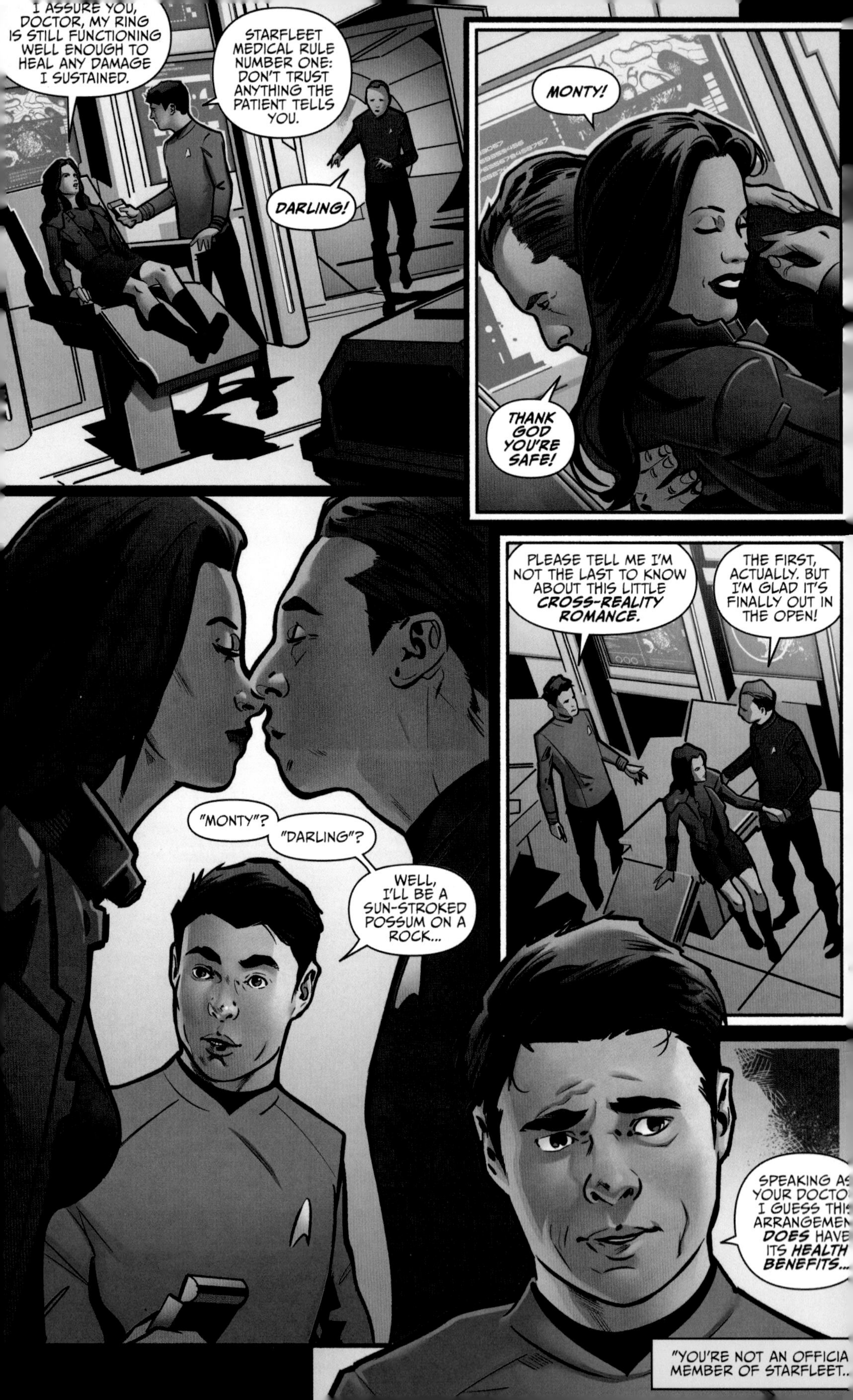
I ASSURE YOU, DOCTOR, MY RING IS STILL FUNCTIONING WELL ENOUGH TO HEAL ANY DAMAGE I SUSTAINED.
STARFLEET MEDICAL RULE NUMBER ONE: DON'T TRUST ANYTHING THE PATIENT TELLS YOU.
DARLING!
MONTY!
THANK GOD YOU'RE SAFE!
"MONTY"?
"DARLING"?
WELL, I'LL BE A SUN-STROKED POSSUM ON A ROCK...
PLEASE TELL ME I'M NOT THE LAST TO KNOW ABOUT THIS LITTLE CROSS-REALITY ROMANCE.
THE FIRST, ACTUALLY. BUT I'M GLAD IT'S FINALLY OUT IN THE OPEN!
SPEAKING AS YOUR DOCTO I GUESS THIS ARRANGEMEN DOES HAVE ITS HEALTH BENEFITS...
"YOU'RE NOT AN OFFICIA MEMBER OF STARFLEET..

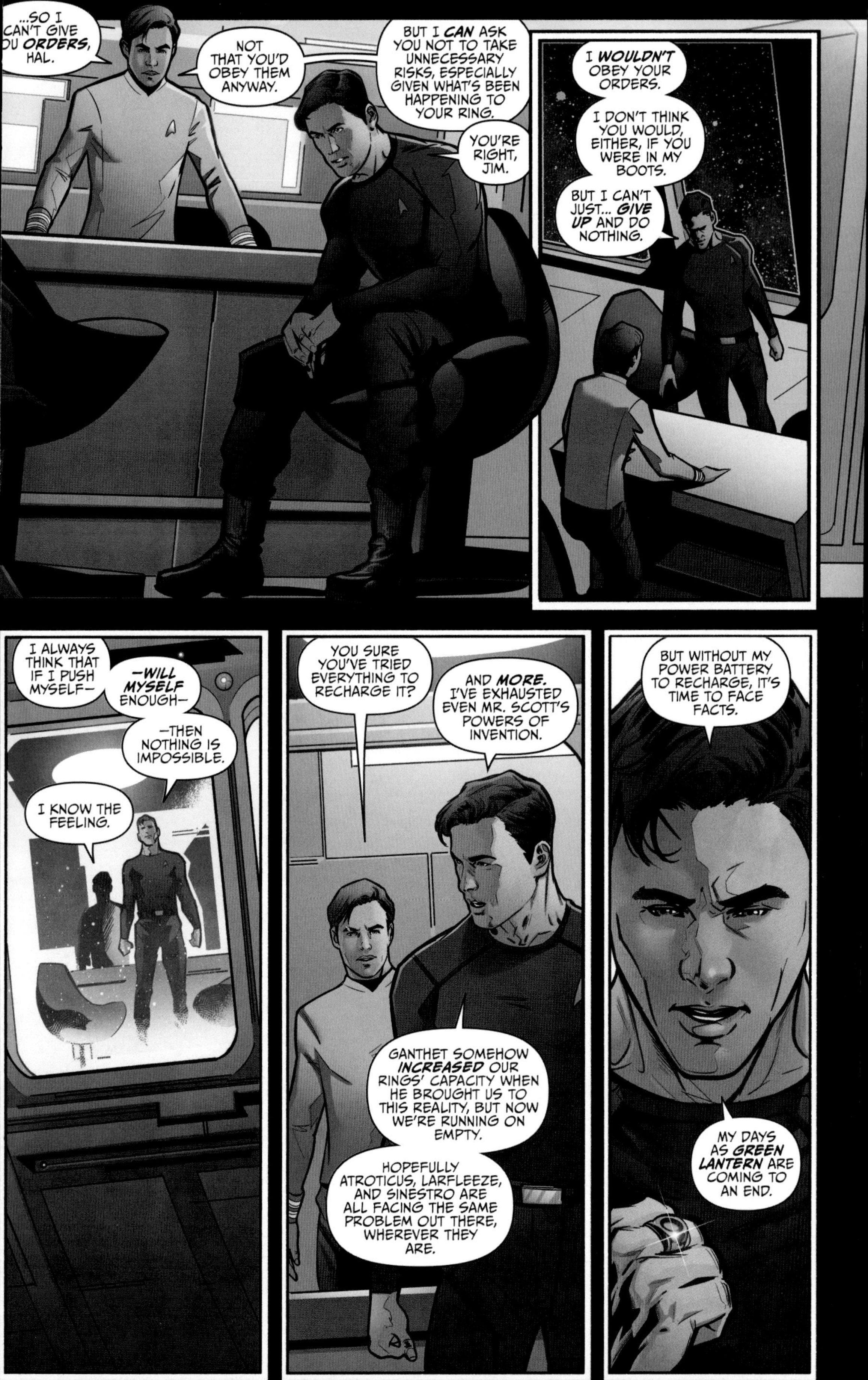
...SO I CAN'T GIVE YOU ORDERS, HAL.
NOT THAT YOU'D OBEY THEM ANYWAY.
BUT I CAN ASK YOU NOT TO TAKE UNNECESSARY RISKS, ESPECIALLY GIVEN WHAT'S BEEN HAPPENING TO YOUR RING.
YOU'RE RIGHT, JIM.
I WOULDN'T OBEY YOUR ORDERS.
I DON'T THINK YOU WOULD, EITHER, IF YOU WERE IN MY BOOTS.
BUT I CAN'T JUST... GIVE UP AND DO NOTHING.
I ALWAYS THINK THAT IF I PUSH MYSELF—
—WILL MYSELF ENOUGH—
—THEN NOTHING IS IMPOSSIBLE.
I KNOW THE FEELING.
YOU SURE YOU'VE TRIED EVERYTHING TO RECHARGE IT?
AND MORE. I'VE EXHAUSTED EVEN MR. SCOTT'S POWERS OF INVENTION.
GANTHET SOMEHOW INCREASED OUR RINGS' CAPACITY WHEN HE BROUGHT US TO THIS REALITY, BUT NOW WE'RE RUNNING ON EMPTY.
HOPEFULLY ATROTICUS, LARFLEEZE, AND SINESTRO ARE ALL FACING THE SAME PROBLEM OUT THERE, WHEREVER THEY ARE.
BUT WITHOUT MY POWER BATTERY TO RECHARGE, IT'S TIME TO FACE FACTS.
MY DAYS AS GREEN LANTERN ARE COMING TO AN END.

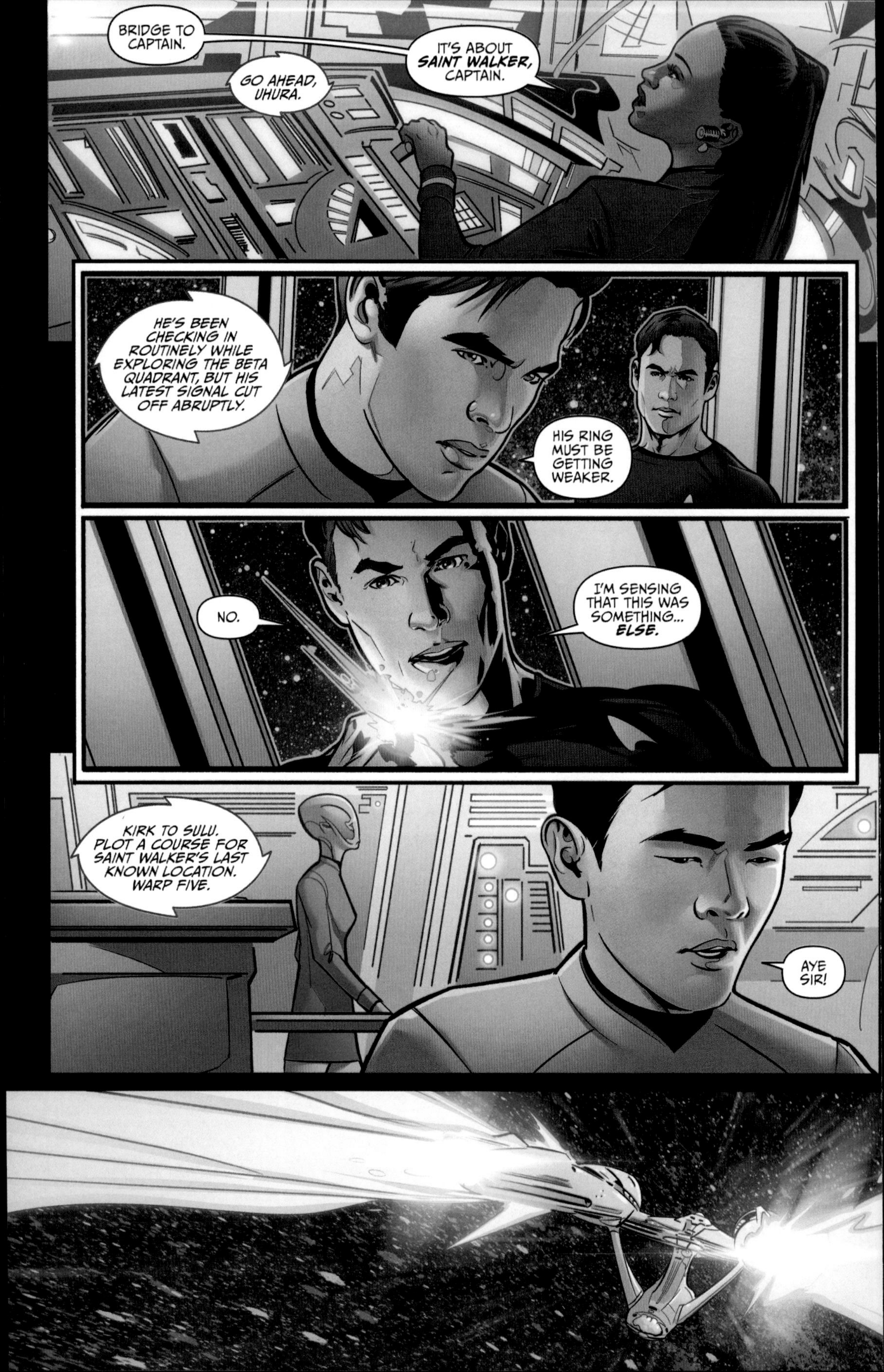
BRIDGE TO CAPTAIN.
GO AHEAD, UHURA.
IT'S ABOUT **SAINT WALKER,** CAPTAIN.
HE'S BEEN CHECKING IN ROUTINELY WHILE EXPLORING THE BETA QUADRANT, BUT HIS LATEST SIGNAL CUT OFF ABRUPTLY.
HIS RING MUST BE GETTING WEAKER.
NO.
I'M SENSING THAT THIS WAS SOMETHING... **ELSE.**
KIRK TO SULU. PLOT A COURSE FOR SAINT WALKER'S LAST KNOWN LOCATION. WARP FIVE.
AYE SIR!

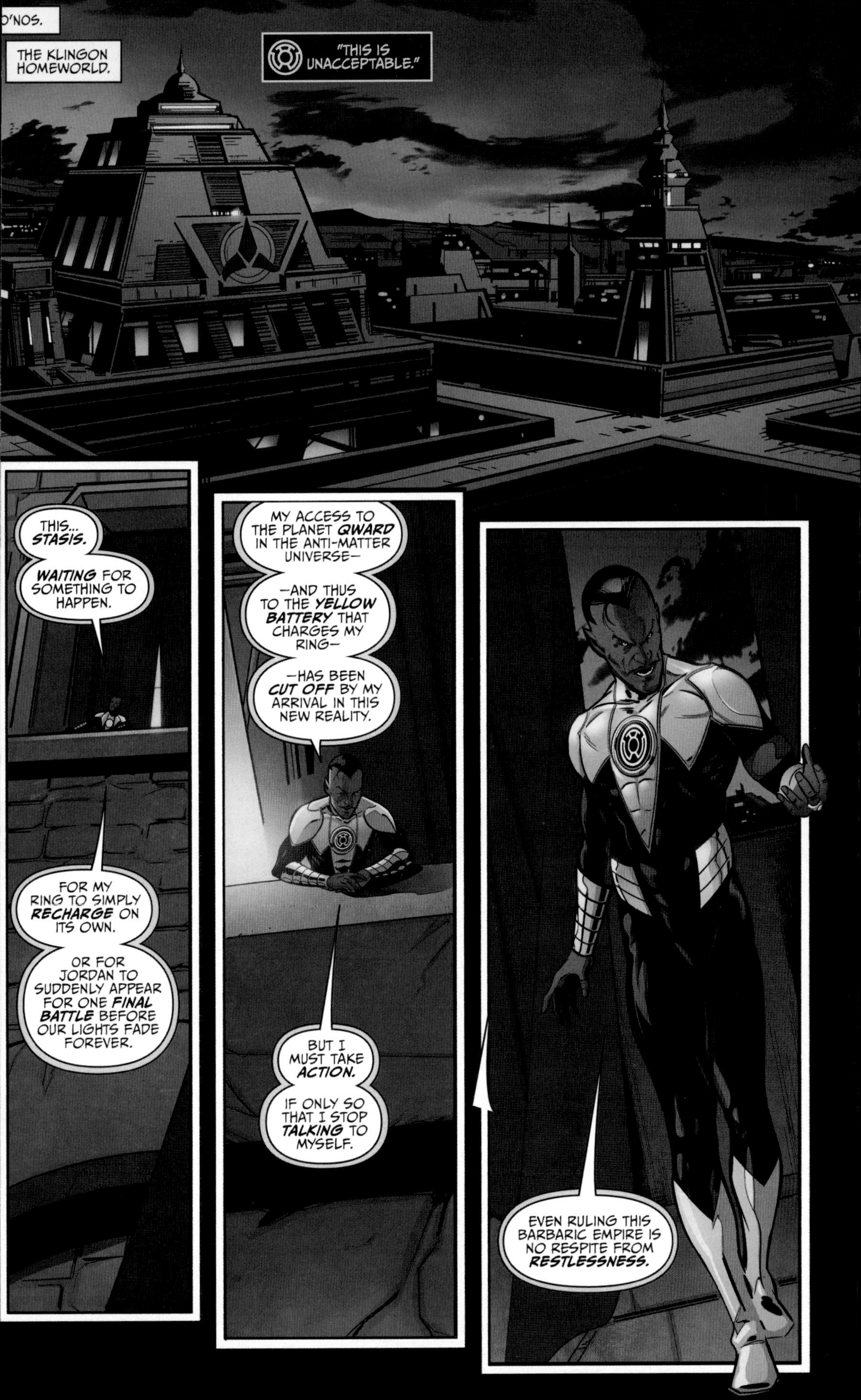

Q'NOS.
THE KLINGON HOMEWORLD.
"THIS IS UNACCEPTABLE."
THIS... STASIS.
WAITING FOR SOMETHING TO HAPPEN.
FOR MY RING TO SIMPLY RECHARGE ON ITS OWN.
OR FOR JORDAN TO SUDDENLY APPEAR FOR ONE FINAL BATTLE BEFORE OUR LIGHTS FADE FOREVER.
MY ACCESS TO THE PLANET QWARD IN THE ANTI-MATTER UNIVERSE—
—AND THUS TO THE YELLOW BATTERY THAT CHARGES MY RING—
—HAS BEEN CUT OFF BY MY ARRIVAL IN THIS NEW REALITY.
BUT I MUST TAKE ACTION.
IF ONLY SO THAT I STOP TALKING TO MYSELF.
EVEN RULING THIS BARBARIC EMPIRE IS NO RESPITE FROM RESTLESSNESS.

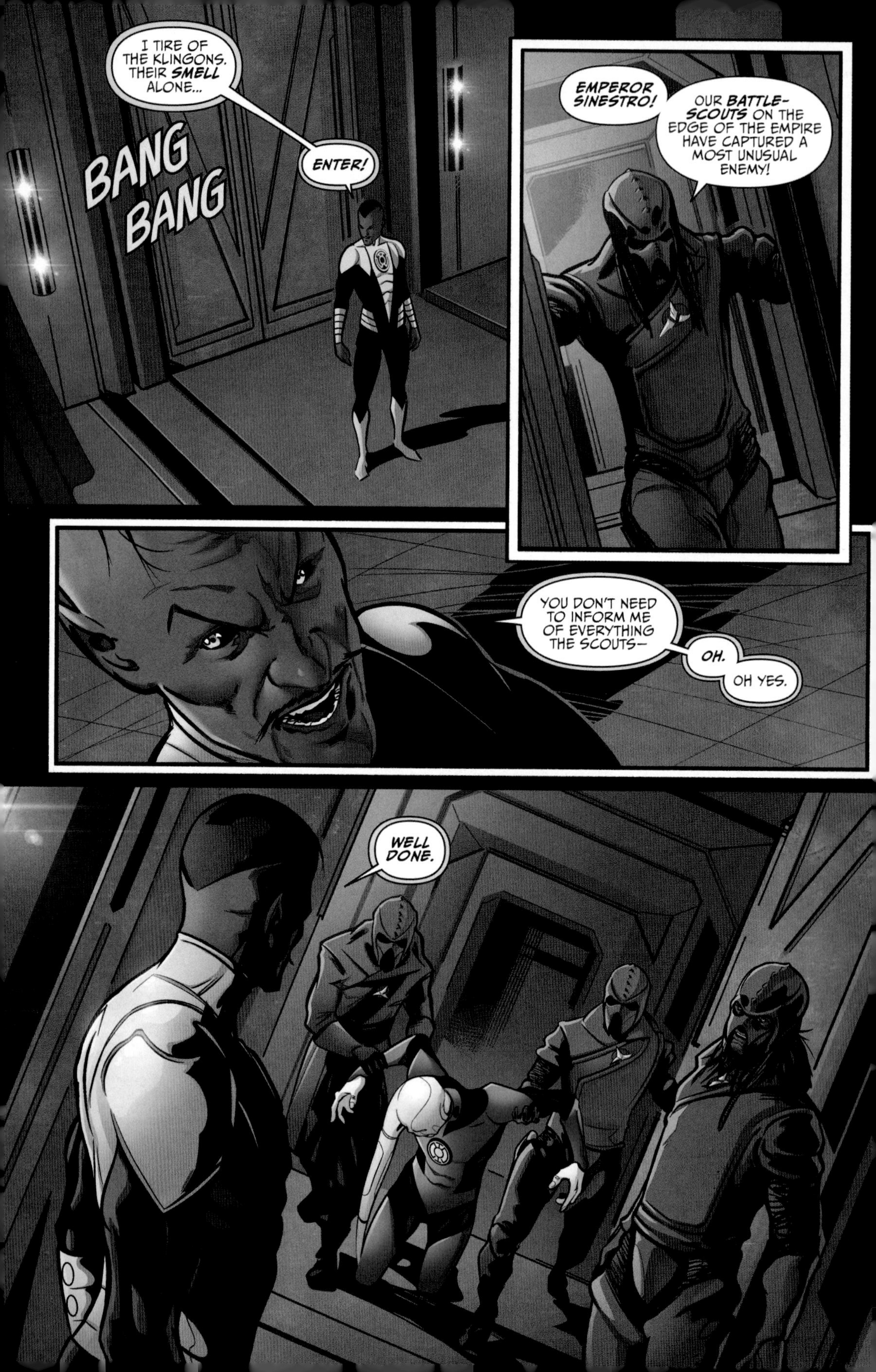
I TIRE OF THE KLINGONS. THEIR SMELL ALONE...
BANG BANG
ENTER!
EMPEROR SINESTRO!
OUR BATTLE-SCOUTS ON THE EDGE OF THE EMPIRE HAVE CAPTURED A MOST UNUSUAL ENEMY!
YOU DON'T NEED TO INFORM ME OF EVERYTHING THE SCOUTS—
OH.
OH YES.
WELL DONE.

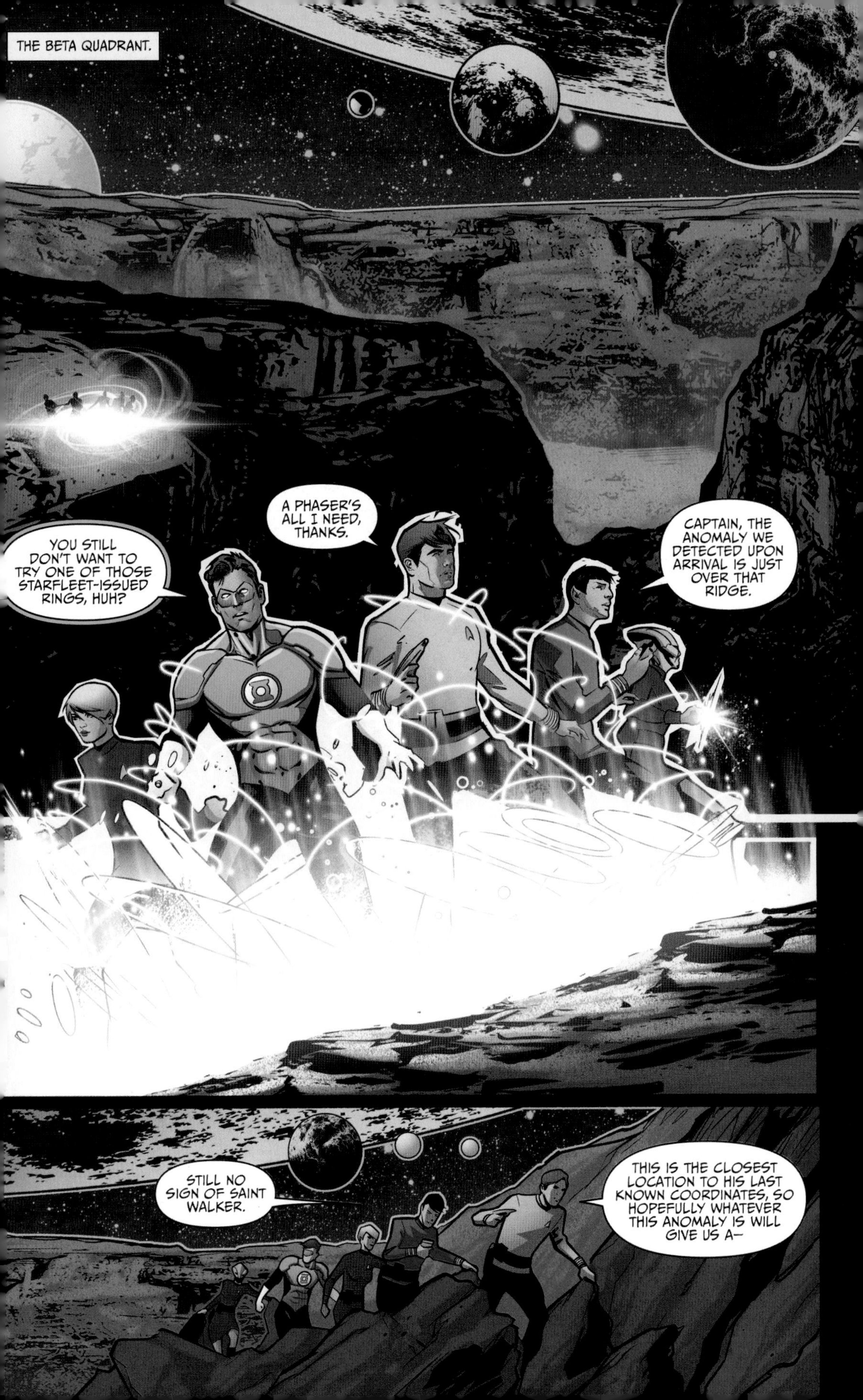
THE BETA QUADRANT.
YOU STILL DON'T WANT TO TRY ONE OF THOSE STARFLEET-ISSUED RINGS, HUH?
A PHASER'S ALL I NEED, THANKS.
CAPTAIN, THE ANOMALY WE DETECTED UPON ARRIVAL IS JUST OVER THAT RIDGE.
STILL NO SIGN OF SAINT WALKER.
THIS IS THE CLOSEST LOCATION TO HIS LAST KNOWN COORDINATES, SO HOPEFULLY WHATEVER THIS ANOMALY IS WILL GIVE US A—

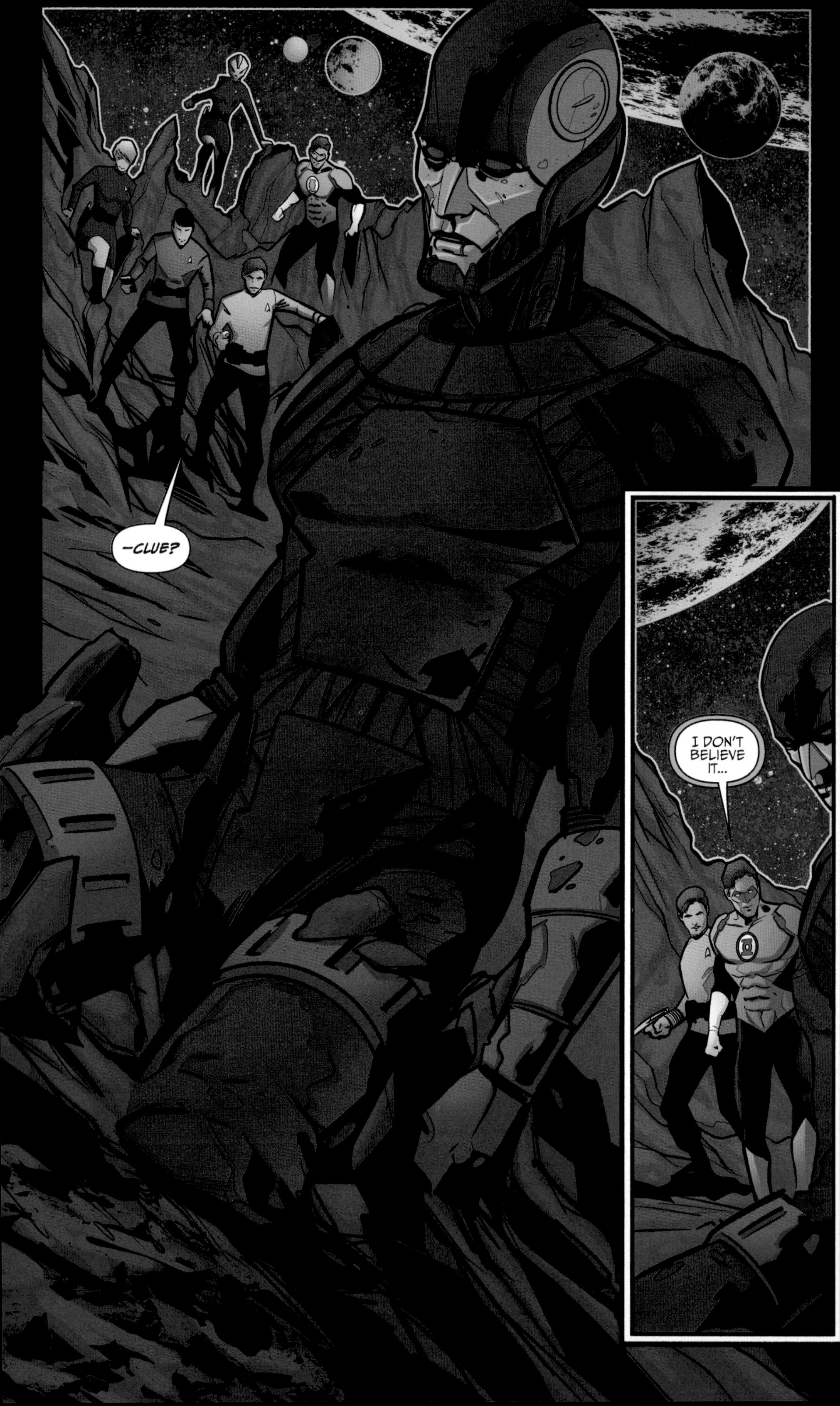
—CLUE?
I DON'T BELIEVE IT...

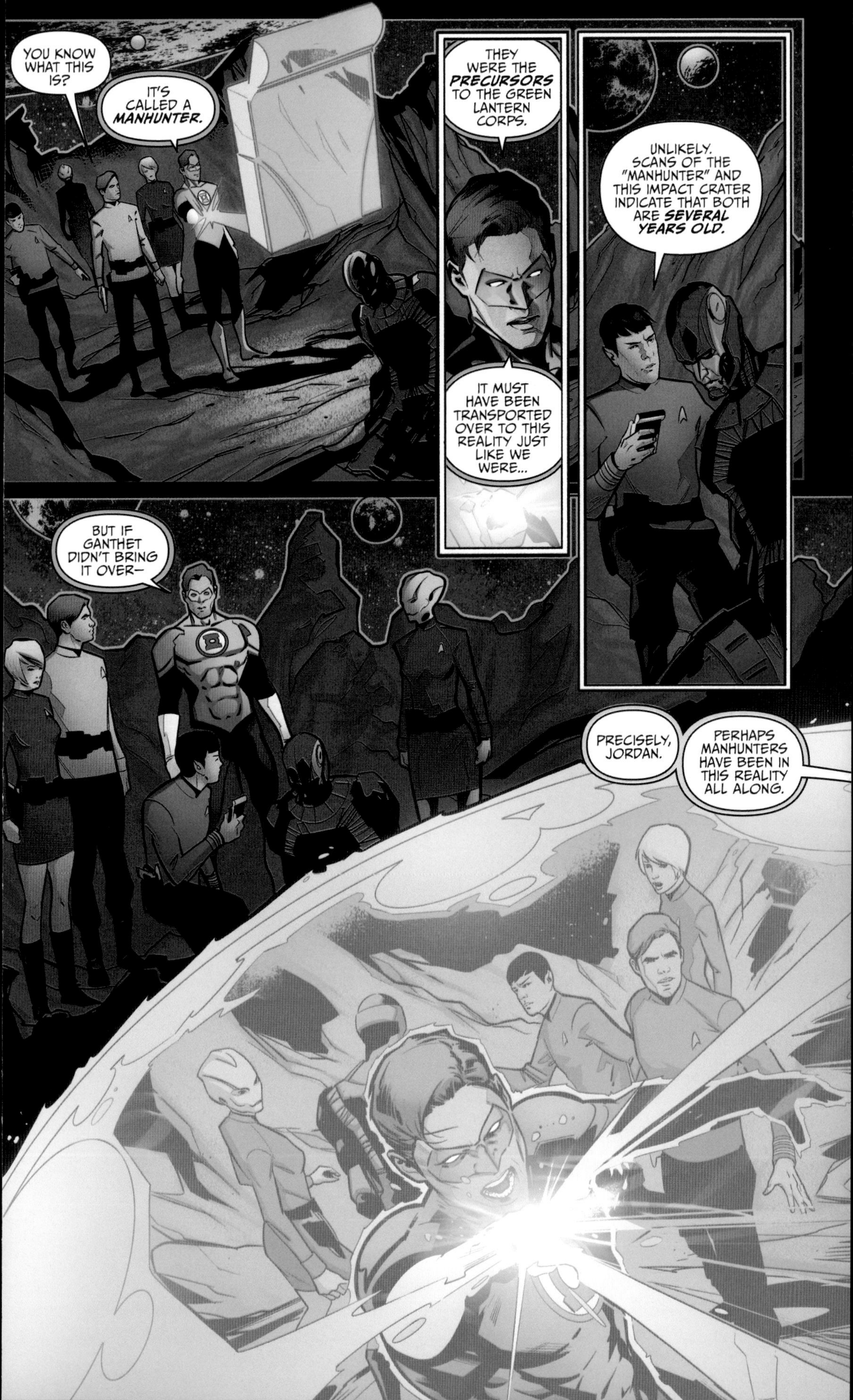
YOU KNOW WHAT THIS IS?
IT'S CALLED A MANHUNTER.
THEY WERE THE PRECURSORS TO THE GREEN LANTERN CORPS.
IT MUST HAVE BEEN TRANSPORTED OVER TO THIS REALITY JUST LIKE WE WERE...
UNLIKELY. SCANS OF THE "MANHUNTER" AND THIS IMPACT CRATER INDICATE THAT BOTH ARE SEVERAL YEARS OLD.
BUT IF GANTHET DIDN'T BRING IT OVER—
PRECISELY, JORDAN.
PERHAPS MANHUNTERS HAVE BEEN IN THIS REALITY ALL ALONG.

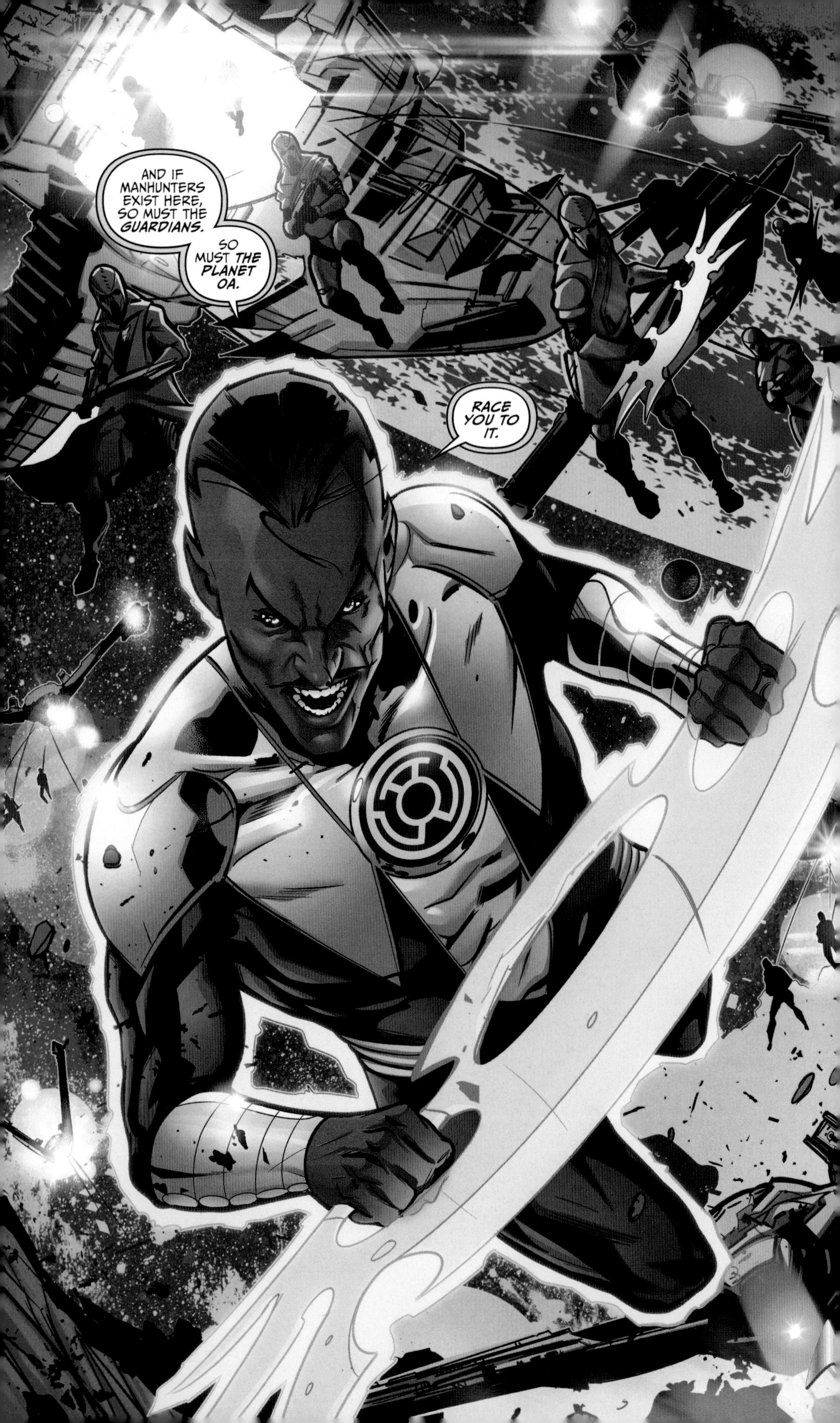
AND IF MANHUNTERS EXIST HERE, SO MUST THE GUARDIANS.
SO MUST THE PLANET OA.
RACE YOU TO IT.

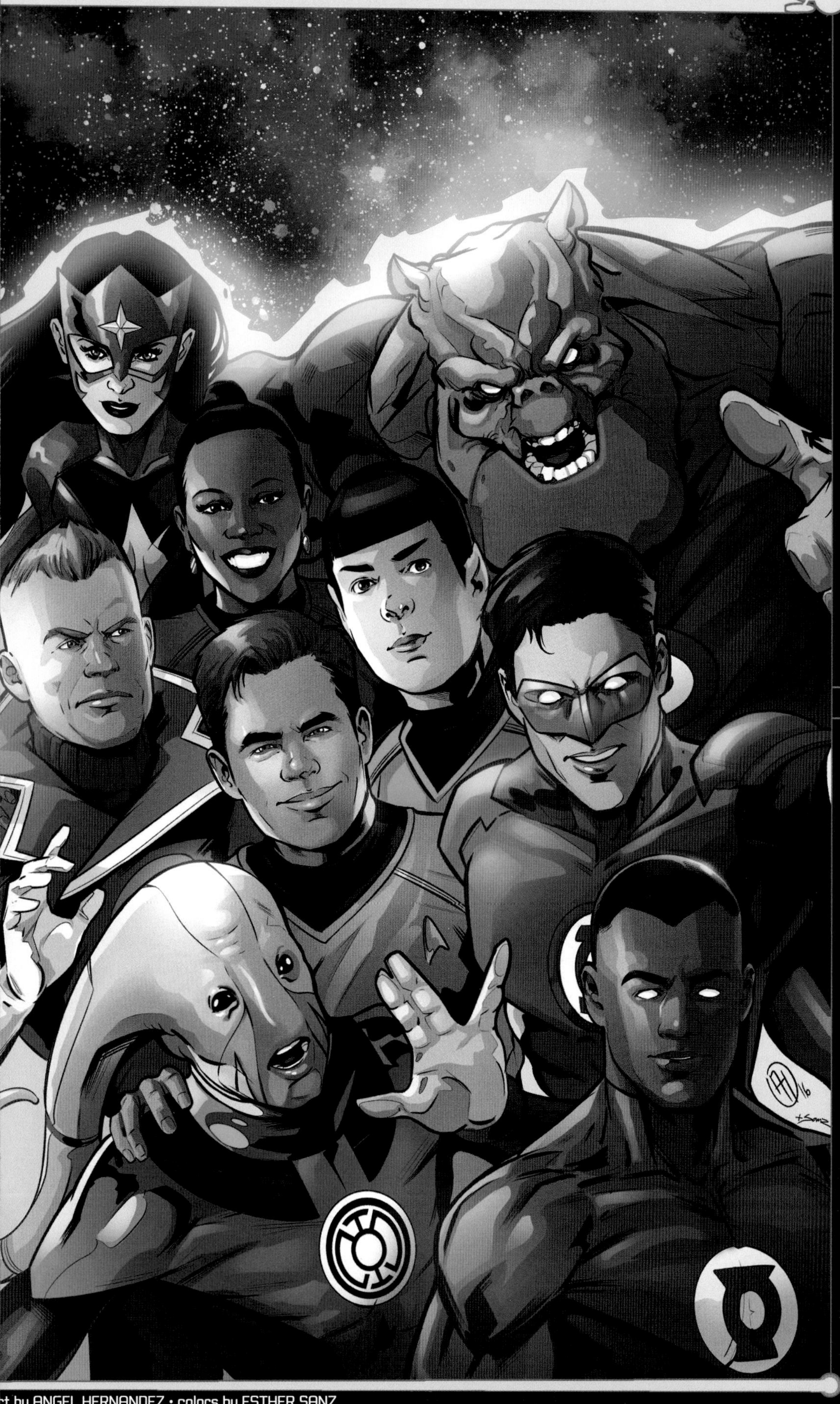

rt by ANGEL HERNANDEZ • colors by ESTHER SANZ

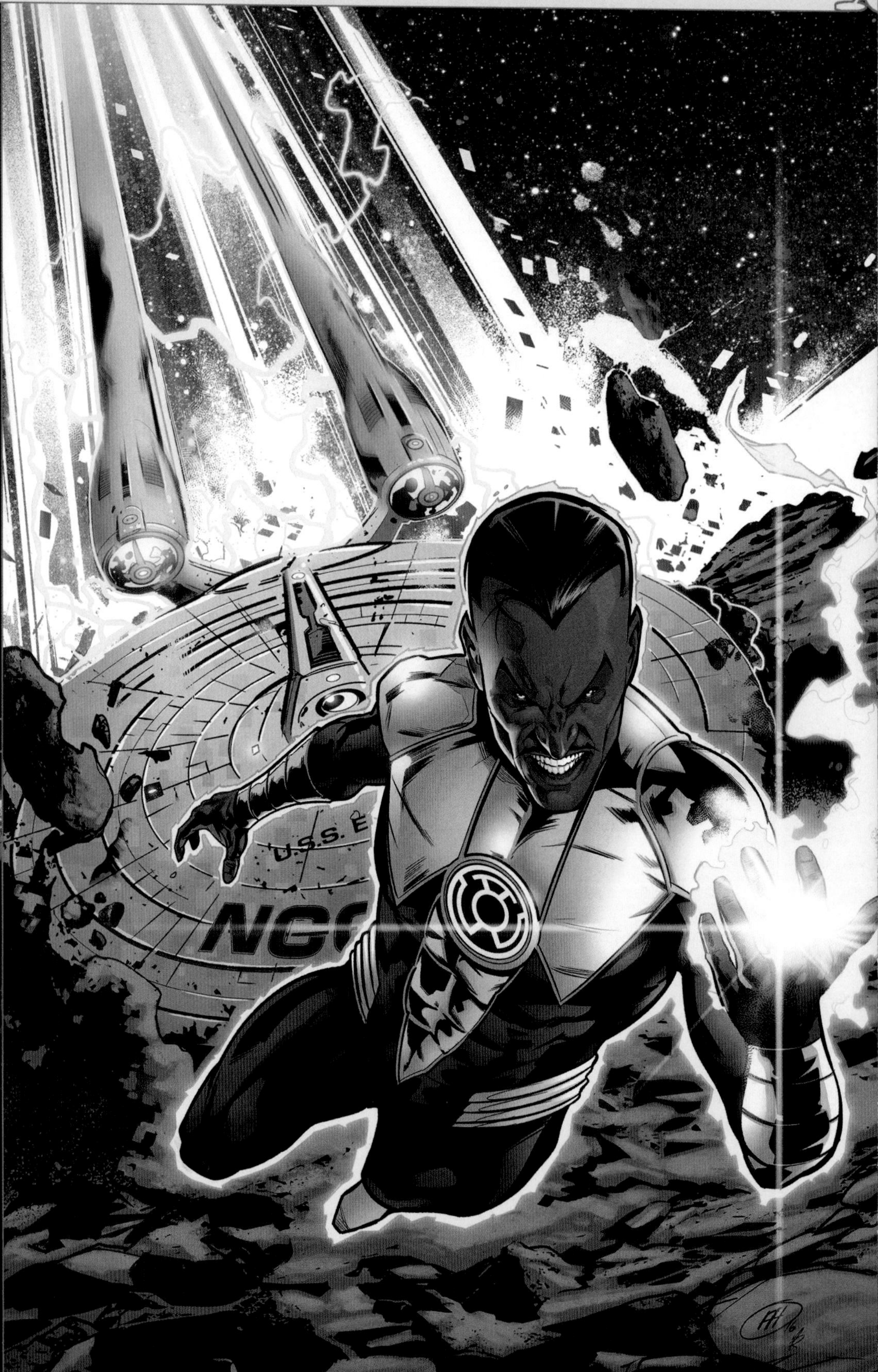
U.S.S. E
NCC

art by ANGEL HERNANDEZ • colors by MARK ROBERTS

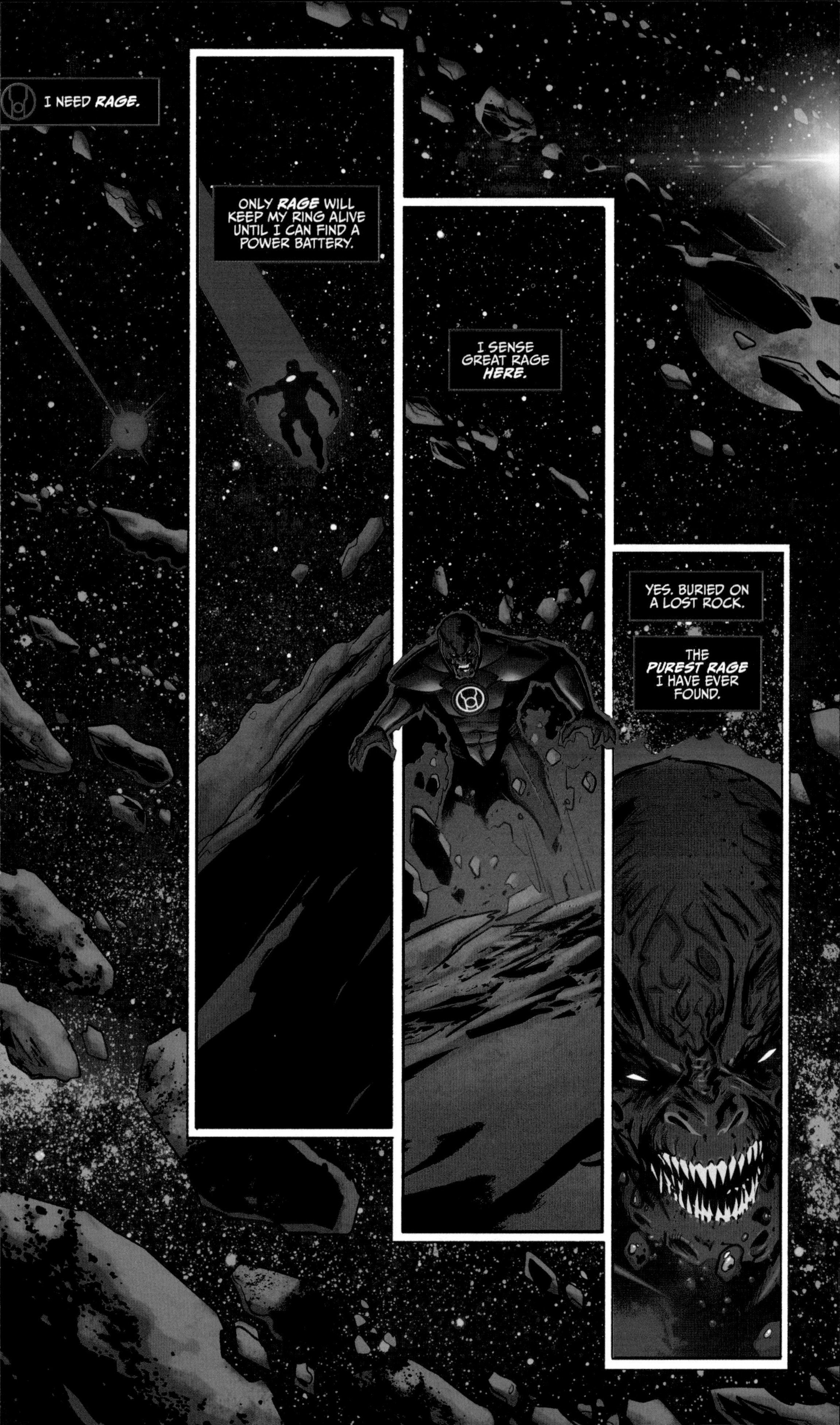
I NEED RAGE.
ONLY RAGE WILL KEEP MY RING ALIVE UNTIL I CAN FIND A POWER BATTERY.
I SENSE GREAT RAGE HERE.
YES. BURIED ON A LOST ROCK.
THE PUREST RAGE I HAVE EVER FOUND.

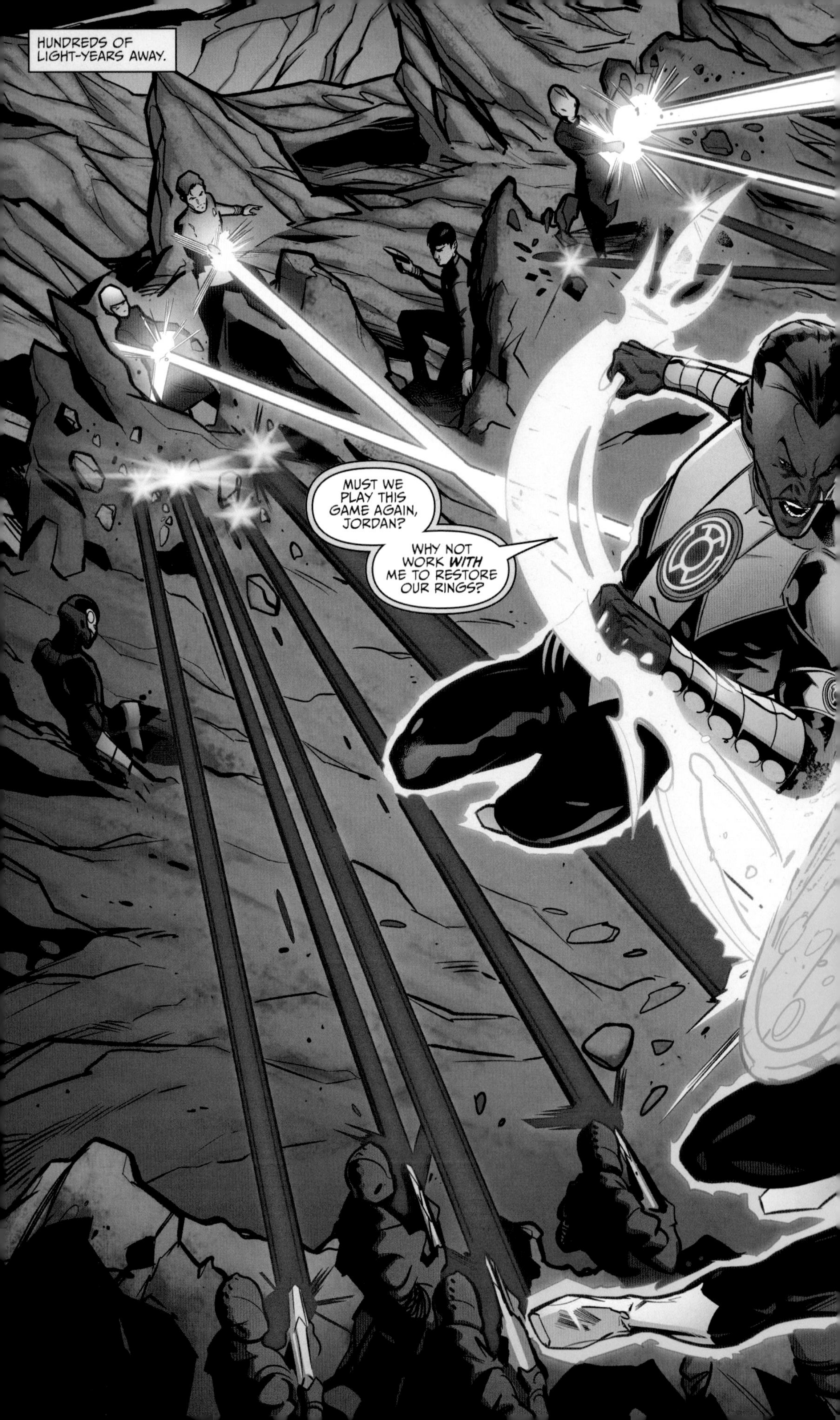
HUNDREDS OF LIGHT-YEARS AWAY.
MUST WE PLAY THIS GAME AGAIN, JORDAN?
WHY NOT WORK WITH ME TO RESTORE OUR RINGS?

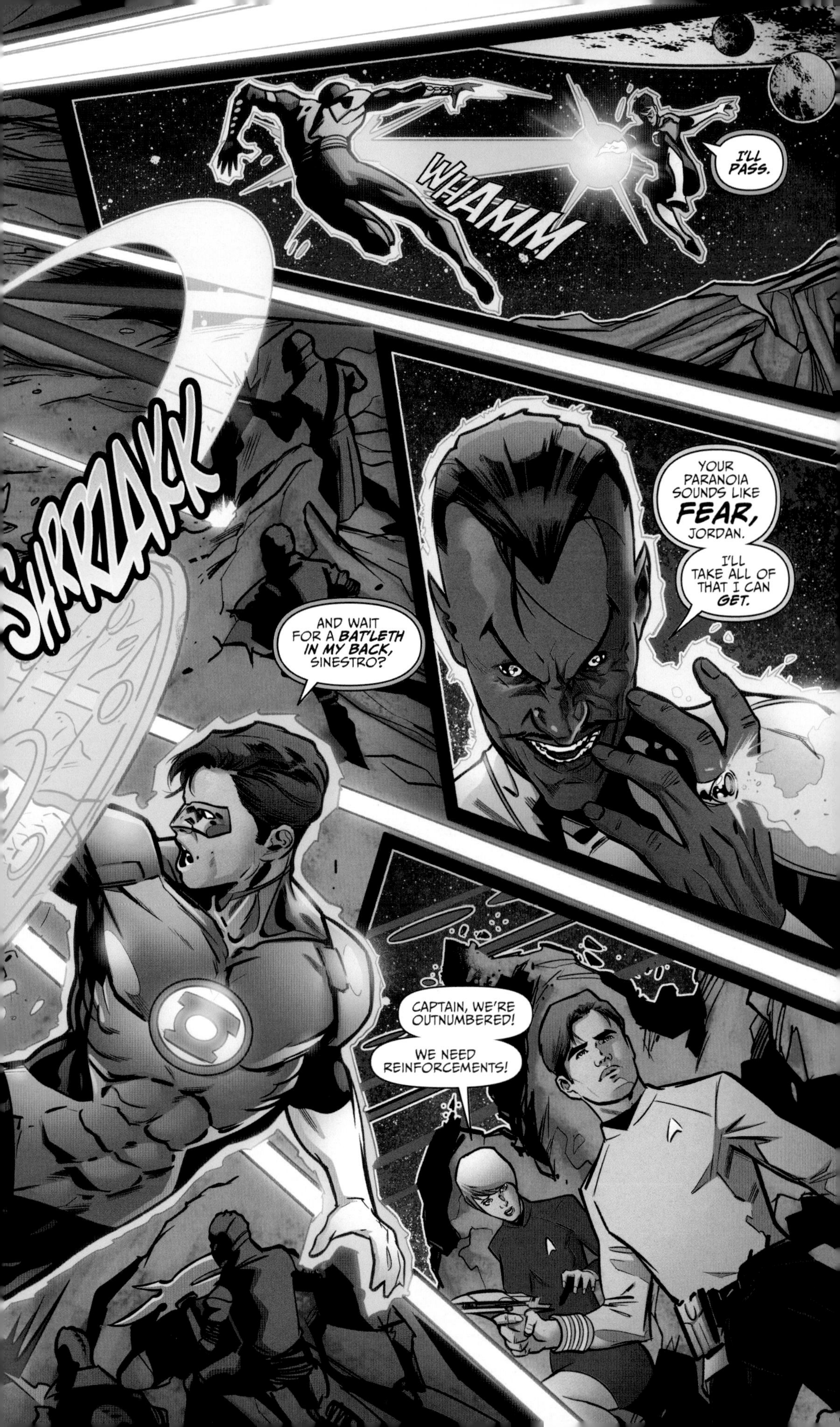
WHAMM
I'LL PASS.
SHRRZAKK
AND WAIT FOR A BAT'LETH IN MY BACK, SINESTRO?
YOUR PARANOIA SOUNDS LIKE FEAR, JORDAN.
I'LL TAKE ALL OF THAT I CAN GET.
CAPTAIN, WE'RE OUTNUMBERED!
WE NEED REINFORCEMENTS!

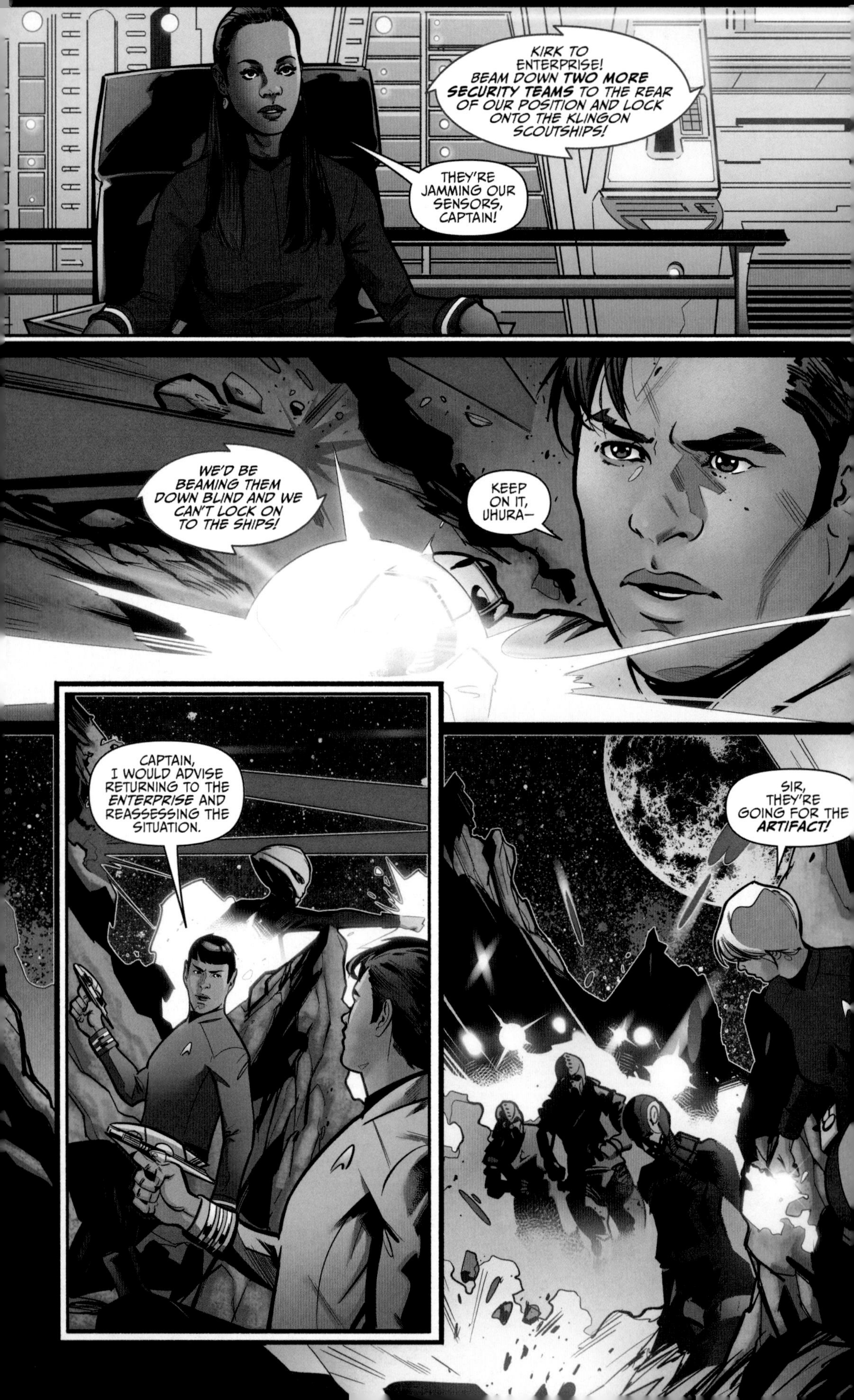
KIRK TO ENTERPRISE! BEAM DOWN **TWO MORE SECURITY TEAMS** TO THE REAR OF OUR POSITION AND LOCK ONTO THE KLINGON SCOUTSHIPS!
THEY'RE JAMMING OUR SENSORS, CAPTAIN!
KEEP ON IT, UHURA—
WE'D BE BEAMING THEM DOWN BLIND AND WE CAN'T LOCK ON TO THE SHIPS!
CAPTAIN, I WOULD ADVISE RETURNING TO THE *ENTERPRISE* AND REASSESSING THE SITUATION.
SIR, THEY'RE GOING FOR THE ***ARTIFACT!***

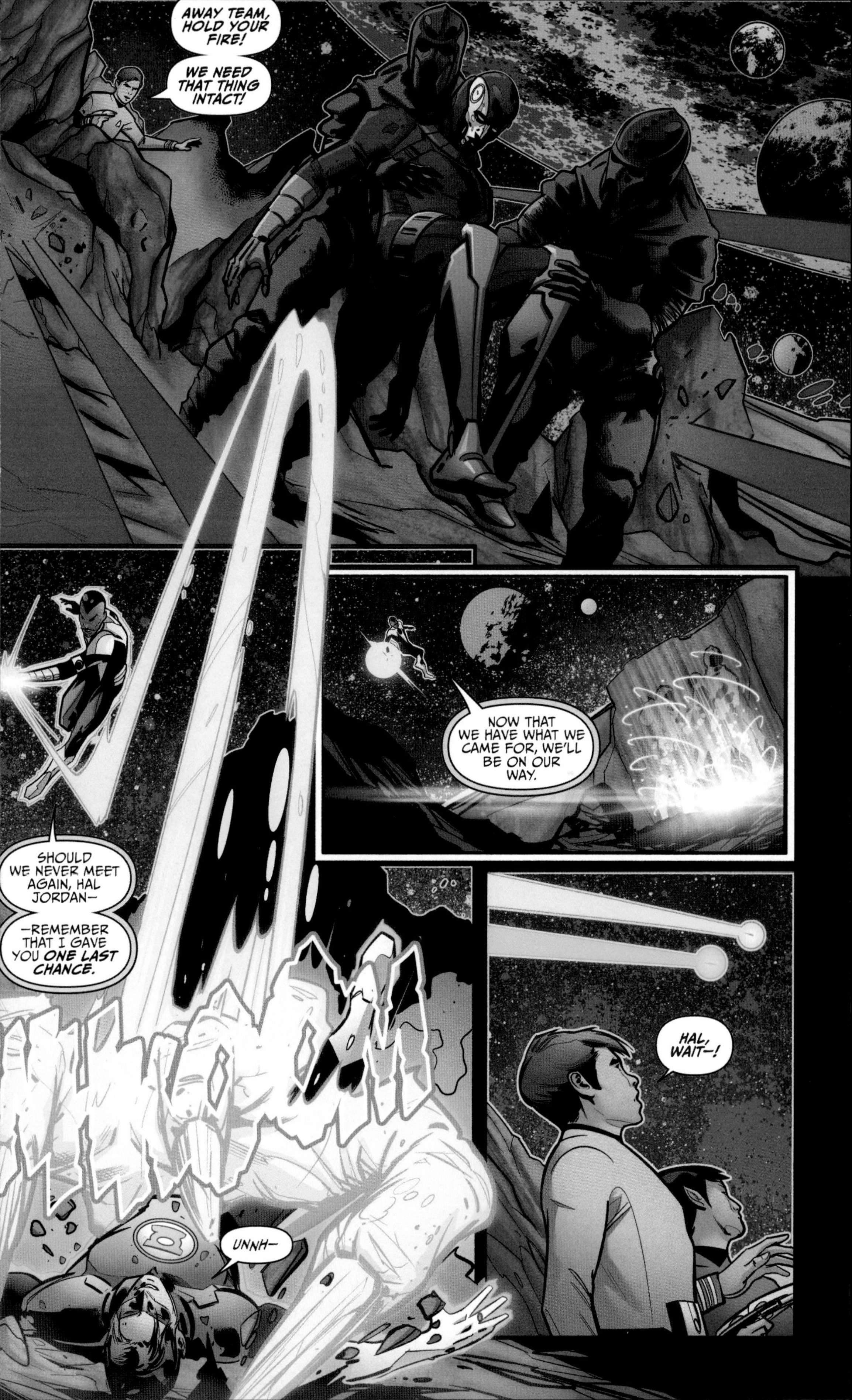
AWAY TEAM, HOLD YOUR FIRE!
WE NEED THAT THING INTACT!
NOW THAT WE HAVE WHAT WE CAME FOR, WE'LL BE ON OUR WAY.
SHOULD WE NEVER MEET AGAIN, HAL JORDAN—
—REMEMBER THAT I GAVE YOU ONE LAST CHANCE.
HAL, WAIT—!
UNNH—

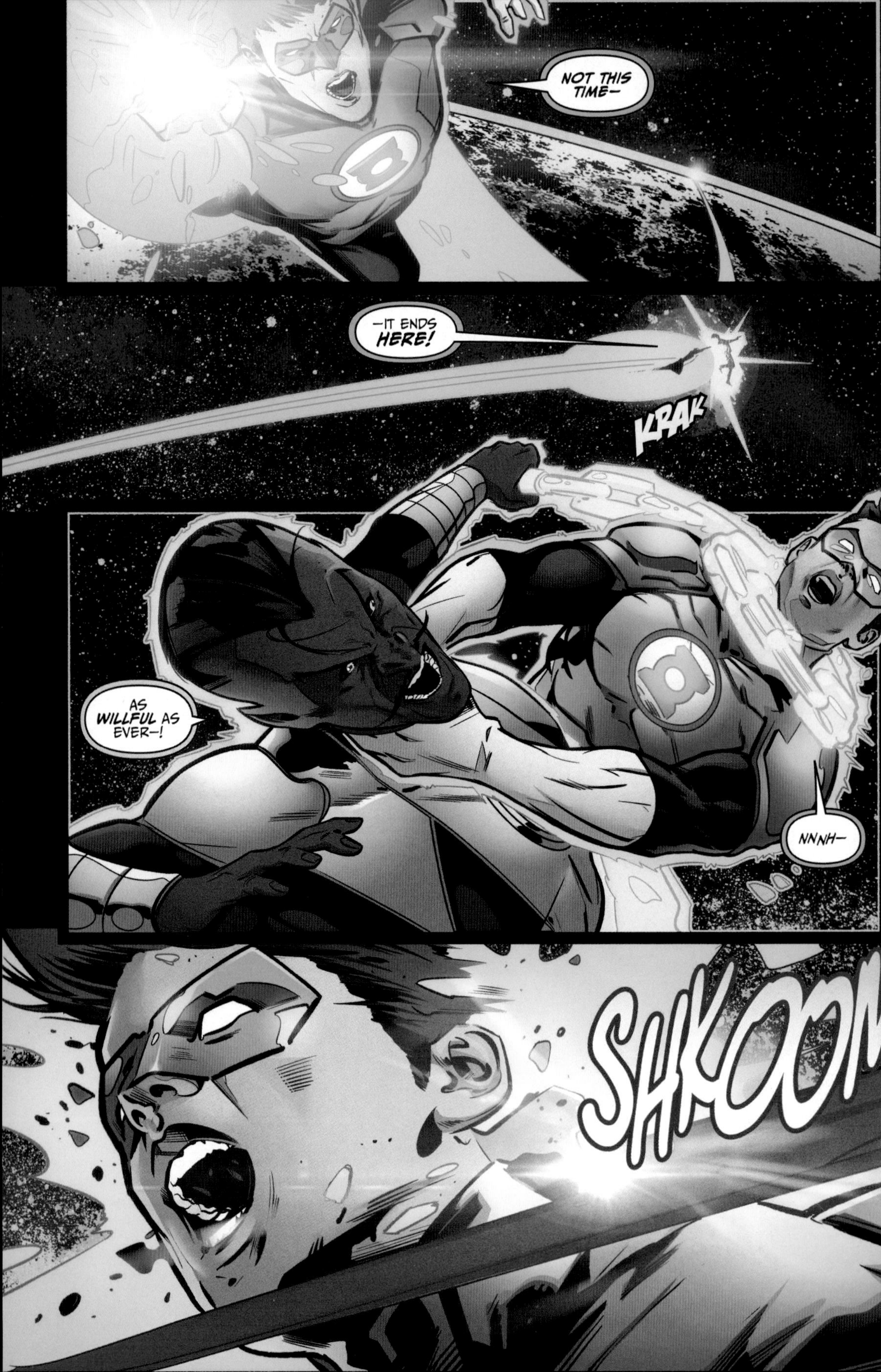
NOT THIS TIME—
—IT ENDS HERE!
KRAK
AS WILLFUL AS EVER—!
NNNH—
SHKOOM

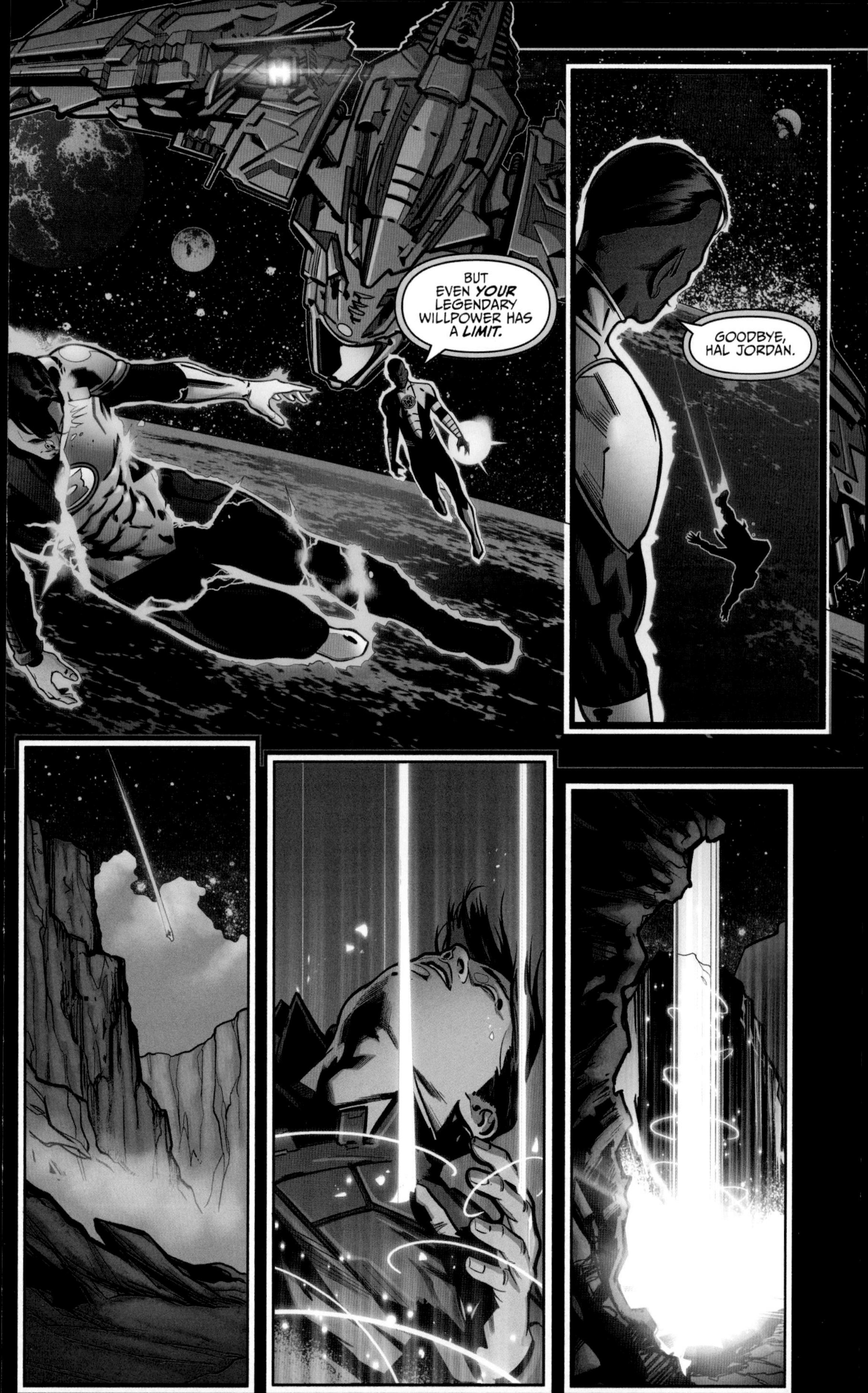
BUT EVEN YOUR LEGENDARY WILLPOWER HAS A LIMIT.
GOODBYE, HAL JORDAN.

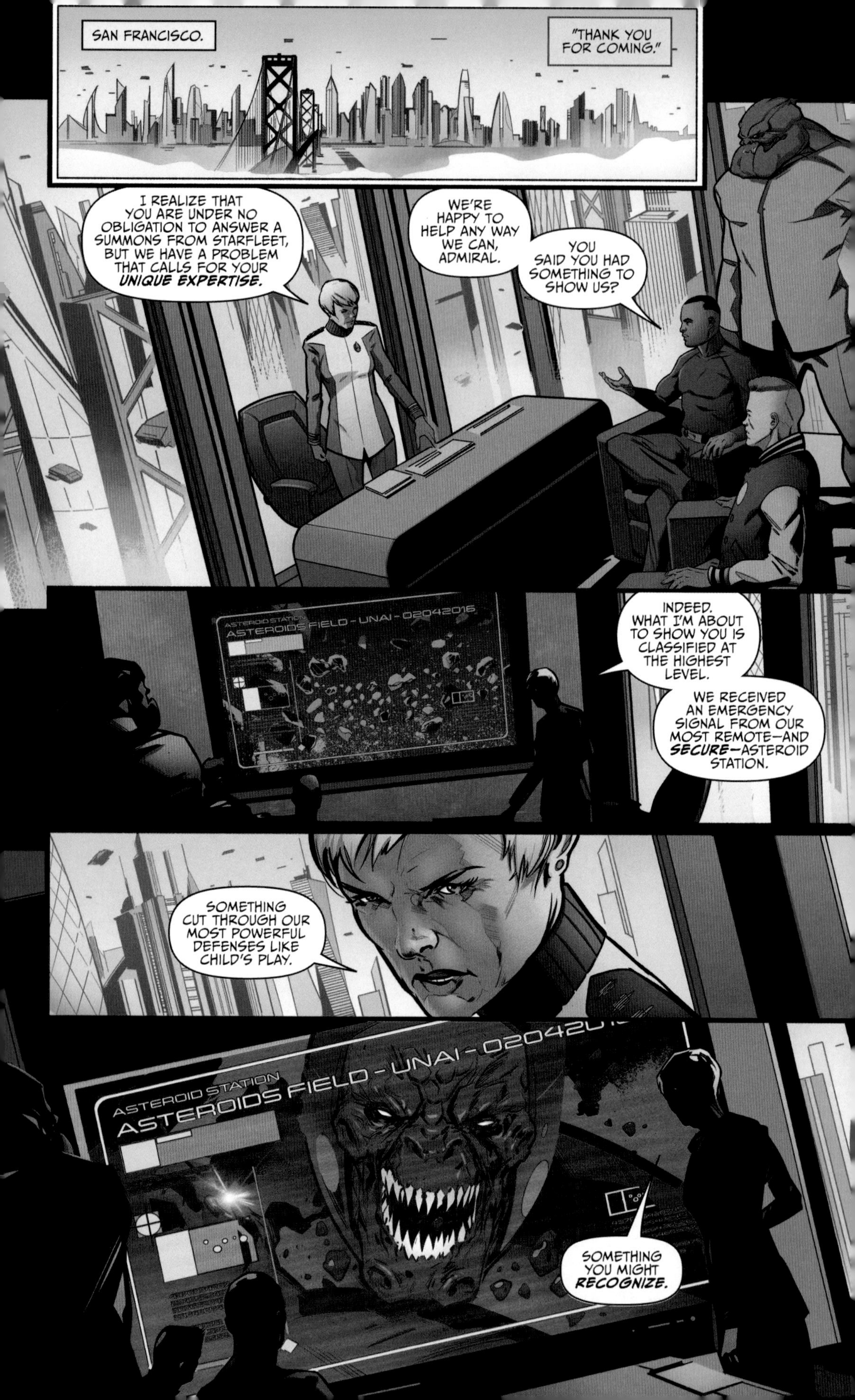
SAN FRANCISCO.
"THANK YOU FOR COMING."
I REALIZE THAT YOU ARE UNDER NO OBLIGATION TO ANSWER A SUMMONS FROM STARFLEET, BUT WE HAVE A PROBLEM THAT CALLS FOR YOUR UNIQUE EXPERTISE.
WE'RE HAPPY TO HELP ANY WAY WE CAN, ADMIRAL.
YOU SAID YOU HAD SOMETHING TO SHOW US?
ASTEROID STATION
ASTEROIDS FIELD - UNAI - 02042016
INDEED. WHAT I'M ABOUT TO SHOW YOU IS CLASSIFIED AT THE HIGHEST LEVEL.
WE RECEIVED AN EMERGENCY SIGNAL FROM OUR MOST REMOTE—AND SECURE—ASTEROID STATION.
SOMETHING CUT THROUGH OUR MOST POWERFUL DEFENSES LIKE CHILD'S PLAY.
ASTEROID STATION
ASTEROIDS FIELD - UNAI - 020420
SOMETHING YOU MIGHT RECOGNIZE.

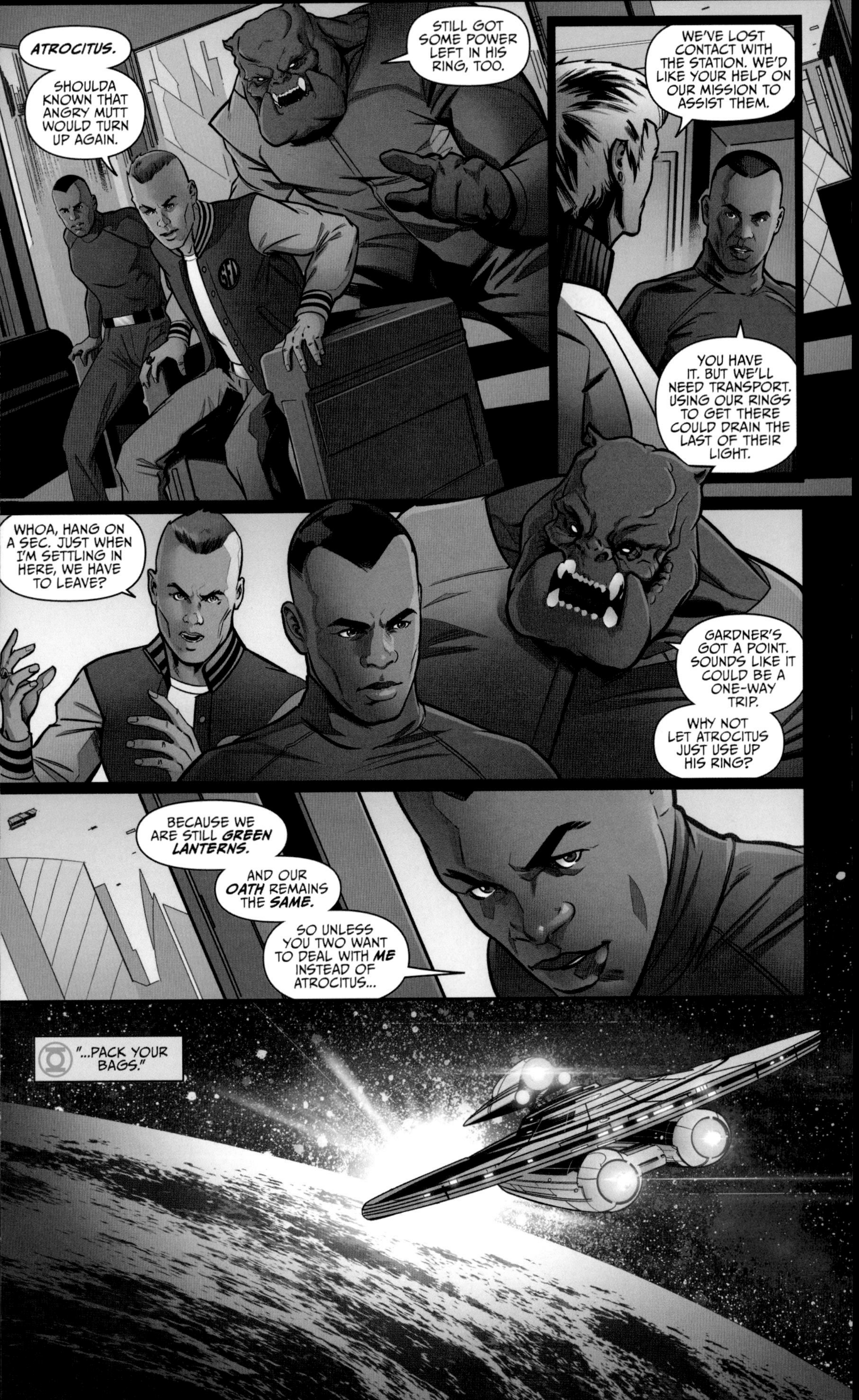
ATROCITUS.
SHOULDA KNOWN THAT ANGRY MUTT WOULD TURN UP AGAIN.
STILL GOT SOME POWER LEFT IN HIS RING, TOO.
WE'VE LOST CONTACT WITH THE STATION. WE'D LIKE YOUR HELP ON OUR MISSION TO ASSIST THEM.
YOU HAVE IT. BUT WE'LL NEED TRANSPORT. USING OUR RINGS TO GET THERE COULD DRAIN THE LAST OF THEIR LIGHT.
WHOA, HANG ON A SEC. JUST WHEN I'M SETTLING IN HERE, WE HAVE TO LEAVE?
GARDNER'S GOT A POINT. SOUNDS LIKE IT COULD BE A ONE-WAY TRIP.
WHY NOT LET ATROCITUS JUST USE UP HIS RING?
BECAUSE WE ARE STILL GREEN LANTERNS.
AND OUR OATH REMAINS THE SAME.
SO UNLESS YOU TWO WANT TO DEAL WITH ME INSTEAD OF ATROCITUS...
"...PACK YOUR BAGS."

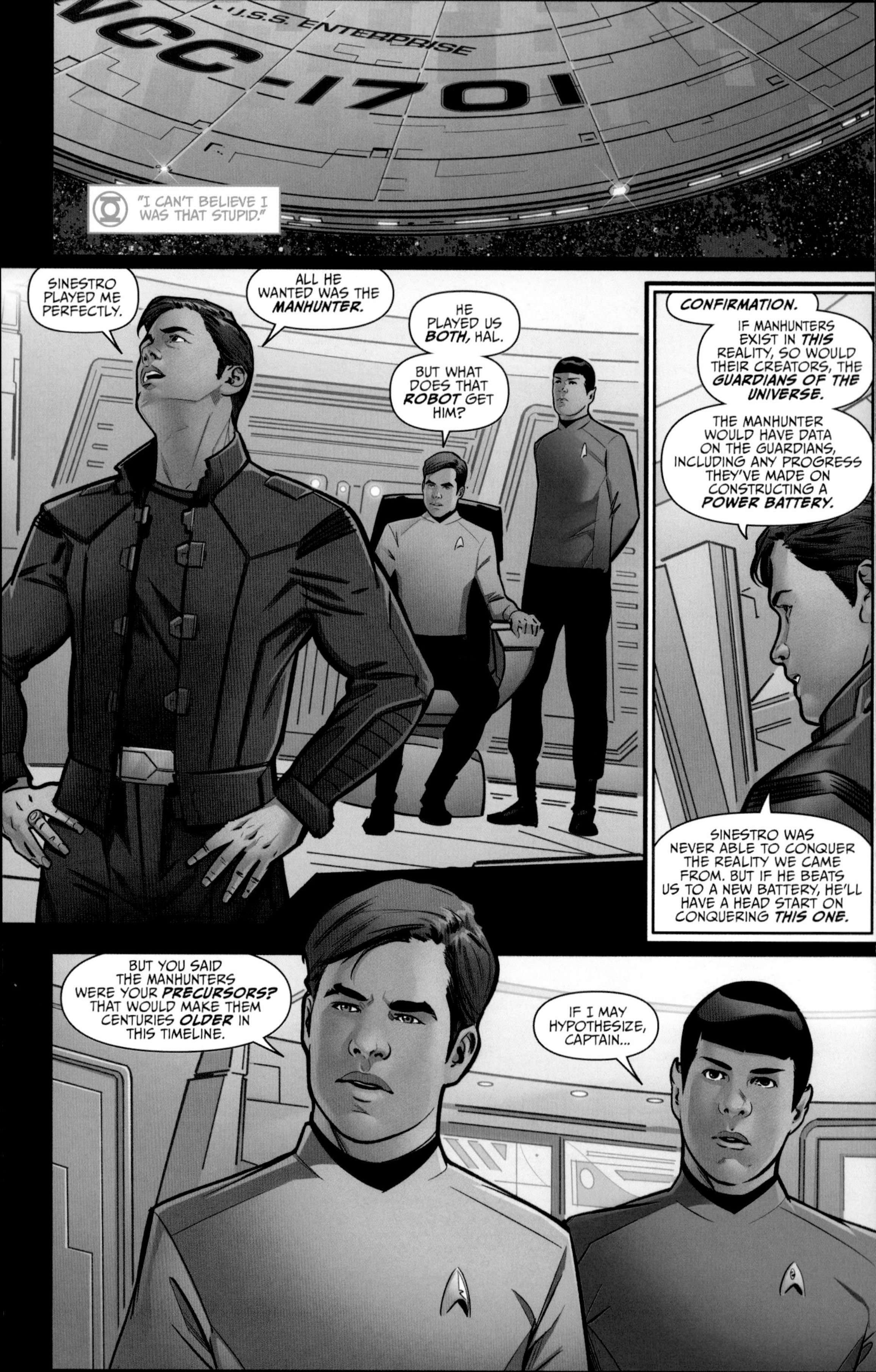
U.S.S. ENTERPRISE
NCC-1701
"I CAN'T BELIEVE I WAS THAT STUPID."
SINESTRO PLAYED ME PERFECTLY.
ALL HE WANTED WAS THE MANHUNTER.
HE PLAYED US BOTH, HAL.
BUT WHAT DOES THAT ROBOT GET HIM?
CONFIRMATION.
IF MANHUNTERS EXIST IN THIS REALITY, SO WOULD THEIR CREATORS, THE GUARDIANS OF THE UNIVERSE.
THE MANHUNTER WOULD HAVE DATA ON THE GUARDIANS, INCLUDING ANY PROGRESS THEY'VE MADE ON CONSTRUCTING A POWER BATTERY.
SINESTRO WAS NEVER ABLE TO CONQUER THE REALITY WE CAME FROM. BUT IF HE BEATS US TO A NEW BATTERY, HE'LL HAVE A HEAD START ON CONQUERING THIS ONE.
BUT YOU SAID THE MANHUNTERS WERE YOUR PRECURSORS? THAT WOULD MAKE THEM CENTURIES OLDER IN THIS TIMELINE.
IF I MAY HYPOTHESIZE, CAPTAIN...

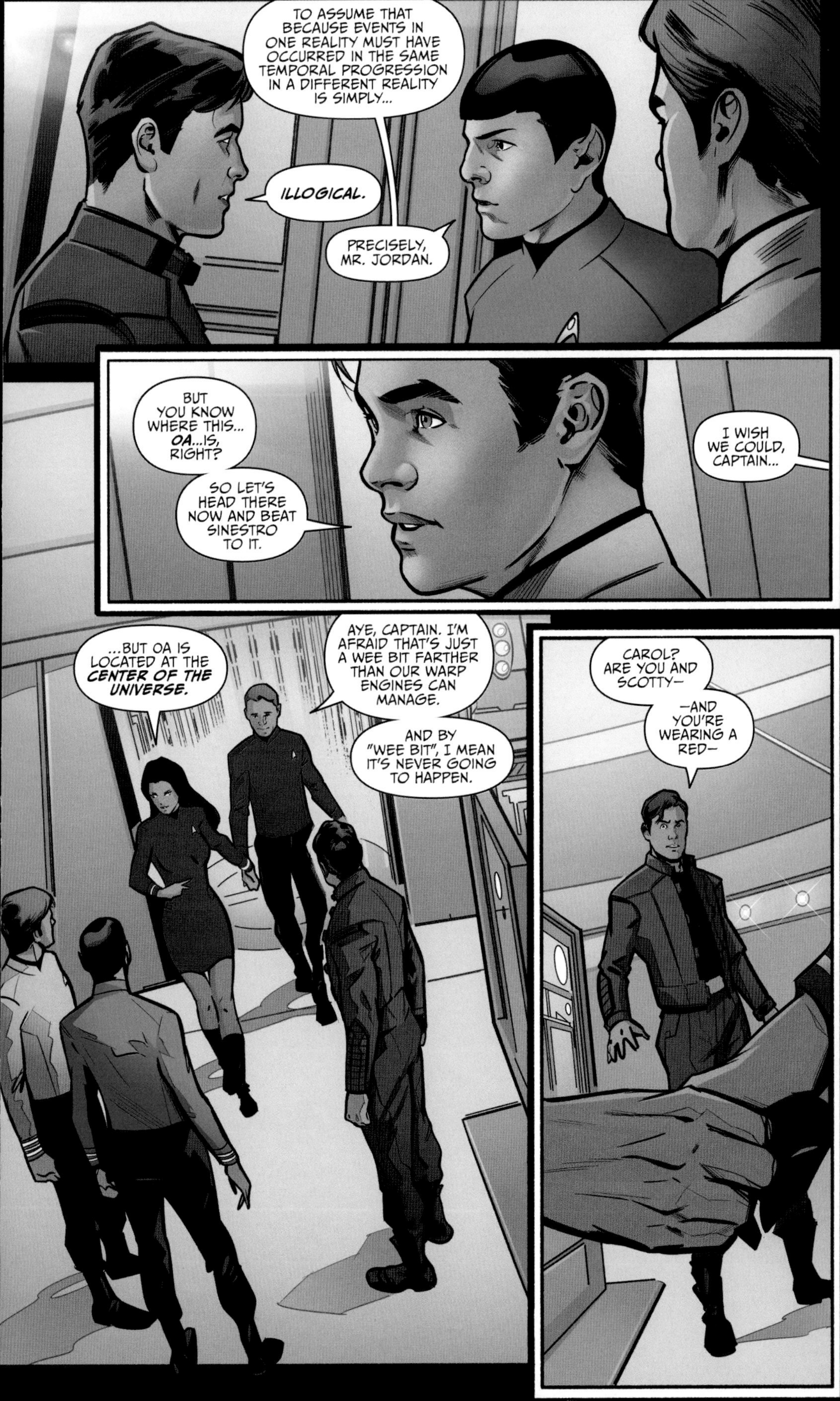
TO ASSUME THAT BECAUSE EVENTS IN ONE REALITY MUST HAVE OCCURRED IN THE SAME TEMPORAL PROGRESSION IN A DIFFERENT REALITY IS SIMPLY...
ILLOGICAL.
PRECISELY, MR. JORDAN.
BUT YOU KNOW WHERE THIS... OA...IS, RIGHT?
SO LET'S HEAD THERE NOW AND BEAT SINESTRO TO IT.
I WISH WE COULD, CAPTAIN...
...BUT OA IS LOCATED AT THE CENTER OF THE UNIVERSE.
AYE, CAPTAIN. I'M AFRAID THAT'S JUST A WEE BIT FARTHER THAN OUR WARP ENGINES CAN MANAGE.
AND BY "WEE BIT", I MEAN IT'S NEVER GOING TO HAPPEN.
CAROL? ARE YOU AND SCOTTY—
—AND YOU'RE WEARING A RED—

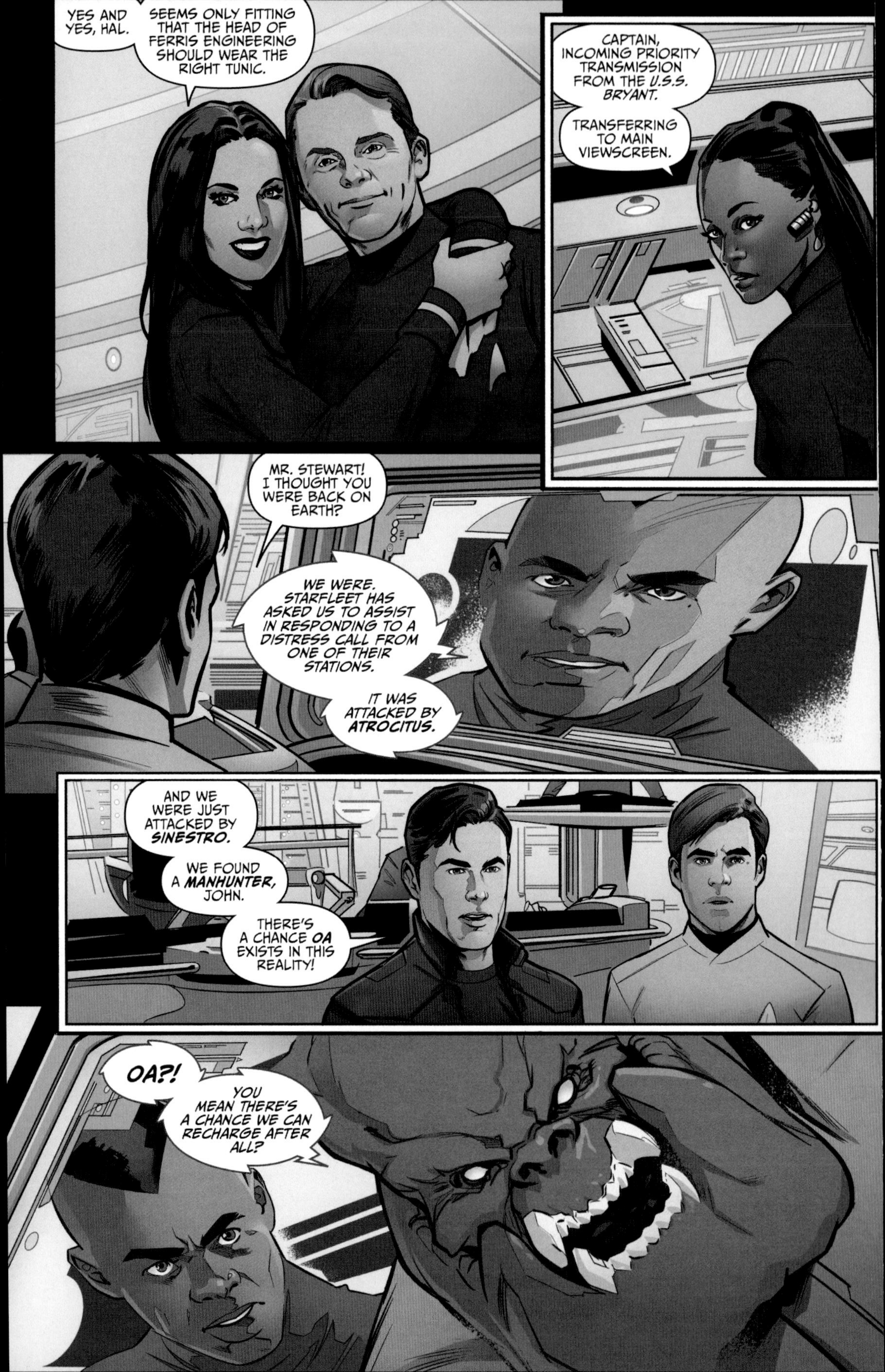
YES AND YES, HAL.
SEEMS ONLY FITTING THAT THE HEAD OF FERRIS ENGINEERING SHOULD WEAR THE RIGHT TUNIC.
CAPTAIN, INCOMING PRIORITY TRANSMISSION FROM THE U.S.S. BRYANT.
TRANSFERRING TO MAIN VIEWSCREEN.
MR. STEWART! I THOUGHT YOU WERE BACK ON EARTH?
WE WERE. STARFLEET HAS ASKED US TO ASSIST IN RESPONDING TO A DISTRESS CALL FROM ONE OF THEIR STATIONS.
IT WAS ATTACKED BY ATROCITUS.
AND WE WERE JUST ATTACKED BY SINESTRO.
WE FOUND A MANHUNTER, JOHN.
THERE'S A CHANCE OA EXISTS IN THIS REALITY!
OA?!
YOU MEAN THERE'S A CHANCE WE CAN RECHARGE AFTER ALL?

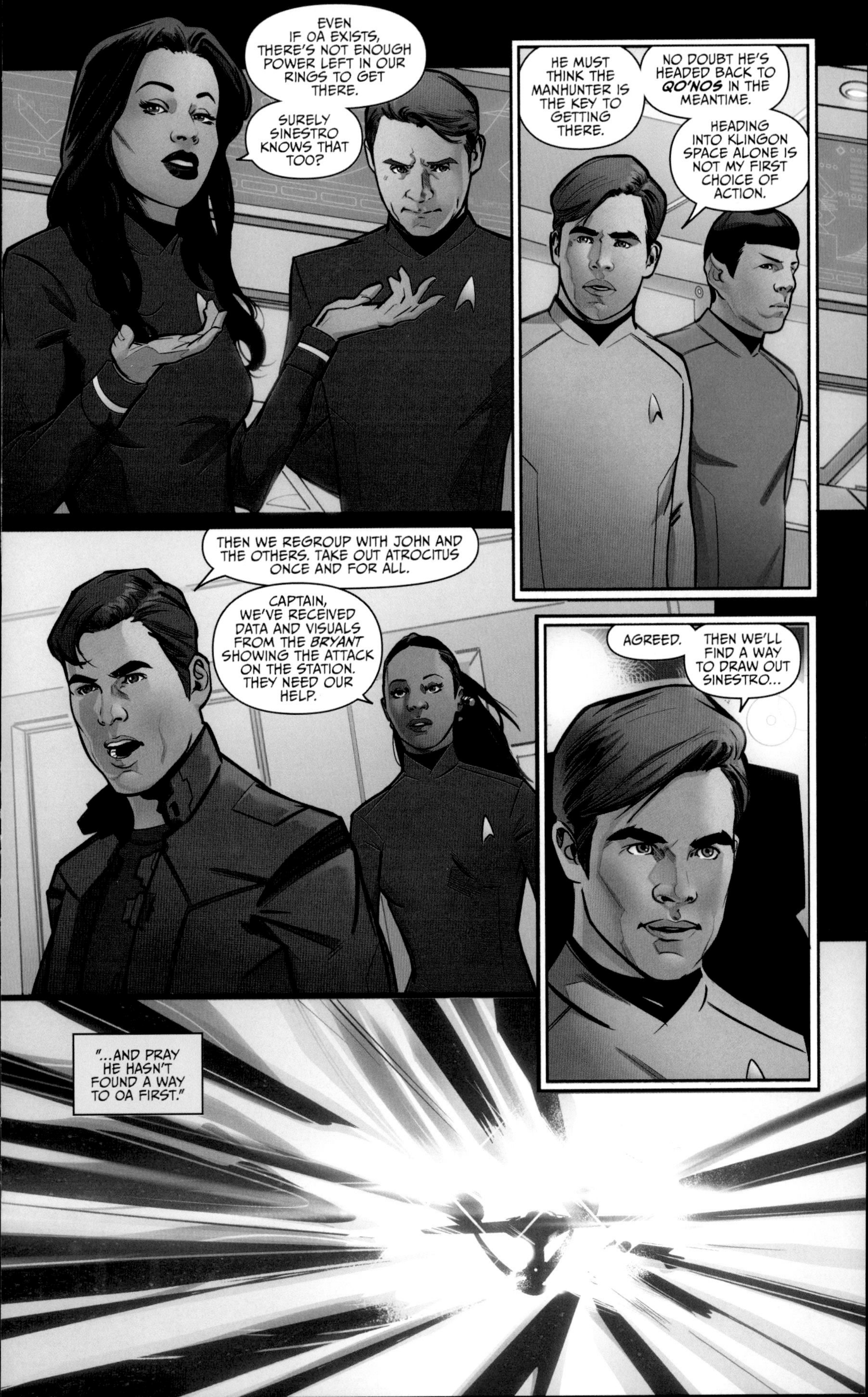
EVEN IF OA EXISTS, THERE'S NOT ENOUGH POWER LEFT IN OUR RINGS TO GET THERE.
SURELY SINESTRO KNOWS THAT TOO?
HE MUST THINK THE MANHUNTER IS THE KEY TO GETTING THERE.
NO DOUBT HE'S HEADED BACK TO *QO'NOS* IN THE MEANTIME.
HEADING INTO KLINGON SPACE ALONE IS NOT MY FIRST CHOICE OF ACTION.
THEN WE REGROUP WITH JOHN AND THE OTHERS. TAKE OUT ATROCITUS ONCE AND FOR ALL.
CAPTAIN, WE'VE RECEIVED DATA AND VISUALS FROM THE *BRYANT* SHOWING THE ATTACK ON THE STATION. THEY NEED OUR HELP.
AGREED.
THEN WE'LL FIND A WAY TO DRAW OUT SINESTRO...
"...AND PRAY HE HASN'T FOUND A WAY TO OA FIRST."

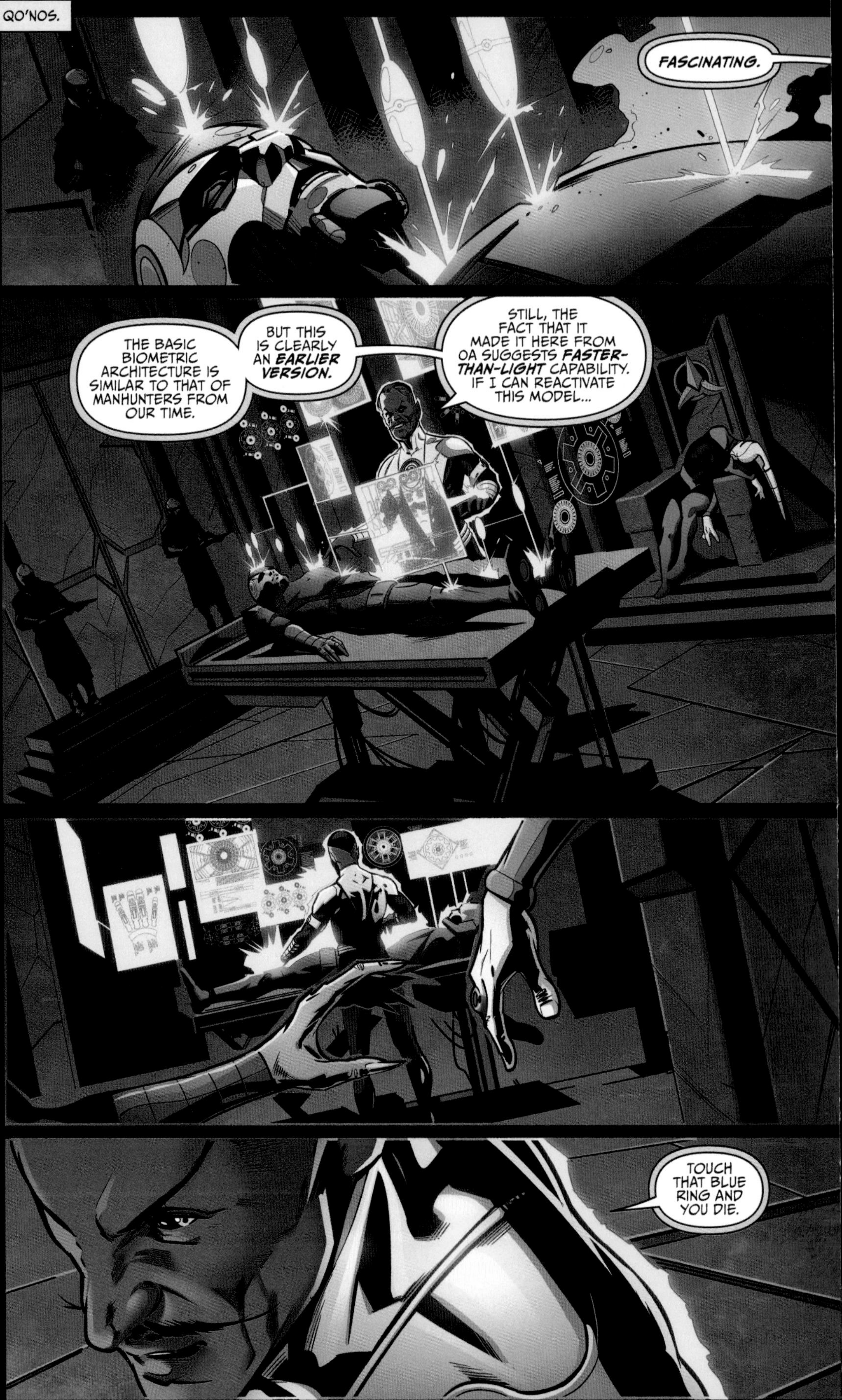
QO'NOS.
FASCINATING.
THE BASIC BIOMETRIC ARCHITECTURE IS SIMILAR TO THAT OF MANHUNTERS FROM OUR TIME.
BUT THIS IS CLEARLY AN ***EARLIER VERSION.***
STILL, THE FACT THAT IT MADE IT HERE FROM OA SUGGESTS ***FASTER-THAN-LIGHT*** CAPABILITY. IF I CAN REACTIVATE THIS MODEL...
TOUCH THAT BLUE RING AND YOU DIE.

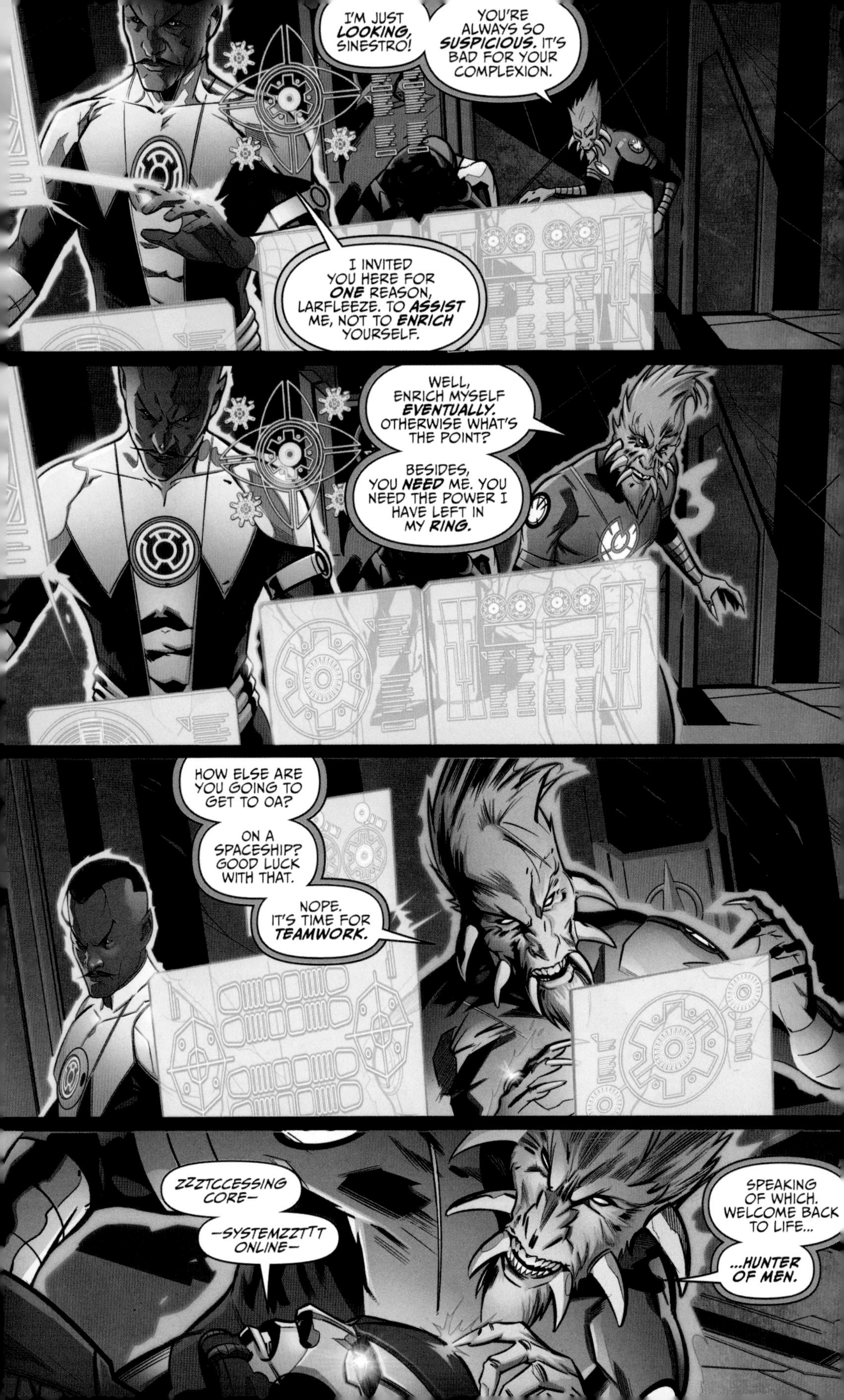
I'M JUST LOOKING, SINESTRO!
YOU'RE ALWAYS SO SUSPICIOUS. IT'S BAD FOR YOUR COMPLEXION.
I INVITED YOU HERE FOR ONE REASON, LARFLEEZE. TO ASSIST ME, NOT TO ENRICH YOURSELF.
WELL, ENRICH MYSELF EVENTUALLY. OTHERWISE WHAT'S THE POINT?
BESIDES, YOU NEED ME. YOU NEED THE POWER I HAVE LEFT IN MY RING.
HOW ELSE ARE YOU GOING TO GET TO OA?
ON A SPACESHIP? GOOD LUCK WITH THAT.
NOPE. IT'S TIME FOR TEAMWORK.
ZZZTCCESSING CORE—
—SYSTEMZZZTTT ONLINE—
SPEAKING OF WHICH. WELCOME BACK TO LIFE...
...HUNTER OF MEN.

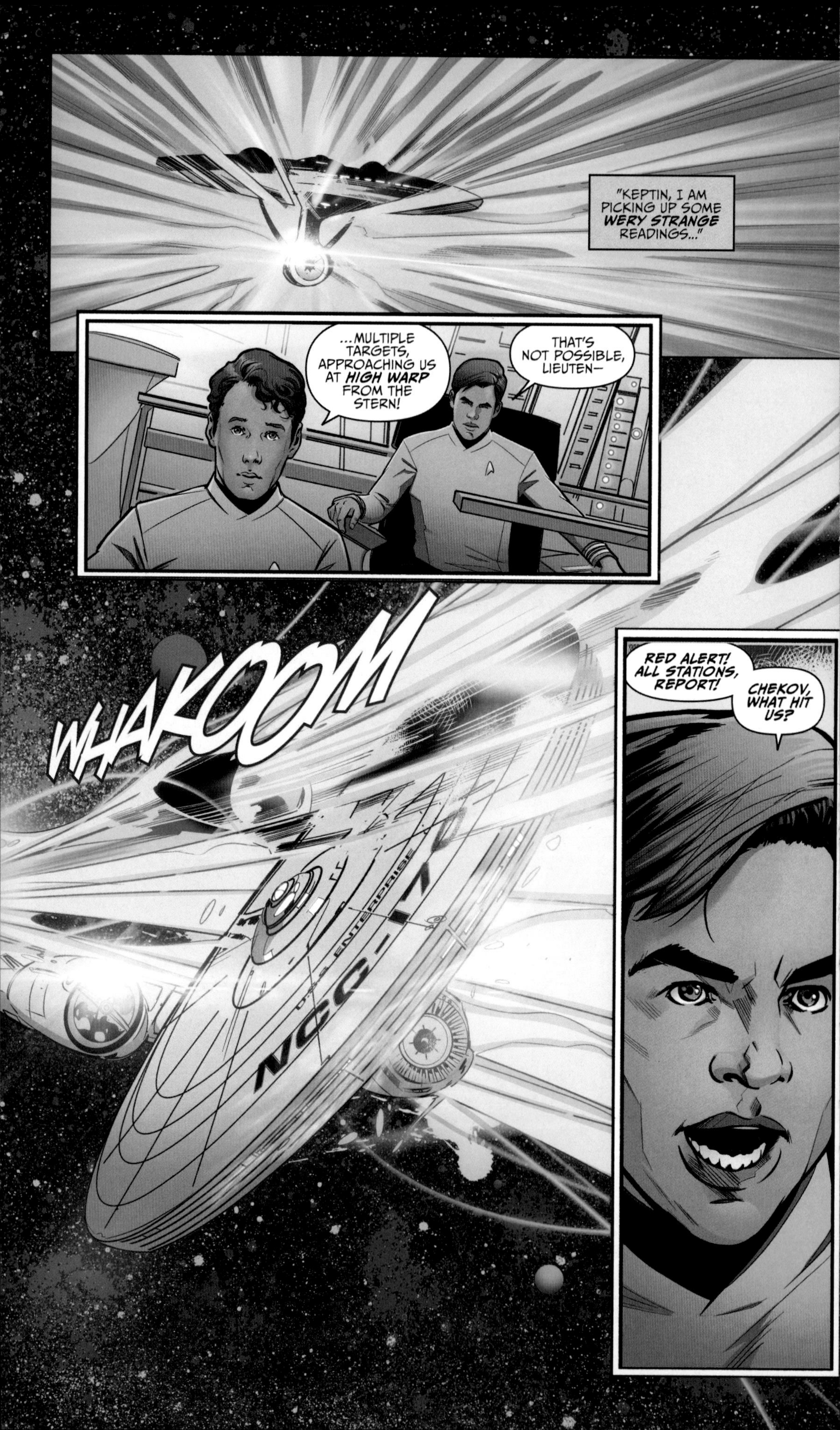
"KEPTIN, I AM PICKING UP SOME WERY STRANGE READINGS..."
...MULTIPLE TARGETS, APPROACHING US AT HIGH WARP FROM THE STERN!
THAT'S NOT POSSIBLE, LIEUTEN—
WHAKOOOM
RED ALERT! ALL STATIONS, REPORT!
CHEKOV, WHAT HIT US?

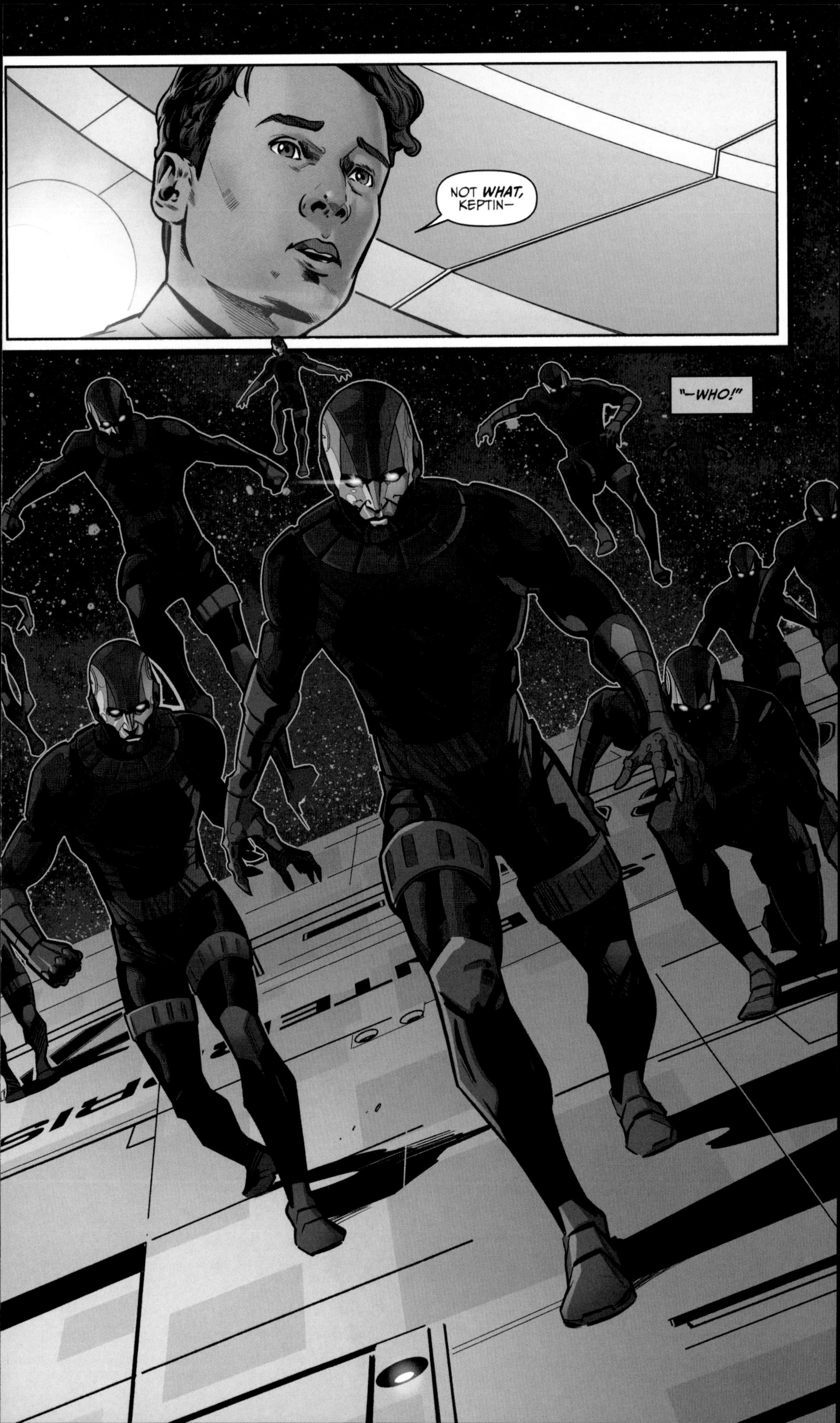
NOT WHAT, KEPTIN—
"—WHO!"

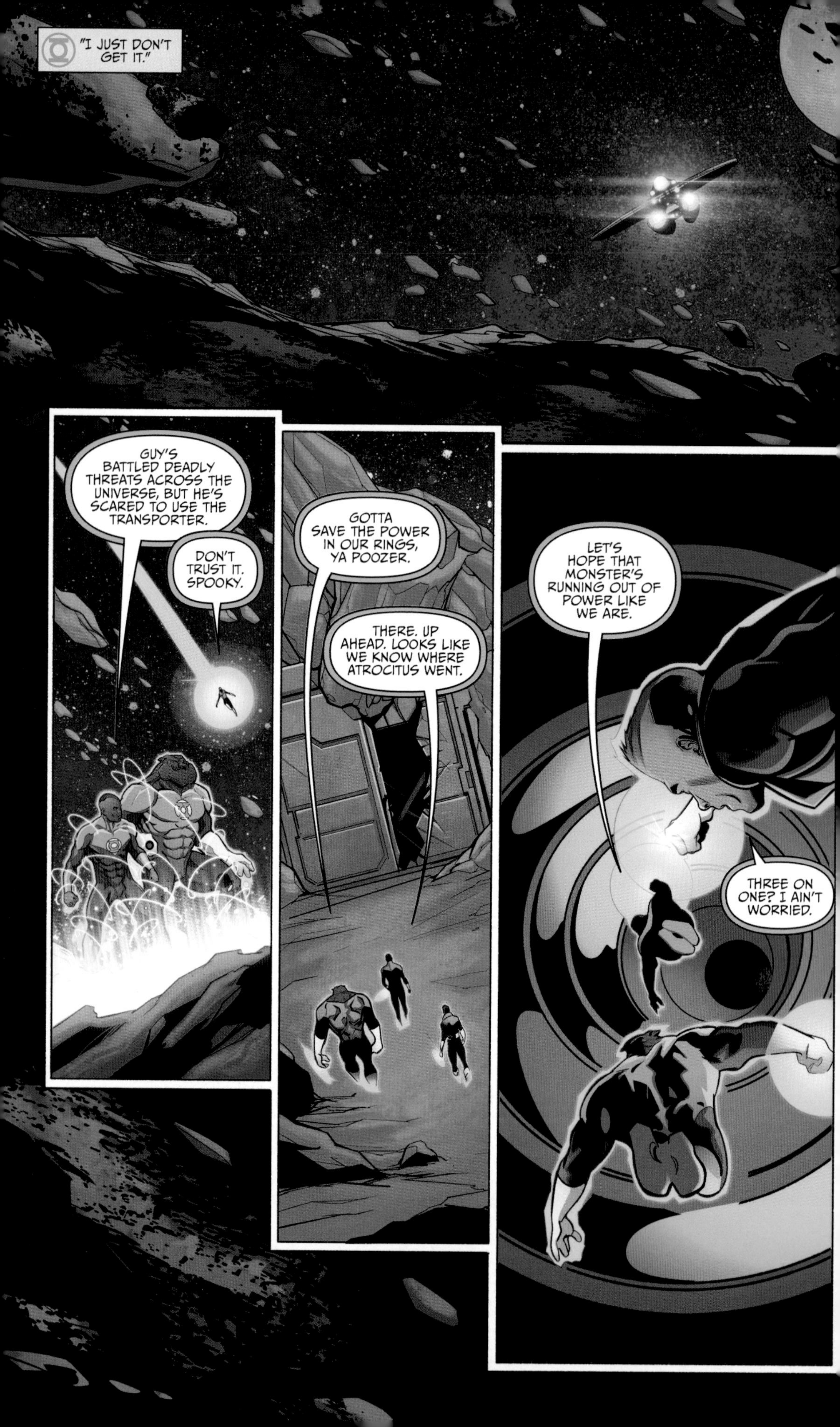
"I JUST DON'T GET IT."
GUY'S BATTLED DEADLY THREATS ACROSS THE UNIVERSE, BUT HE'S SCARED TO USE THE TRANSPORTER.
DON'T TRUST IT. SPOOKY.
GOTTA SAVE THE POWER IN OUR RINGS, YA POOZER.
THERE. UP AHEAD. LOOKS LIKE WE KNOW WHERE ATROCITUS WENT.
LET'S HOPE THAT MONSTER'S RUNNING OUT OF POWER LIKE WE ARE.
THREE ON ONE? I AIN'T WORRIED.

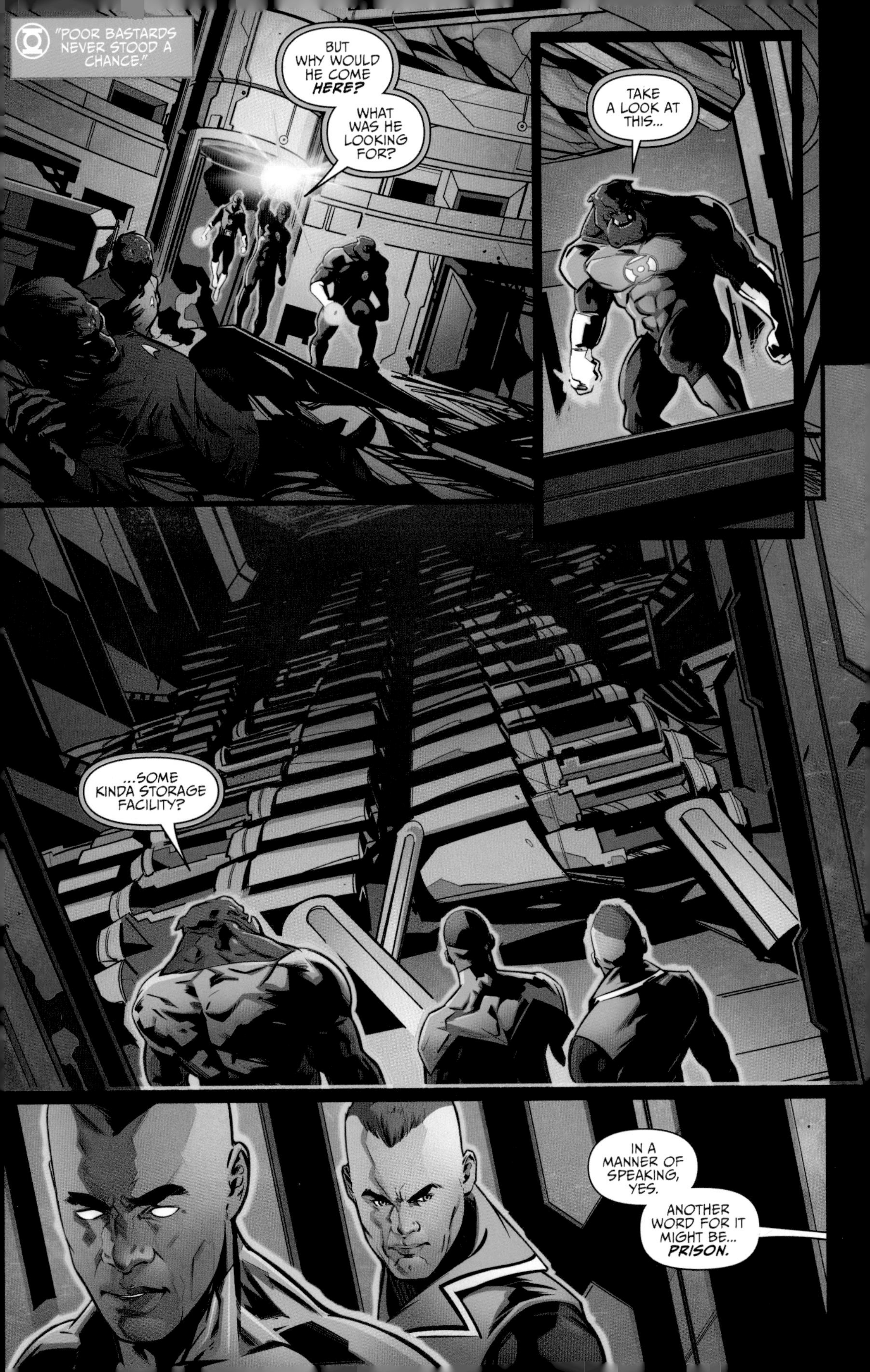
"POOR BASTARDS NEVER STOOD A CHANCE."
BUT WHY WOULD HE COME ***HERE?***
WHAT WAS HE LOOKING FOR?
TAKE A LOOK AT THIS...
...SOME KINDA STORAGE FACILITY?
IN A MANNER OF SPEAKING, YES.
ANOTHER WORD FOR IT MIGHT BE... ***PRISON.***

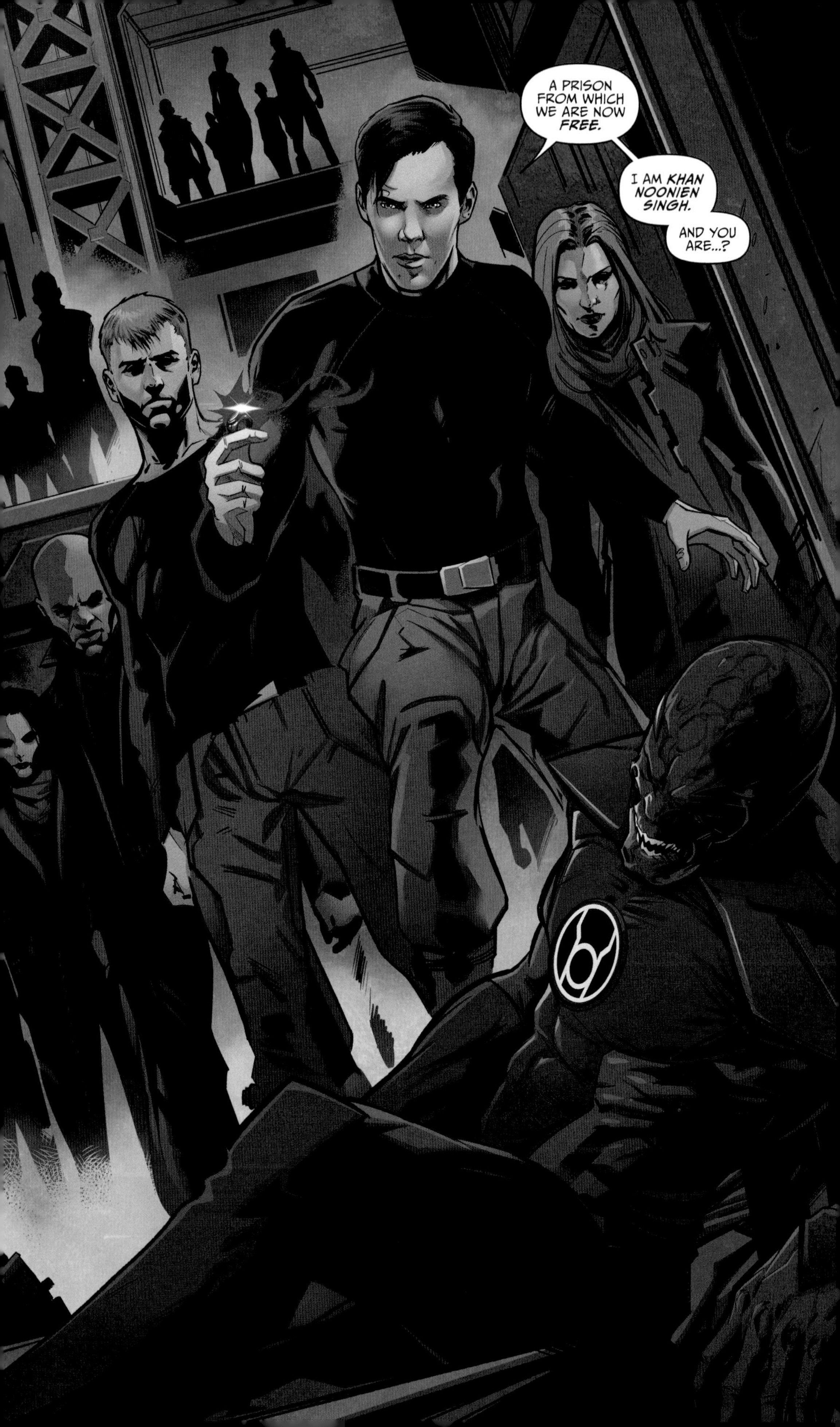
A PRISON FROM WHICH WE ARE NOW FREE.
I AM KHAN NOONIEN SINGH.
AND YOU ARE...?

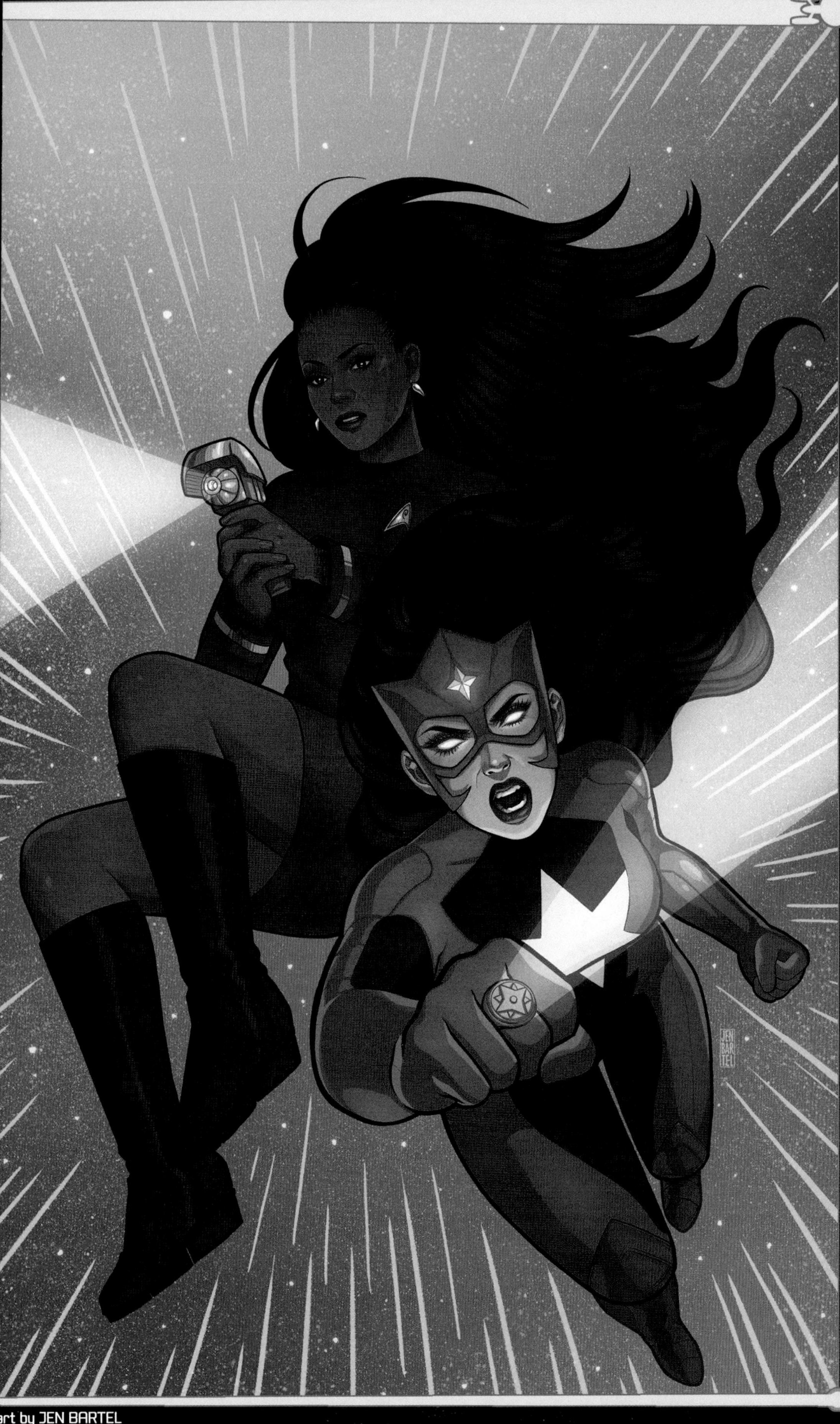
JEN BARTEL
art by JEN BARTEL

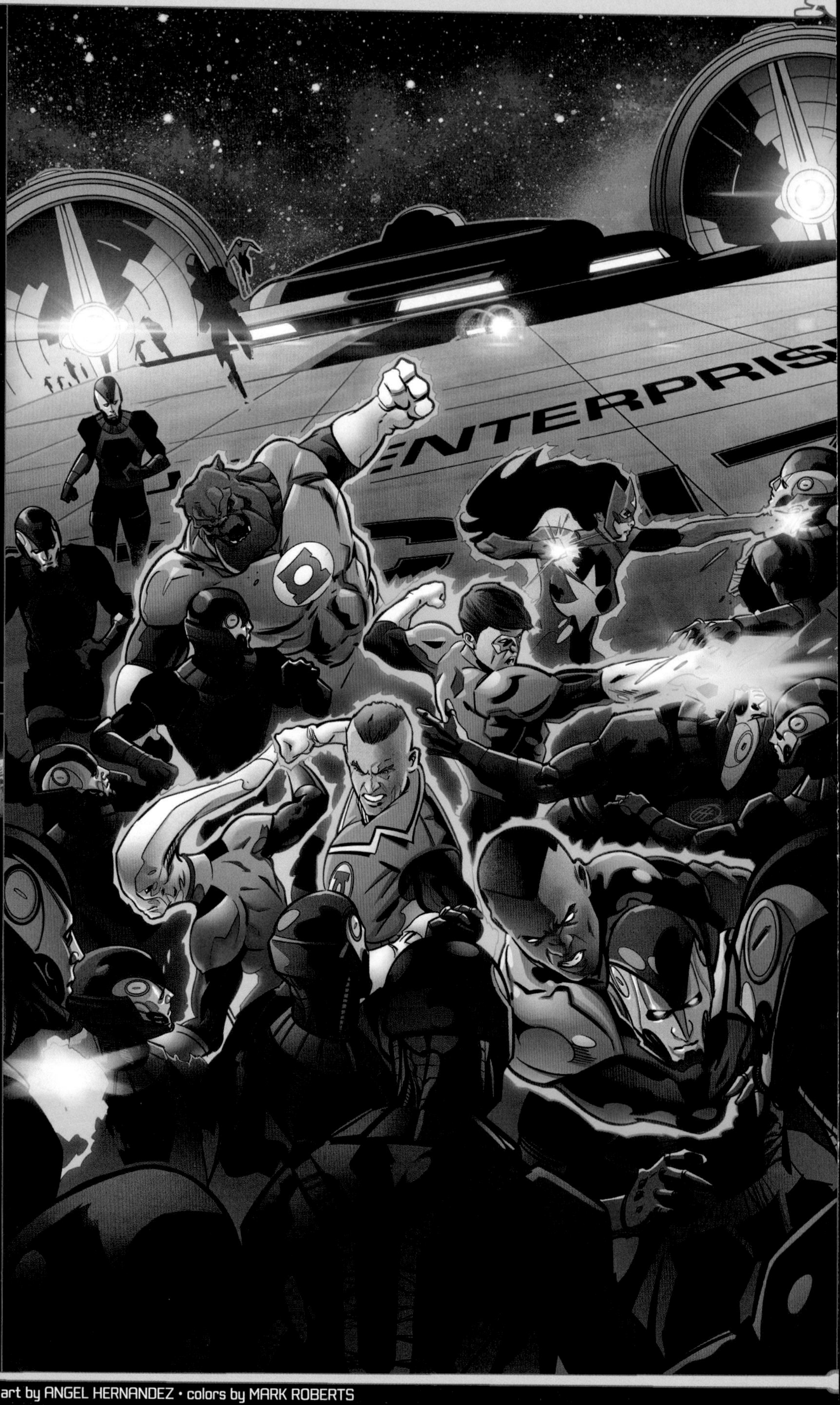
ENTERPRISE

art by ANGEL HERNANDEZ • colors by MARK ROBERTS

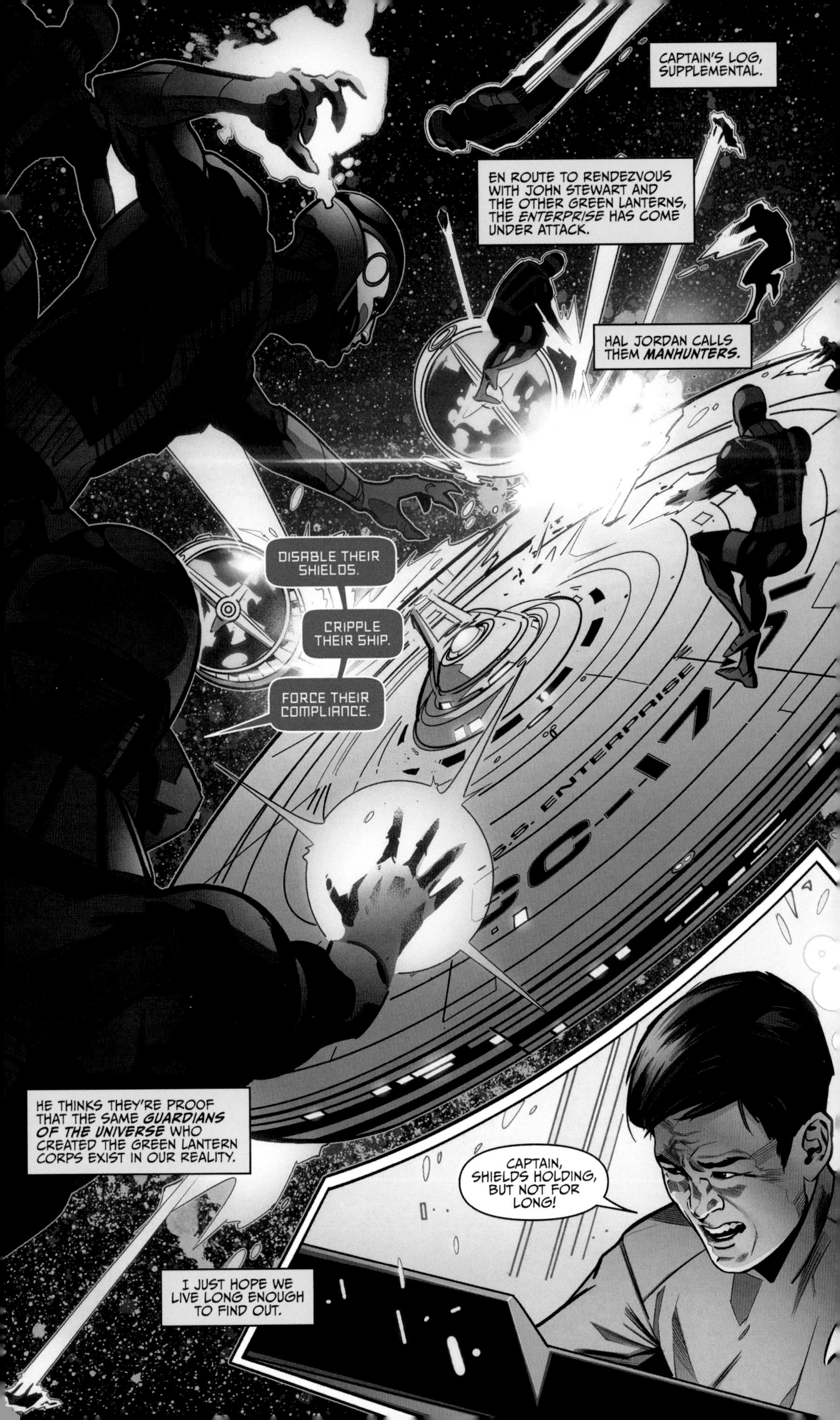

CAPTAIN'S LOG, SUPPLEMENTAL.
EN ROUTE TO RENDEZVOUS WITH JOHN STEWART AND THE OTHER GREEN LANTERNS, THE *ENTERPRISE* HAS COME UNDER ATTACK.
HAL JORDAN CALLS THEM ***MANHUNTERS.***
DISABLE THEIR SHIELDS.
CRIPPLE THEIR SHIP.
FORCE THEIR COMPLIANCE.
U.S.S. ENTERPRISE
NCC-1701
HE THINKS THEY'RE PROOF THAT THE SAME ***GUARDIANS OF THE UNIVERSE*** WHO CREATED THE GREEN LANTERN CORPS EXIST IN OUR REALITY.
CAPTAIN, SHIELDS HOLDING, BUT NOT FOR LONG!
I JUST HOPE WE LIVE LONG ENOUGH TO FIND OUT.

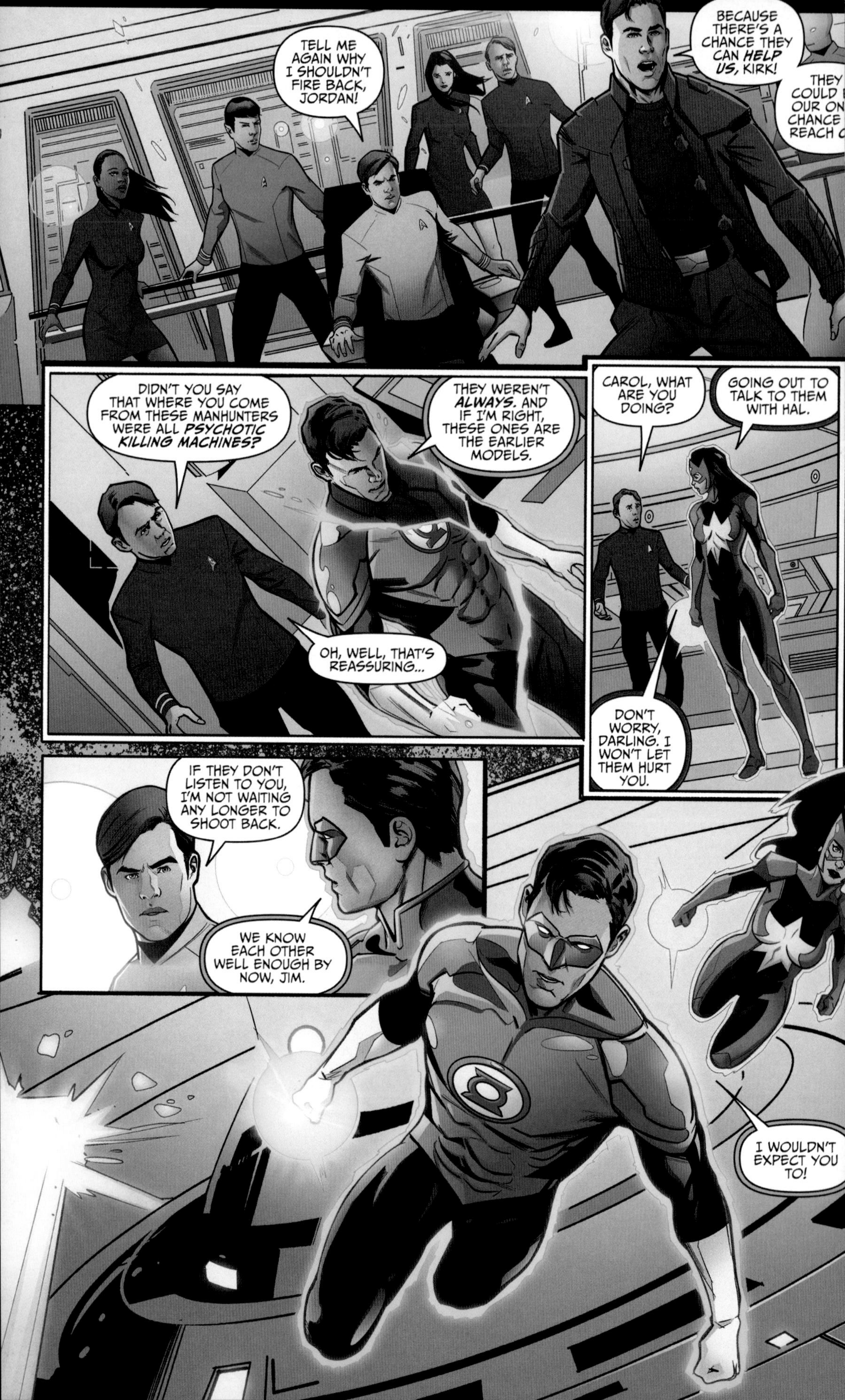
TELL ME AGAIN WHY I SHOULDN'T FIRE BACK, JORDAN!
BECAUSE THERE'S A CHANCE THEY CAN *HELP US*, KIRK!
THEY COULD OUR ON CHANCE REACH
DIDN'T YOU SAY THAT WHERE YOU COME FROM THESE MANHUNTERS WERE ALL *PSYCHOTIC KILLING MACHINES?*
THEY WEREN'T *ALWAYS.* AND IF I'M RIGHT, THESE ONES ARE THE EARLIER MODELS.
OH, WELL, THAT'S REASSURING...
CAROL, WHAT ARE YOU DOING?
GOING OUT TO TALK TO THEM WITH HAL.
DON'T WORRY, DARLING. I WON'T LET THEM HURT YOU.
IF THEY DON'T LISTEN TO YOU, I'M NOT WAITING ANY LONGER TO SHOOT BACK.
WE KNOW EACH OTHER WELL ENOUGH BY NOW, JIM.
I WOULDN'T EXPECT YOU TO!

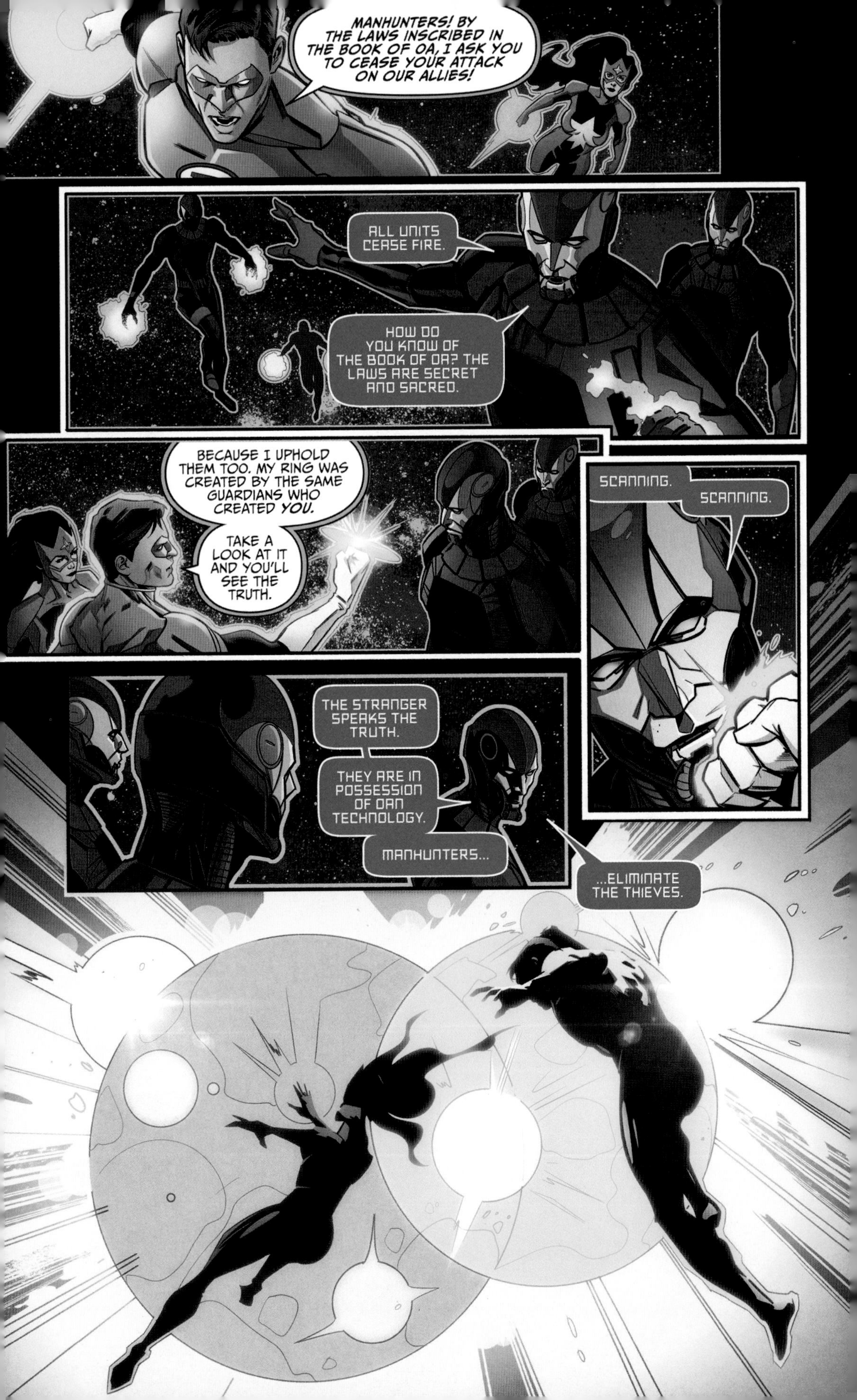
MANHUNTERS! BY THE LAWS INSCRIBED IN THE BOOK OF OA, I ASK YOU TO CEASE YOUR ATTACK ON OUR ALLIES!
ALL UNITS CEASE FIRE.
HOW DO YOU KNOW OF THE BOOK OF OA? THE LAWS ARE SECRET AND SACRED.
BECAUSE I UPHOLD THEM TOO. MY RING WAS CREATED BY THE SAME GUARDIANS WHO CREATED *YOU.*
TAKE A LOOK AT IT AND YOU'LL SEE THE TRUTH.
SCANNING.
SCANNING.
THE STRANGER SPEAKS THE TRUTH.
THEY ARE IN POSSESSION OF OAN TECHNOLOGY.
MANHUNTERS...
...ELIMINATE THE THIEVES.

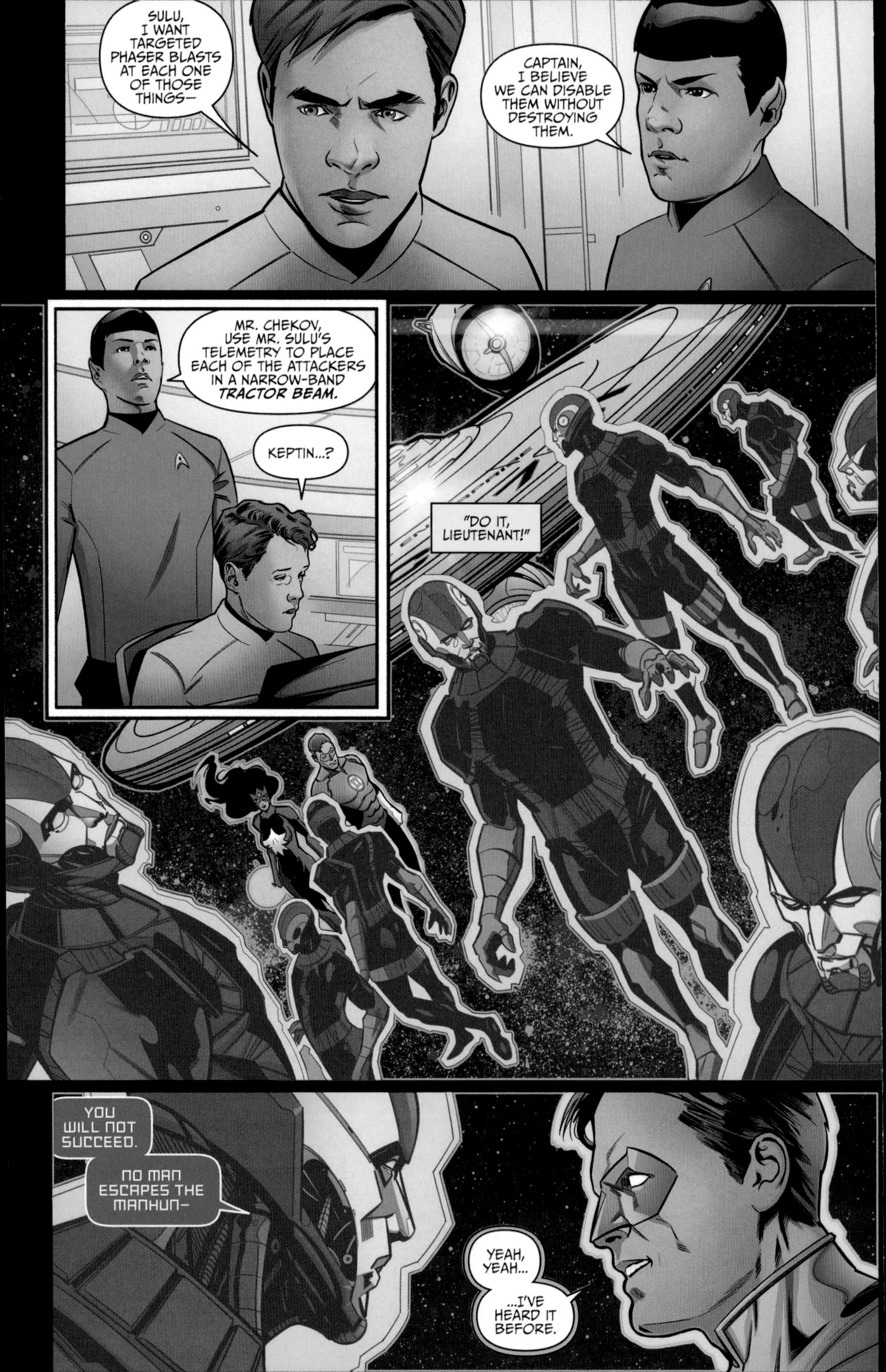
SULU, I WANT TARGETED PHASER BLASTS AT EACH ONE OF THOSE THINGS—
CAPTAIN, I BELIEVE WE CAN DISABLE THEM WITHOUT DESTROYING THEM.
MR. CHEKOV, USE MR. SULU'S TELEMETRY TO PLACE EACH OF THE ATTACKERS IN A NARROW-BAND TRACTOR BEAM.
KEPTIN...?
"DO IT, LIEUTENANT!"
YOU WILL NOT SUCCEED.
NO MAN ESCAPES THE MANHUN—
YEAH, YEAH...
...I'VE HEARD IT BEFORE.

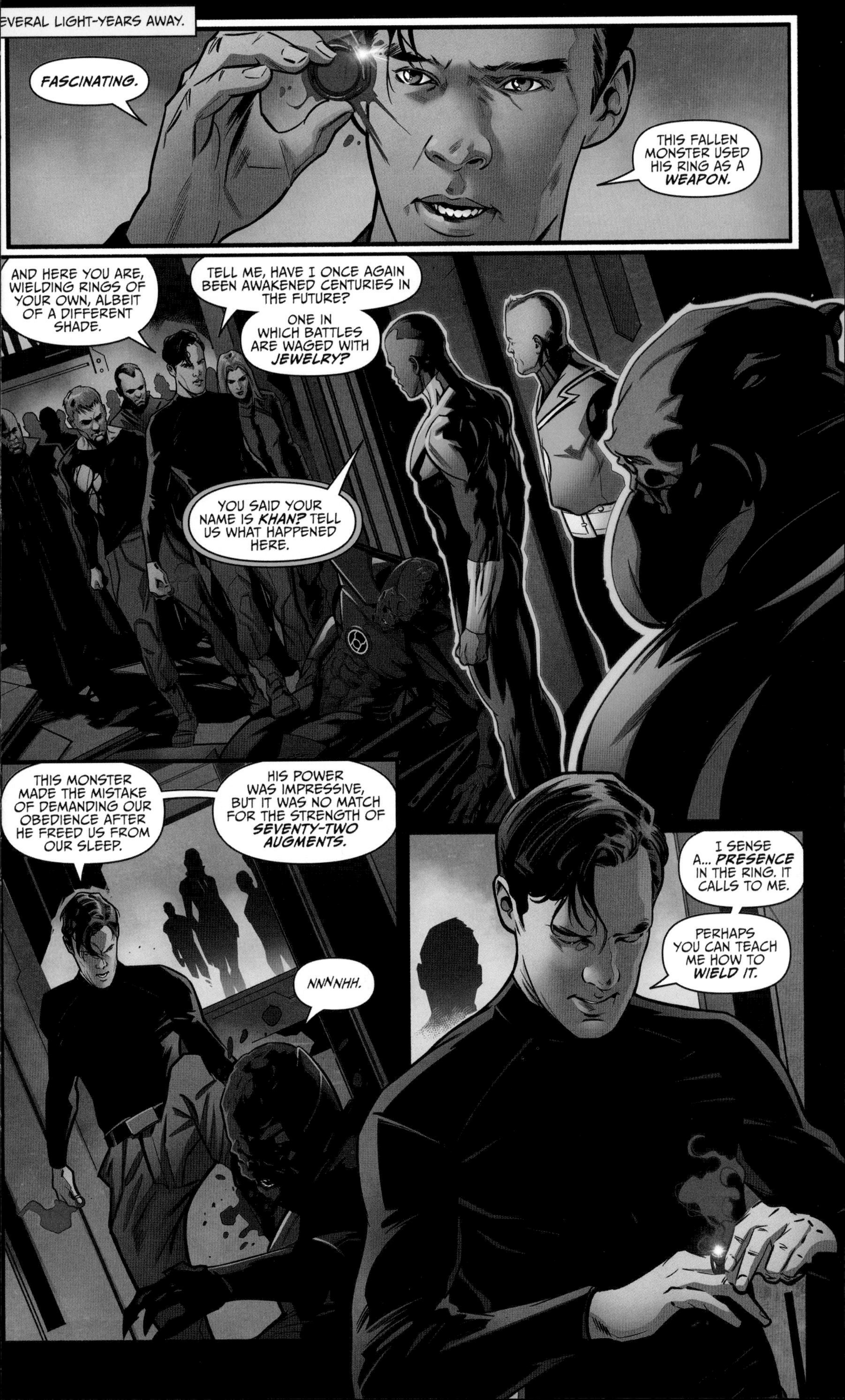
EVERAL LIGHT-YEARS AWAY.
FASCINATING.
THIS FALLEN MONSTER USED HIS RING AS A WEAPON.
AND HERE YOU ARE, WIELDING RINGS OF YOUR OWN, ALBEIT OF A DIFFERENT SHADE.
TELL ME, HAVE I ONCE AGAIN BEEN AWAKENED CENTURIES IN THE FUTURE?
ONE IN WHICH BATTLES ARE WAGED WITH JEWELRY?
YOU SAID YOUR NAME IS KHAN? TELL US WHAT HAPPENED HERE.
THIS MONSTER MADE THE MISTAKE OF DEMANDING OUR OBEDIENCE AFTER HE FREED US FROM OUR SLEEP.
HIS POWER WAS IMPRESSIVE, BUT IT WAS NO MATCH FOR THE STRENGTH OF SEVENTY-TWO AUGMENTS.
NNNNHH.
I SENSE A... PRESENCE IN THE RING. IT CALLS TO ME.
PERHAPS YOU CAN TEACH ME HOW TO WIELD IT.

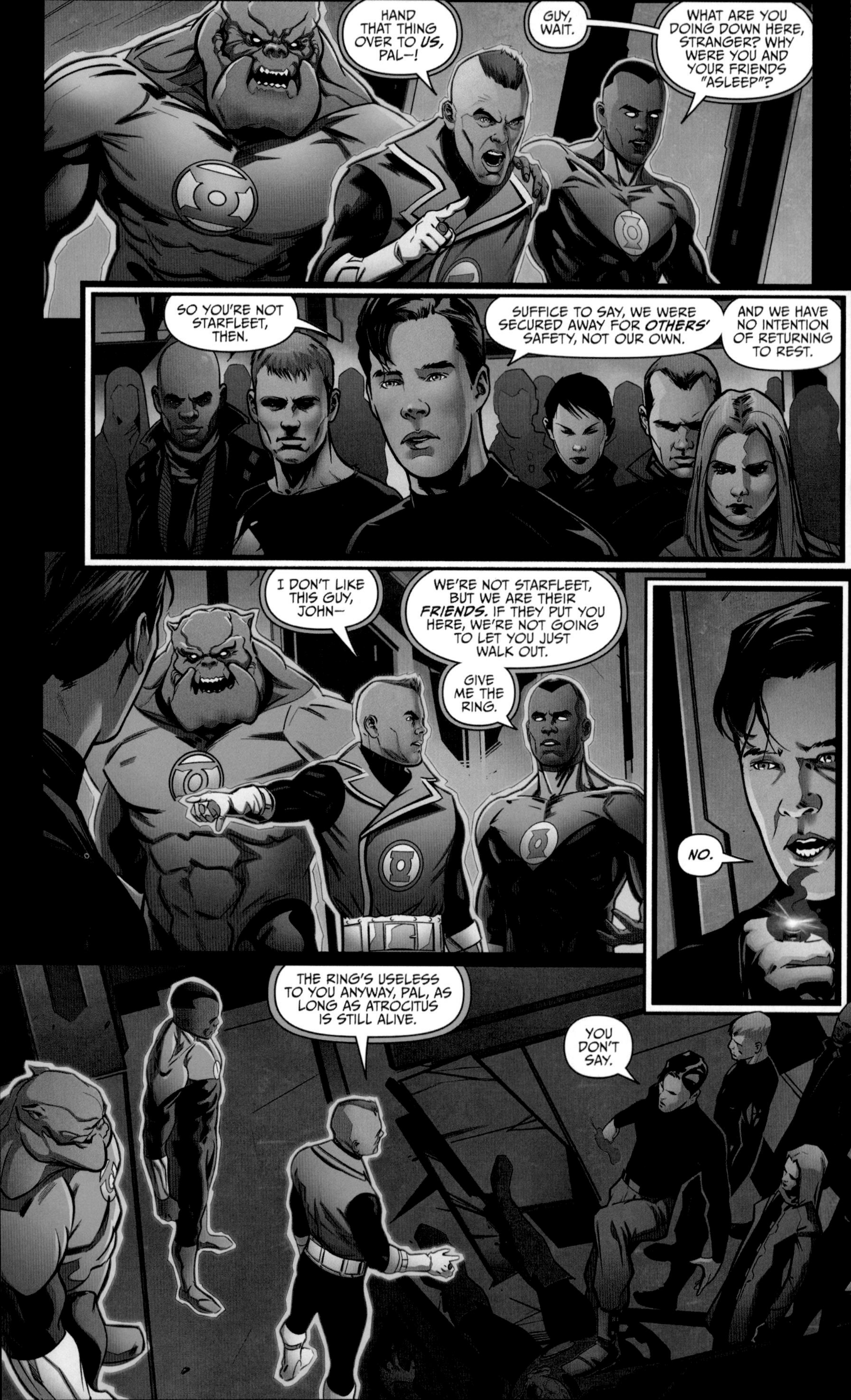
HAND THAT THING OVER TO *US*, PAL--!
GUY, WAIT.
WHAT ARE YOU DOING DOWN HERE, STRANGER? WHY WERE YOU AND YOUR FRIENDS "ASLEEP"?
SO YOU'RE NOT STARFLEET, THEN.
SUFFICE TO SAY, WE WERE SECURED AWAY FOR *OTHERS'* SAFETY, NOT OUR OWN.
AND WE HAVE NO INTENTION OF RETURNING TO REST.
I DON'T LIKE THIS GUY, JOHN--
WE'RE NOT STARFLEET, BUT WE ARE THEIR *FRIENDS.* IF THEY PUT YOU HERE, WE'RE NOT GOING TO LET YOU JUST WALK OUT.
GIVE ME THE RING.
NO.
THE RING'S USELESS TO YOU ANYWAY, PAL, AS LONG AS ATROCITUS IS STILL ALIVE.
YOU DON'T SAY.

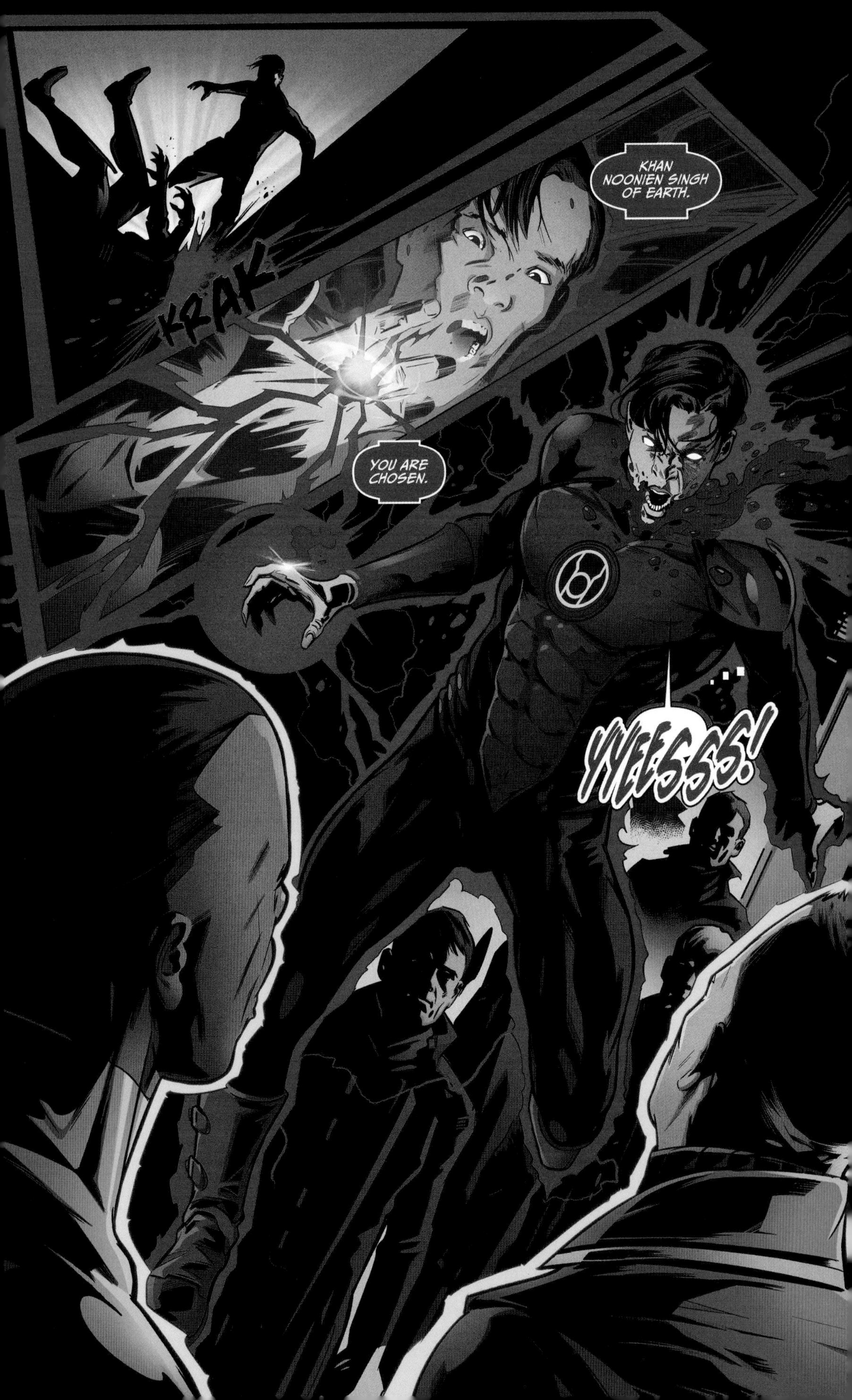
KRAK
KHAN NOONIEN SINGH OF EARTH.
YOU ARE CHOSEN.
YYEESSS!

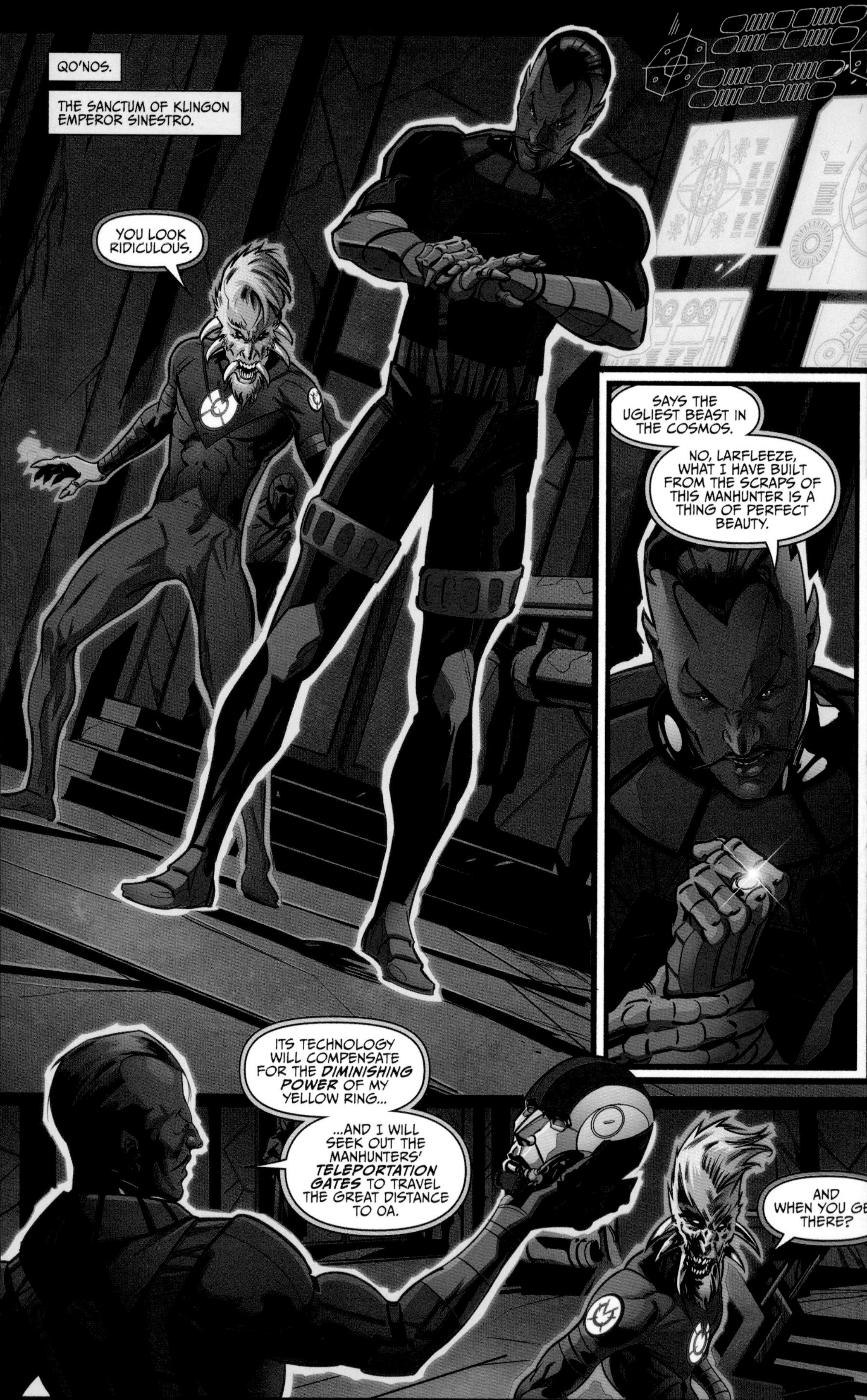
QO'NOS.
THE SANCTUM OF KLINGON EMPEROR SINESTRO.
YOU LOOK RIDICULOUS.
SAYS THE UGLIEST BEAST IN THE COSMOS.
NO, LARFLEEZE, WHAT I HAVE BUILT FROM THE SCRAPS OF THIS MANHUNTER IS A THING OF PERFECT BEAUTY.
ITS TECHNOLOGY WILL COMPENSATE FOR THE DIMINISHING POWER OF MY YELLOW RING...
...AND I WILL SEEK OUT THE MANHUNTERS' TELEPORTATION GATES TO TRAVEL THE GREAT DISTANCE TO OA.
AND WHEN YOU GE THERE?

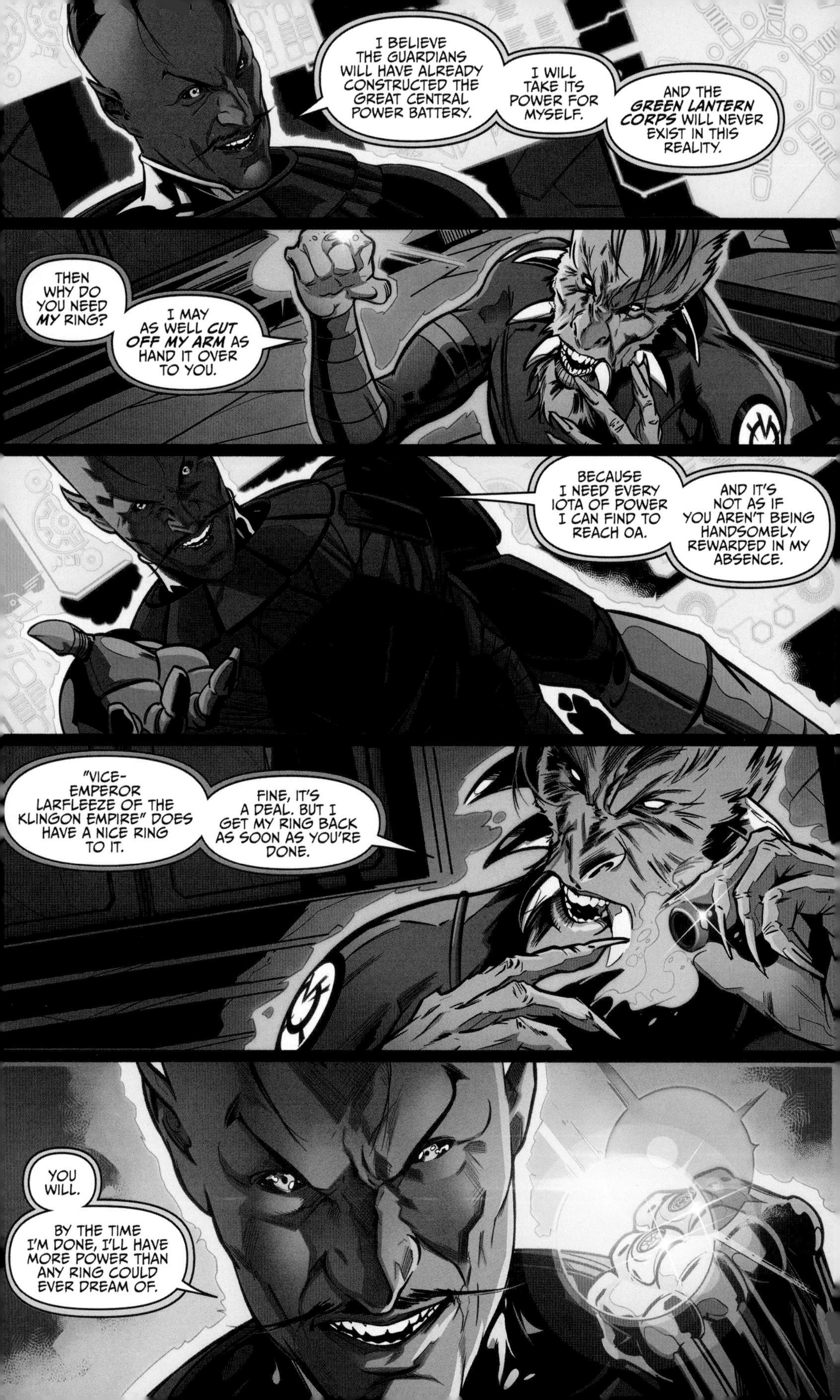
I BELIEVE THE GUARDIANS WILL HAVE ALREADY CONSTRUCTED THE GREAT CENTRAL POWER BATTERY.
I WILL TAKE ITS POWER FOR MYSELF.
AND THE *GREEN LANTERN CORPS* WILL NEVER EXIST IN THIS REALITY.
THEN WHY DO YOU NEED *MY* RING?
I MAY AS WELL *CUT OFF MY ARM* AS HAND IT OVER TO YOU.
BECAUSE I NEED EVERY IOTA OF POWER I CAN FIND TO REACH OA.
AND IT'S NOT AS IF YOU AREN'T BEING HANDSOMELY REWARDED IN MY ABSENCE.
"VICE-EMPEROR LARFLEEZE OF THE KLINGON EMPIRE" DOES HAVE A NICE RING TO IT.
FINE, IT'S A DEAL. BUT I GET MY RING BACK AS SOON AS YOU'RE DONE.
YOU WILL.
BY THE TIME I'M DONE, I'LL HAVE MORE POWER THAN ANY RING COULD EVER DREAM OF.

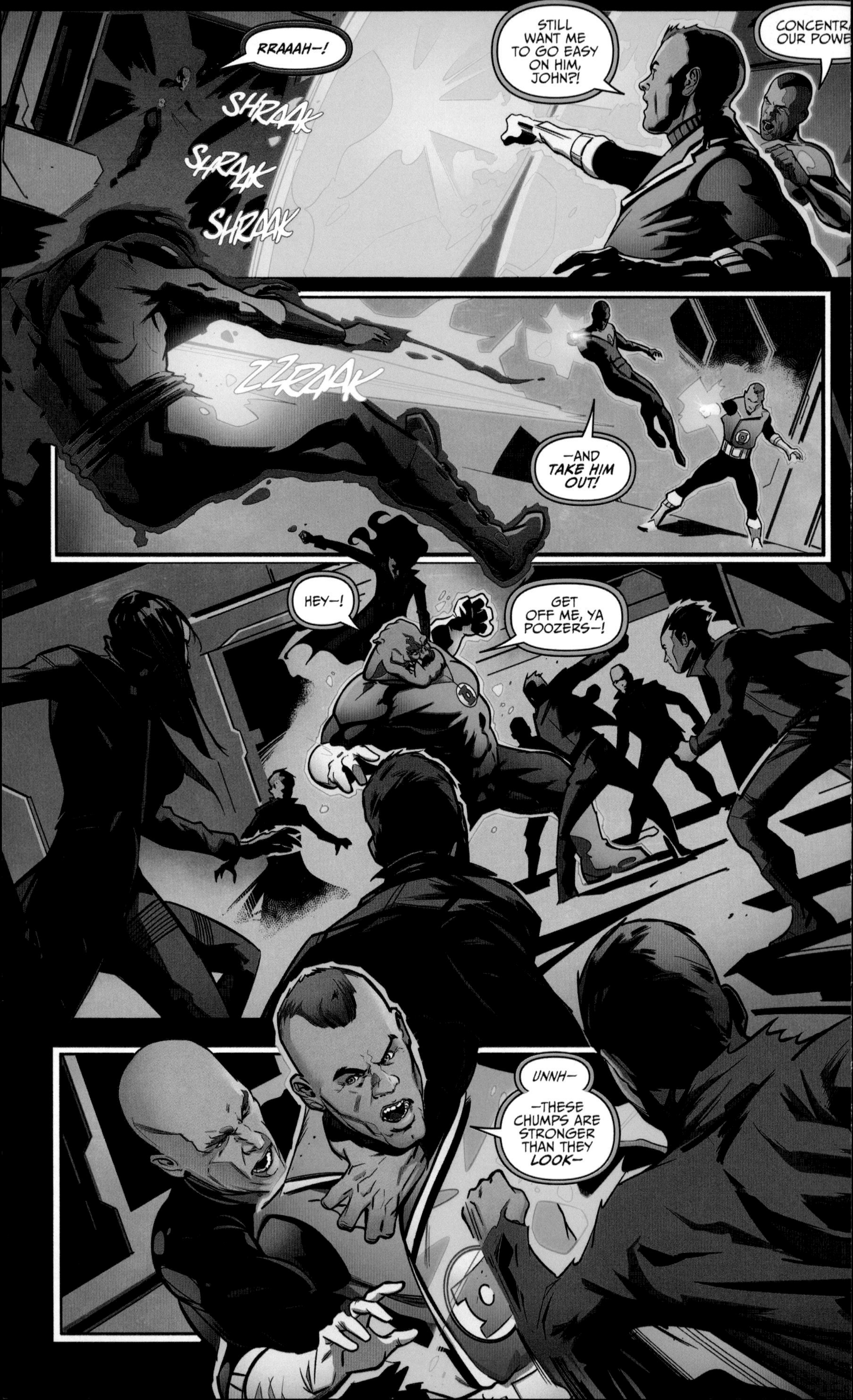

RRAAAH–!
SHRAAK
SHRAAK
SHRAAK
STILL WANT ME TO GO EASY ON HIM, JOHN?!
CONCENTRA OUR POWE
ZZRAAK
–AND TAKE HIM OUT!
HEY–!
GET OFF ME, YA POOZERS–!
UNNH–
–THESE CHUMPS ARE STRONGER THAN THEY LOOK–

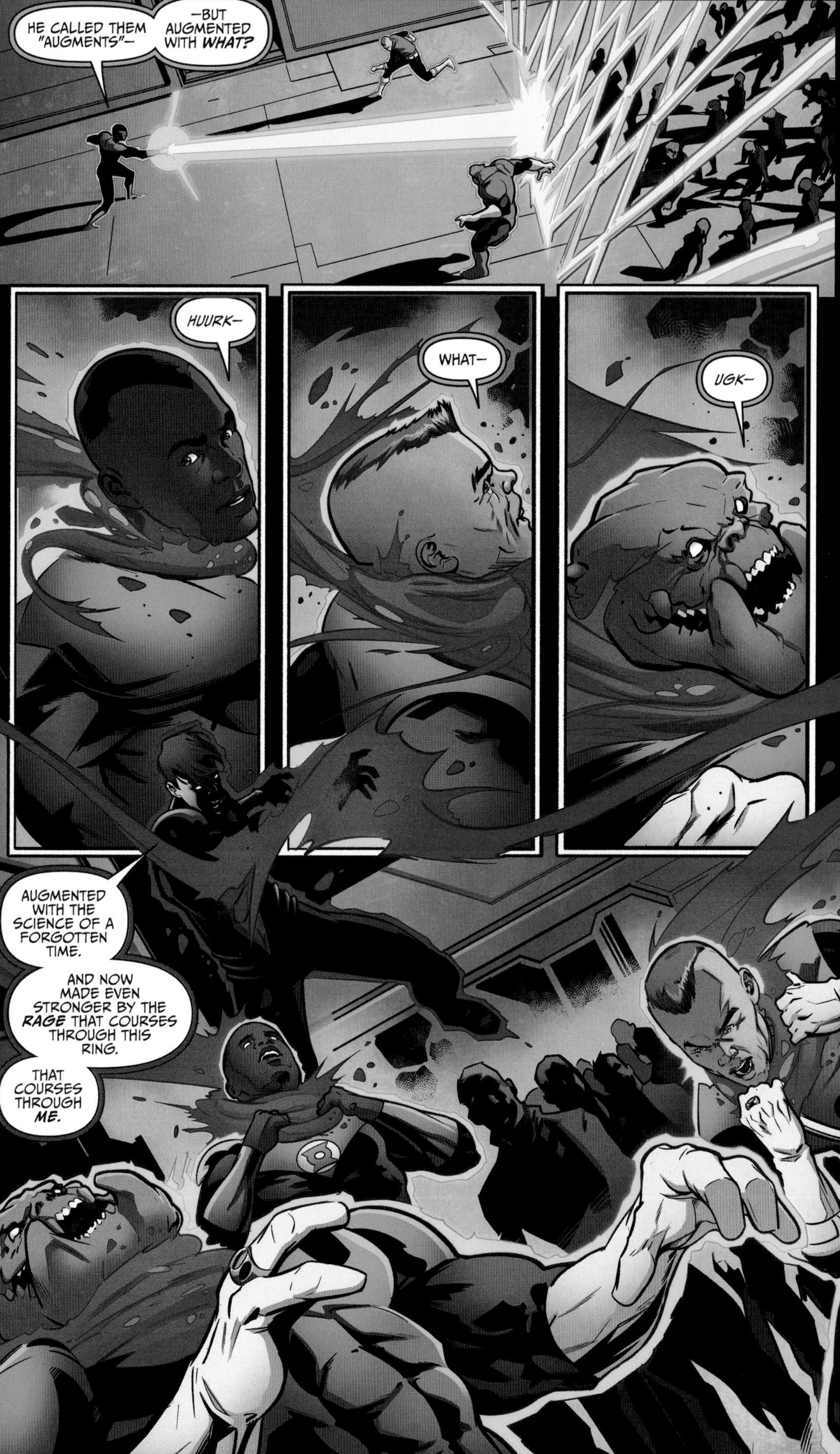

HE CALLED THEM "AUGMENTS"—
—BUT AUGMENTED WITH *WHAT?*
HUURK—
WHAT—
UGK—
AUGMENTED WITH THE SCIENCE OF A FORGOTTEN TIME.
AND NOW MADE EVEN STRONGER BY THE *RAGE* THAT COURSES THROUGH THIS RING.
THAT COURSES THROUGH *ME.*

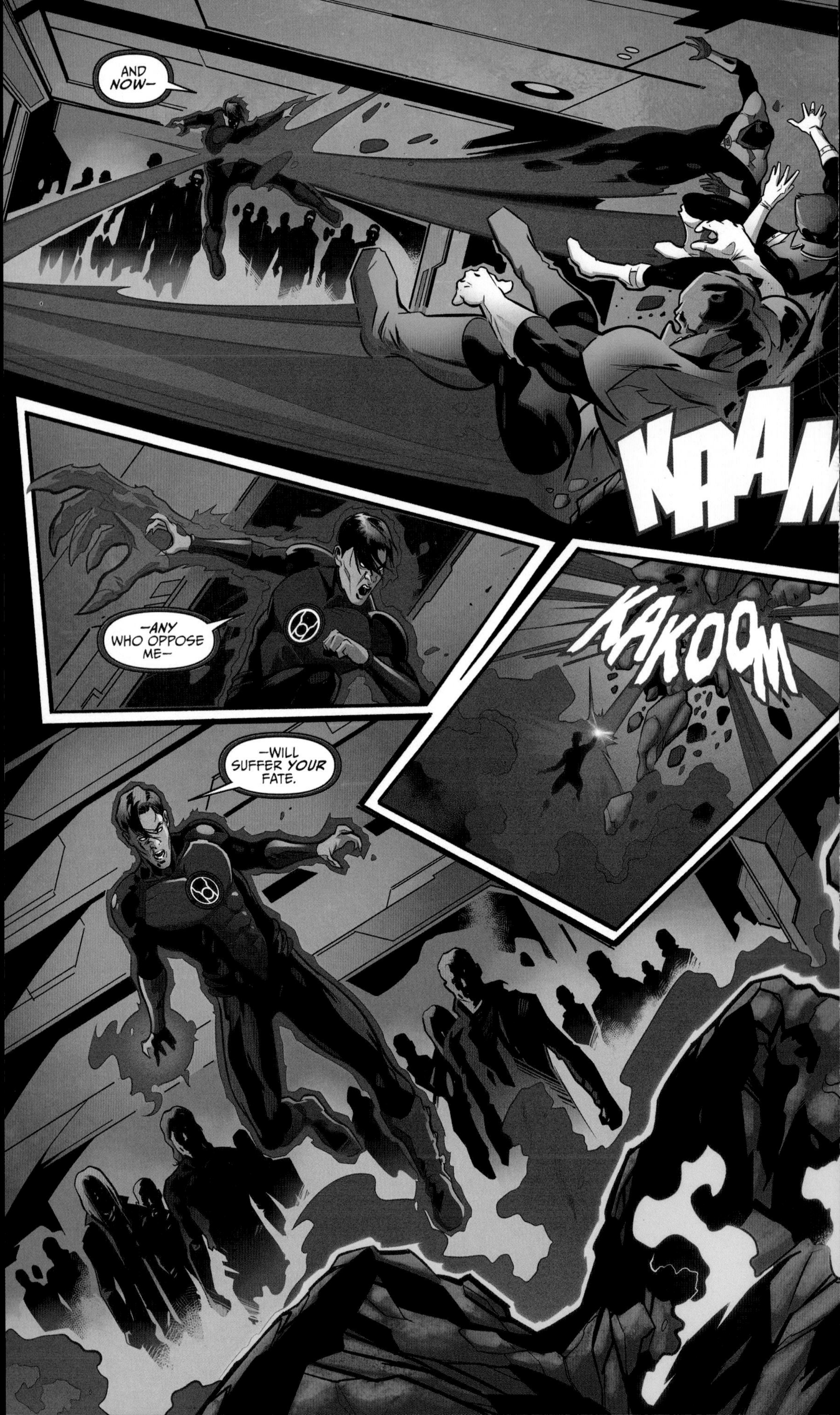
AND NOW—
KRAAM
—ANY WHO OPPOSE ME—
KAKOOM
—WILL SUFFER YOUR FATE.

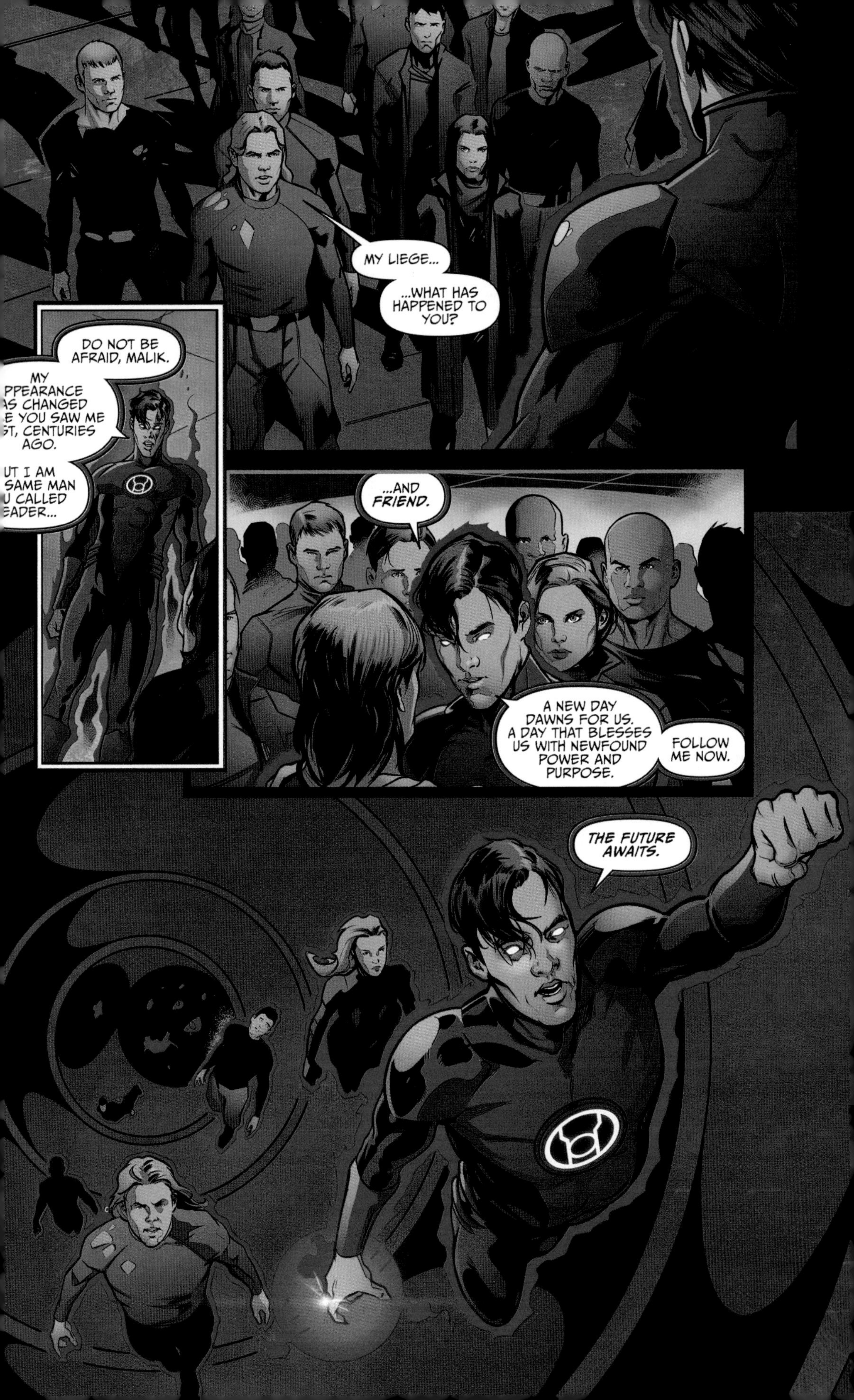
MY LIEGE...
...WHAT HAS HAPPENED TO YOU?
DO NOT BE AFRAID, MALIK.
MY PPEARANCE AS CHANGED E YOU SAW ME ST, CENTURIES AGO.
UT I AM SAME MAN U CALLED EADER...
...AND FRIEND.
A NEW DAY DAWNS FOR US. A DAY THAT BLESSES US WITH NEWFOUND POWER AND PURPOSE.
FOLLOW ME NOW.
THE FUTURE AWAITS.

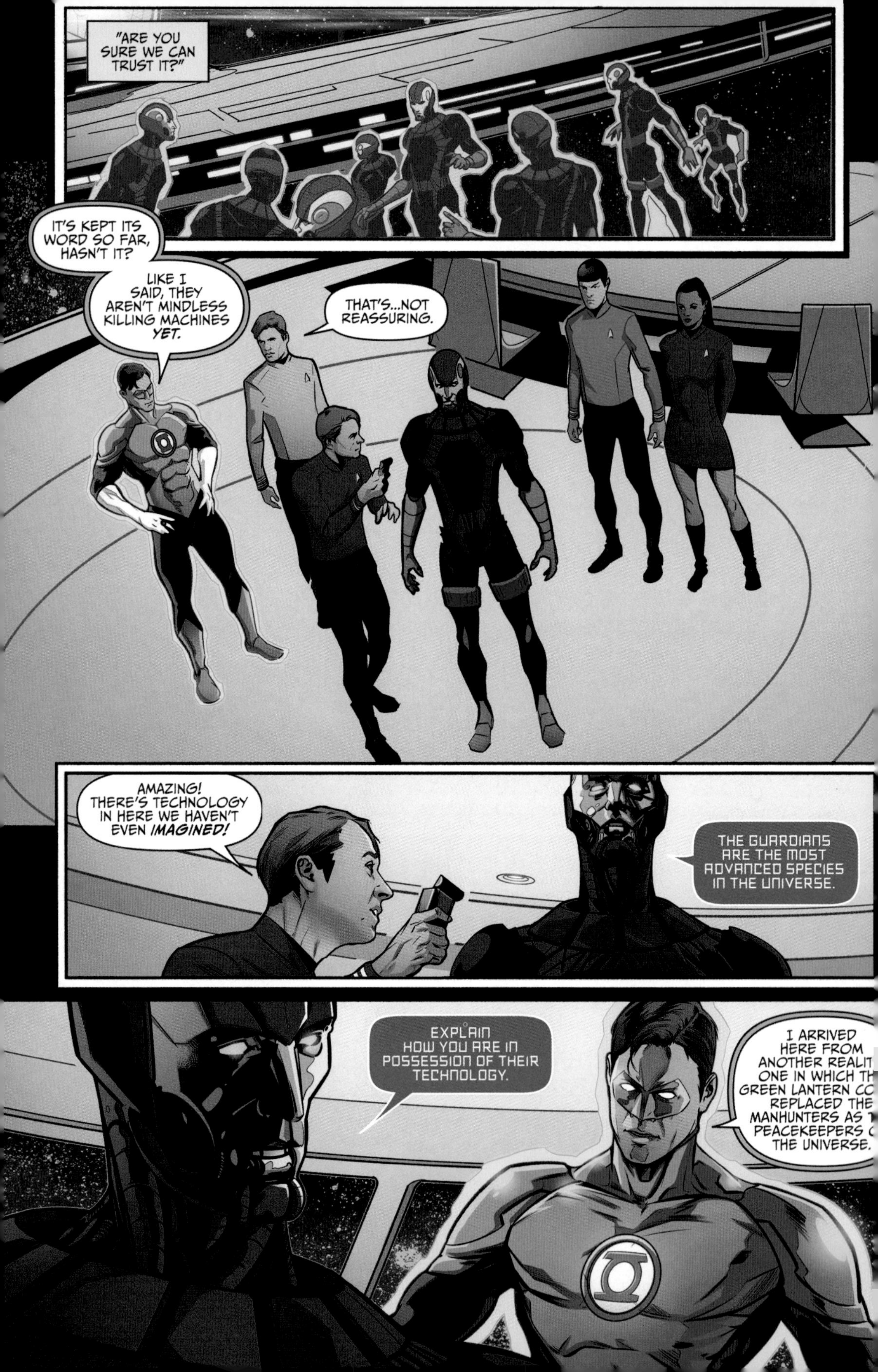
"ARE YOU SURE WE CAN TRUST IT?"
IT'S KEPT ITS WORD SO FAR, HASN'T IT?
LIKE I SAID, THEY AREN'T MINDLESS KILLING MACHINES *YET.*
THAT'S...NOT REASSURING.
AMAZING! THERE'S TECHNOLOGY IN HERE WE HAVEN'T EVEN *IMAGINED!*
THE GUARDIANS ARE THE MOST ADVANCED SPECIES IN THE UNIVERSE.
EXPLAIN HOW YOU ARE IN POSSESSION OF THEIR TECHNOLOGY.
I ARRIVED HERE FROM ANOTHER REALIT ONE IN WHICH TH GREEN LANTERN CO REPLACED THE MANHUNTERS AS T PEACEKEEPERS O THE UNIVERSE.

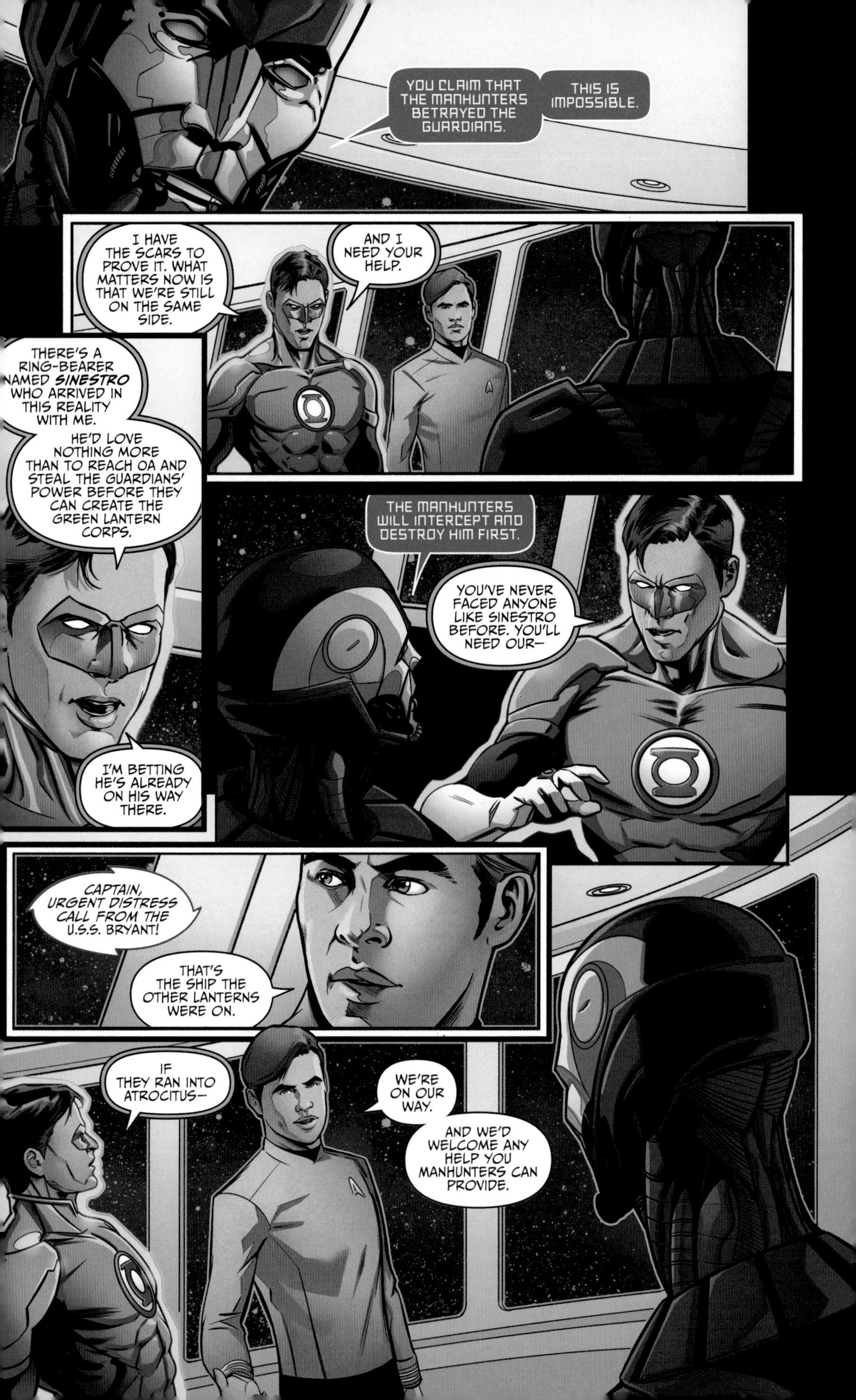
YOU CLAIM THAT THE MANHUNTERS BETRAYED THE GUARDIANS.
THIS IS IMPOSSIBLE.
I HAVE THE SCARS TO PROVE IT. WHAT MATTERS NOW IS THAT WE'RE STILL ON THE SAME SIDE.
AND I NEED YOUR HELP.
THERE'S A RING-BEARER NAMED *SINESTRO* WHO ARRIVED IN THIS REALITY WITH ME.
HE'D LOVE NOTHING MORE THAN TO REACH OA AND STEAL THE GUARDIANS' POWER BEFORE THEY CAN CREATE THE GREEN LANTERN CORPS.
I'M BETTING HE'S ALREADY ON HIS WAY THERE.
THE MANHUNTERS WILL INTERCEPT AND DESTROY HIM FIRST.
YOU'VE NEVER FACED ANYONE LIKE SINESTRO BEFORE. YOU'LL NEED OUR—
CAPTAIN, URGENT DISTRESS CALL FROM THE U.S.S. BRYANT!
THAT'S THE SHIP THE OTHER LANTERNS WERE ON.
IF THEY RAN INTO ATROCITUS—
WE'RE ON OUR WAY.
AND WE'D WELCOME ANY HELP YOU MANHUNTERS CAN PROVIDE.

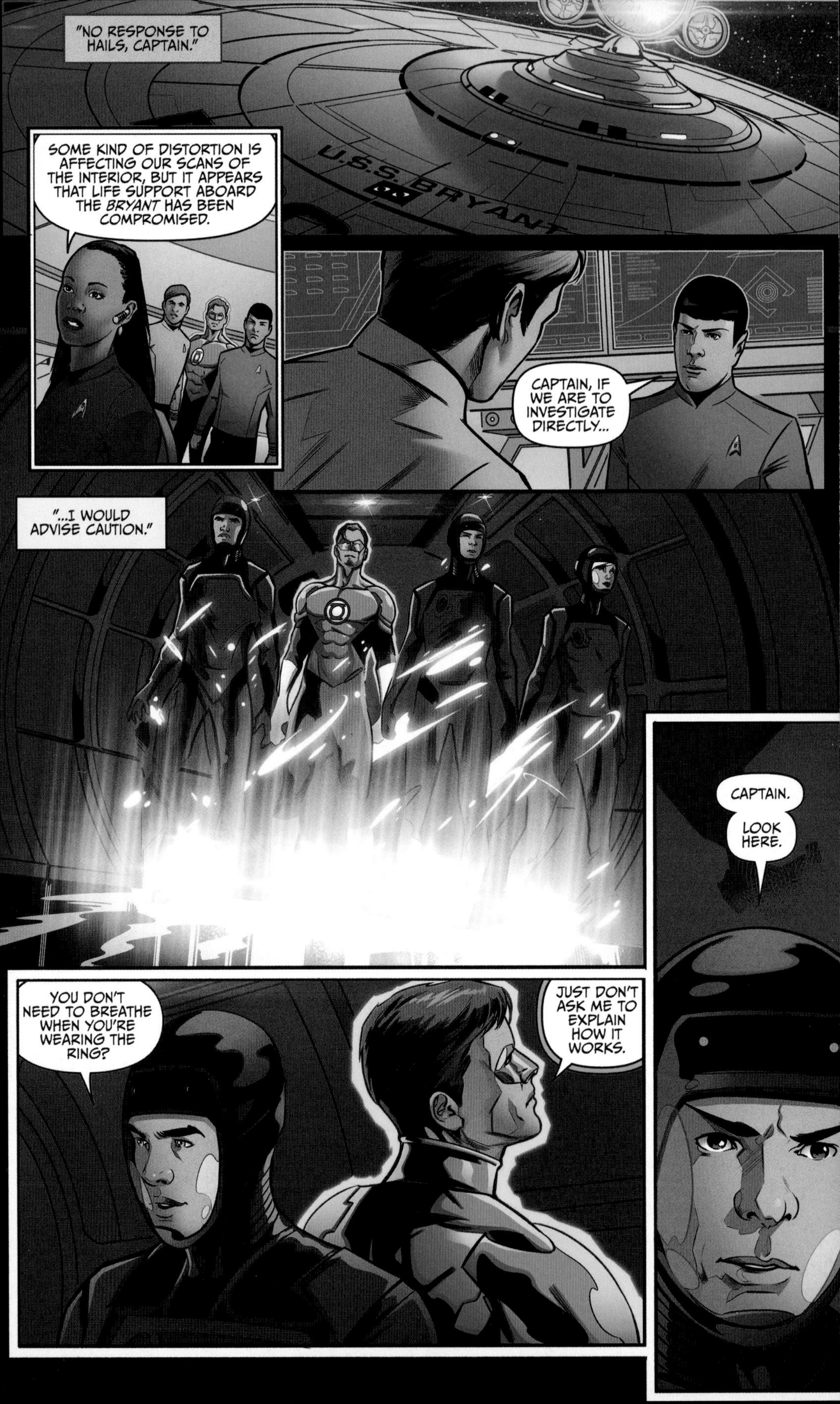
"NO RESPONSE TO HAILS, CAPTAIN."
SOME KIND OF DISTORTION IS AFFECTING OUR SCANS OF THE INTERIOR, BUT IT APPEARS THAT LIFE SUPPORT ABOARD THE *BRYANT* HAS BEEN COMPROMISED.
U.S.S. BRYANT
CAPTAIN, IF WE ARE TO INVESTIGATE DIRECTLY...
"...I WOULD ADVISE CAUTION."
CAPTAIN.
LOOK HERE.
YOU DON'T NEED TO BREATHE WHEN YOU'RE WEARING THE RING?
JUST DON'T ASK ME TO EXPLAIN HOW IT WORKS.

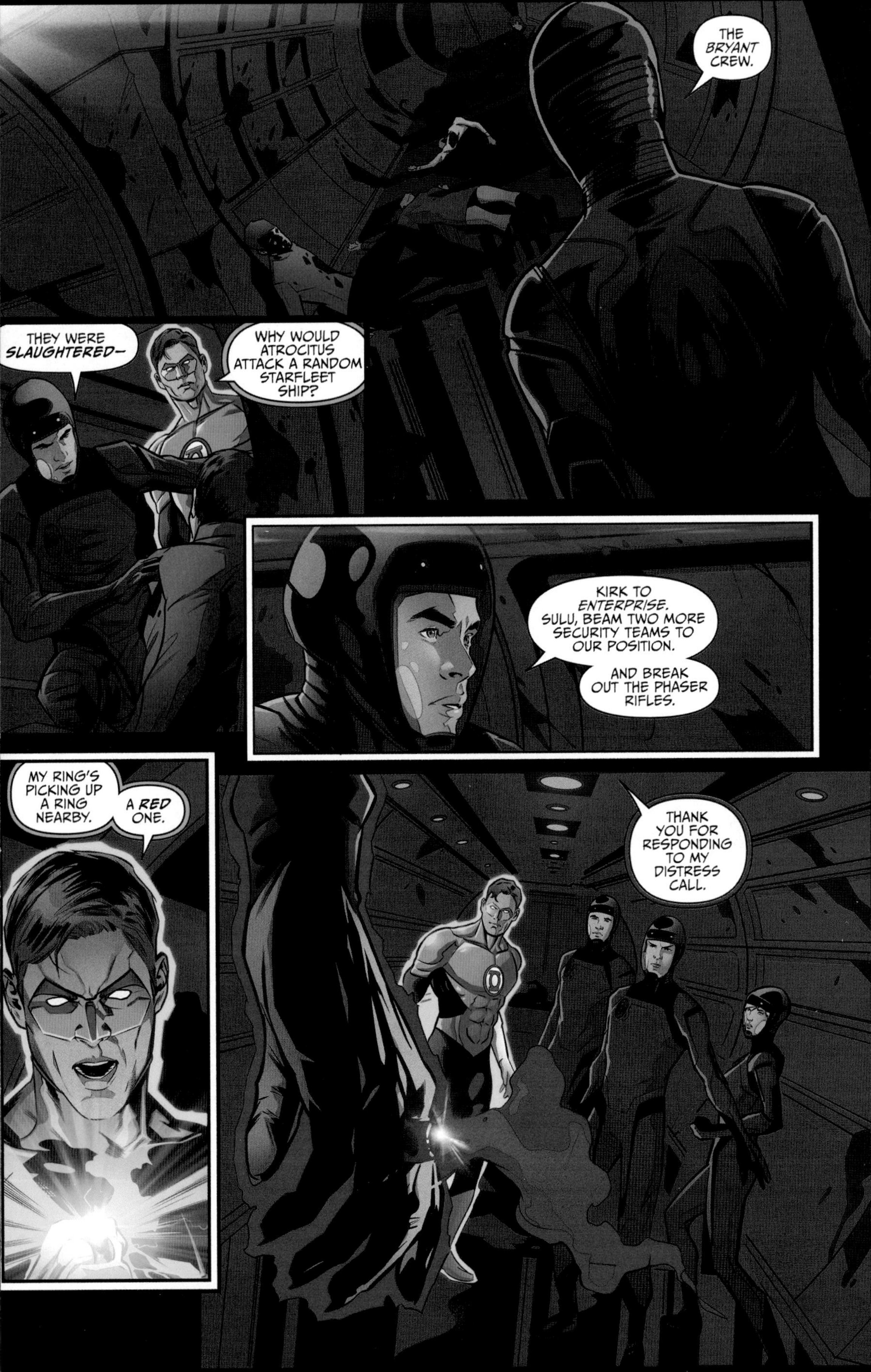
THE *BRYANT* CREW.
THEY WERE *SLAUGHTERED*—
WHY WOULD ATROCITUS ATTACK A RANDOM STARFLEET SHIP?
KIRK TO *ENTERPRISE*. SULU, BEAM TWO MORE SECURITY TEAMS TO OUR POSITION.
AND BREAK OUT THE PHASER RIFLES.
MY RING'S PICKING UP A RING NEARBY.
A *RED* ONE.
THANK YOU FOR RESPONDING TO MY DISTRESS CALL.

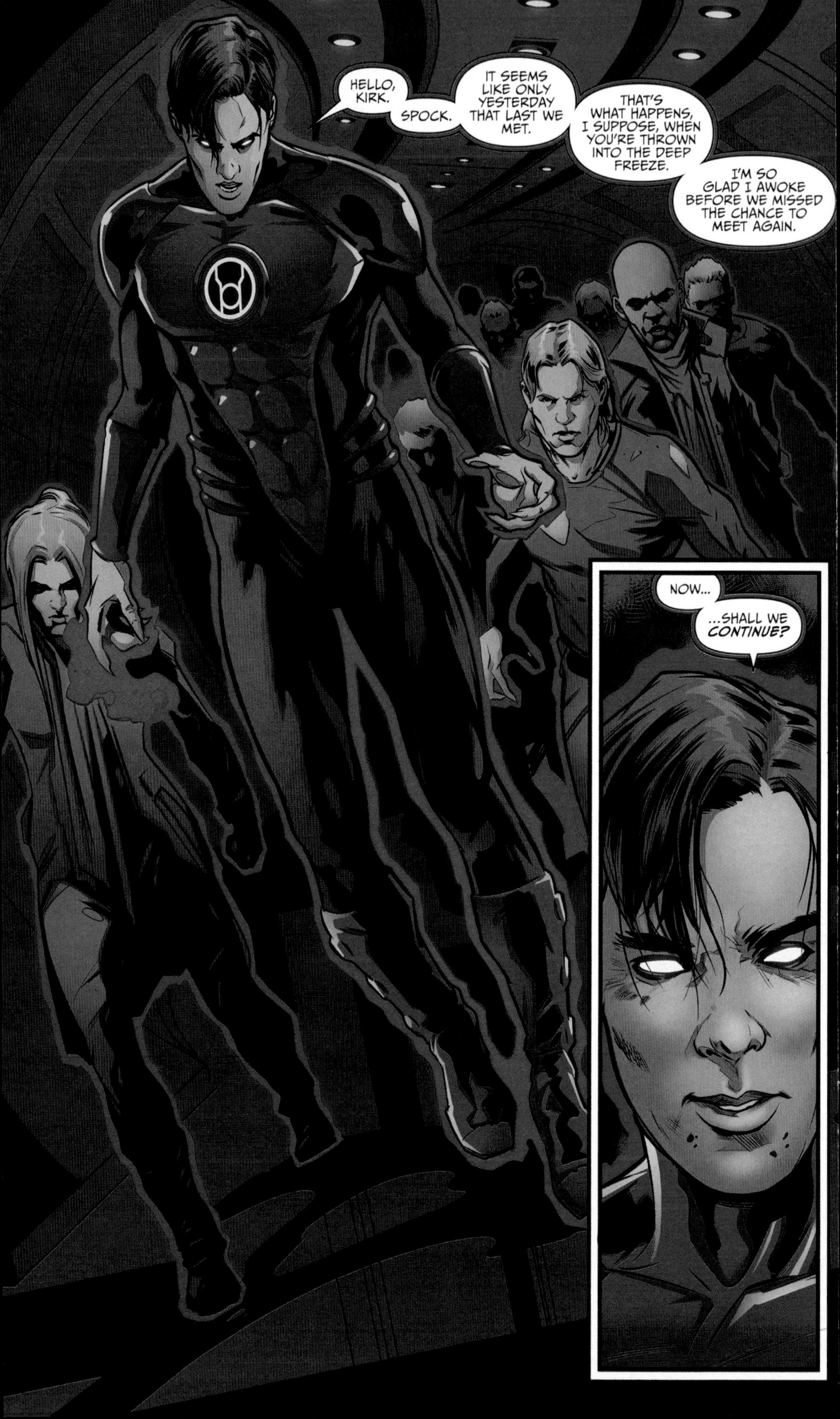
HELLO, KIRK.
SPOCK.
IT SEEMS LIKE ONLY YESTERDAY THAT LAST WE MET.
THAT'S WHAT HAPPENS, I SUPPOSE, WHEN YOU'RE THROWN INTO THE DEEP FREEZE.
I'M SO GLAD I AWOKE BEFORE WE MISSED THE CHANCE TO MEET AGAIN.
NOW...
...SHALL WE *CONTINUE?*

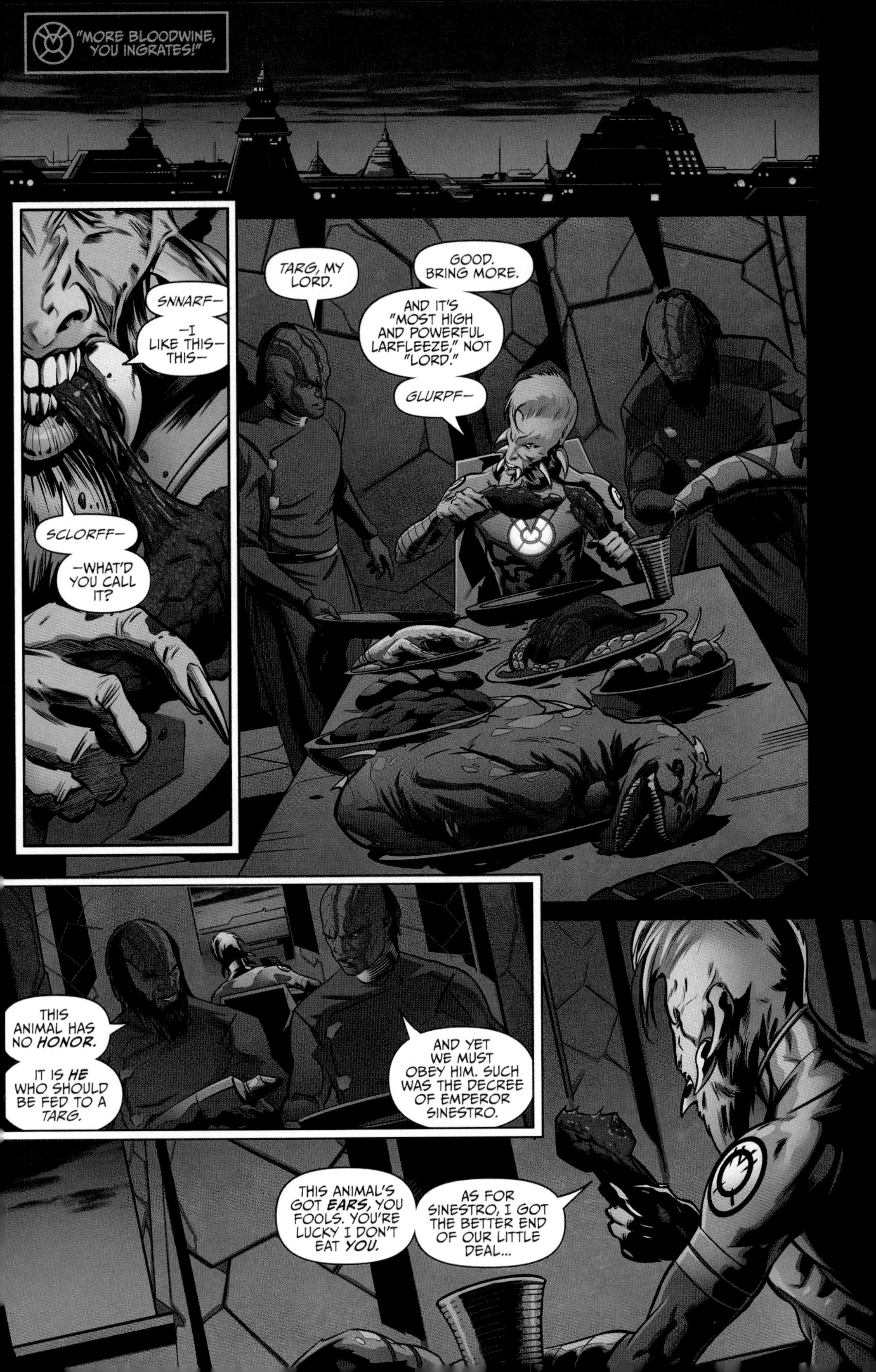
"MORE BLOODWINE, YOU INGRATES!"
SNNARF—
—I LIKE THIS—THIS—
SCLORFF—
—WHAT'D YOU CALL IT?
TARG, MY LORD.
GOOD. BRING MORE.
AND IT'S "MOST HIGH AND POWERFUL LARFLEEZE," NOT "LORD."
GLURPF—
THIS ANIMAL HAS NO HONOR.
IT IS HE WHO SHOULD BE FED TO A TARG.
AND YET WE MUST OBEY HIM. SUCH WAS THE DECREE OF EMPEROR SINESTRO.
THIS ANIMAL'S GOT EARS, YOU FOOLS. YOU'RE LUCKY I DON'T EAT YOU.
AS FOR SINESTRO, I GOT THE BETTER END OF OUR LITTLE DEAL...

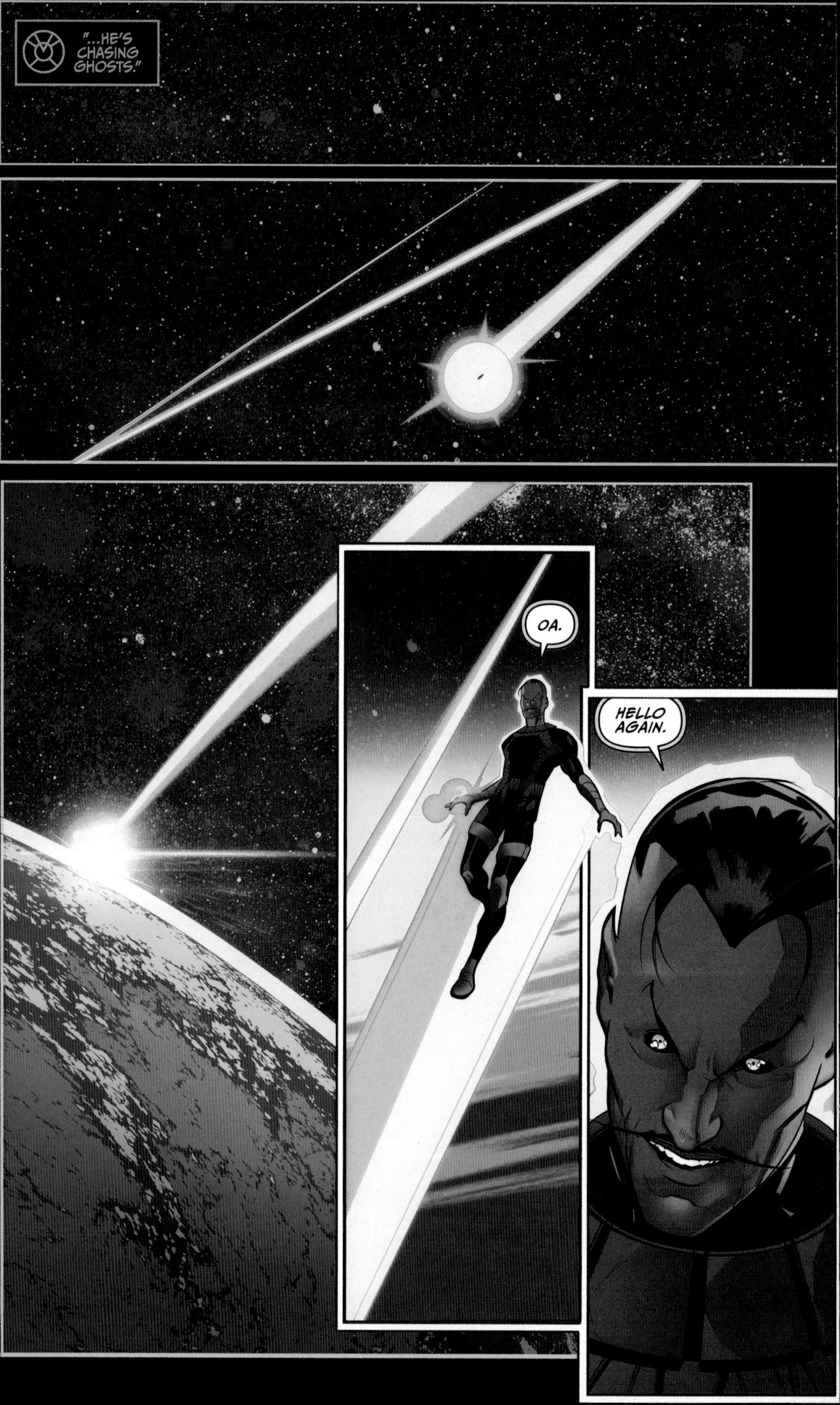
"...HE'S CHASING GHOSTS."
OA.
HELLO AGAIN.

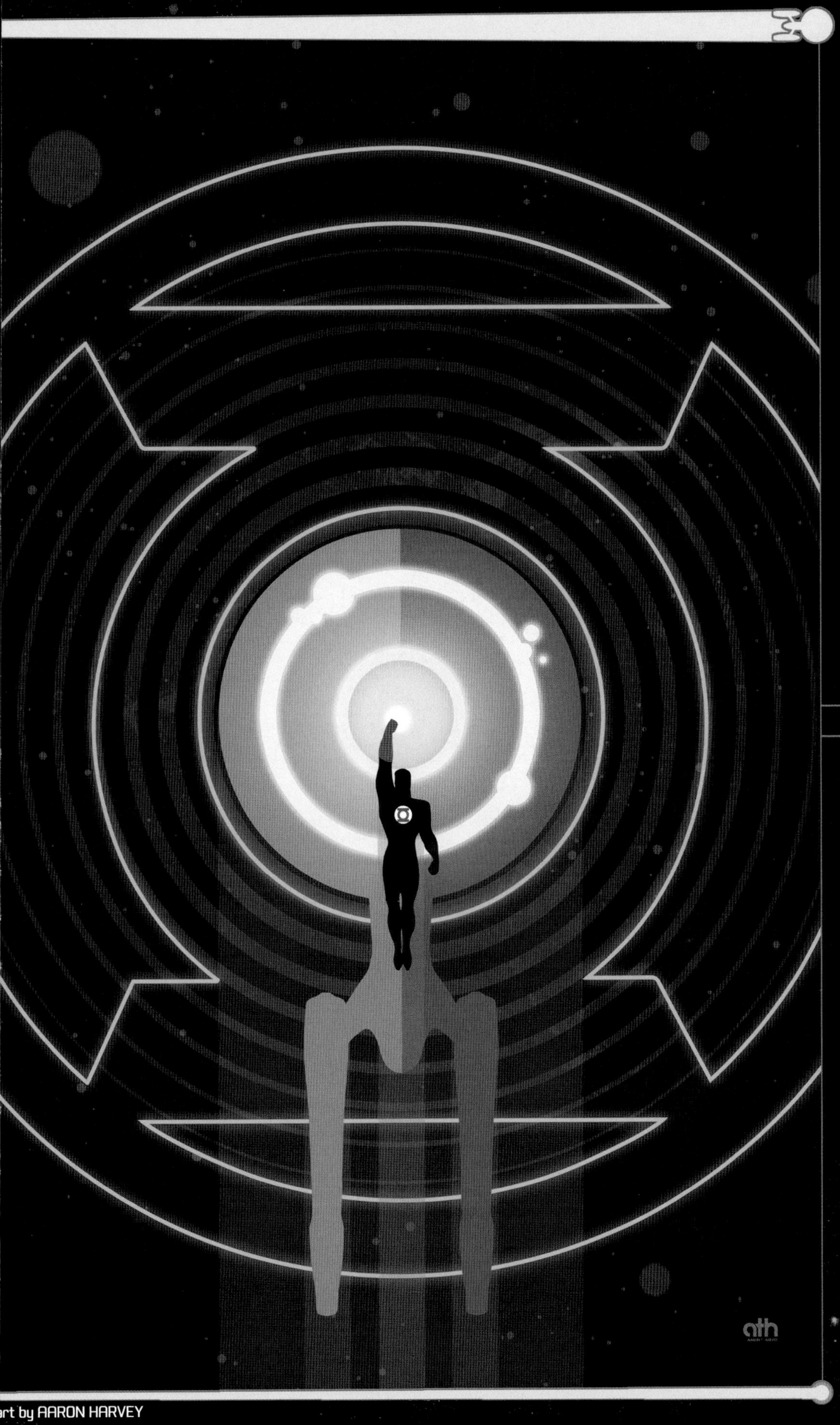

rt by AARON HARVEY

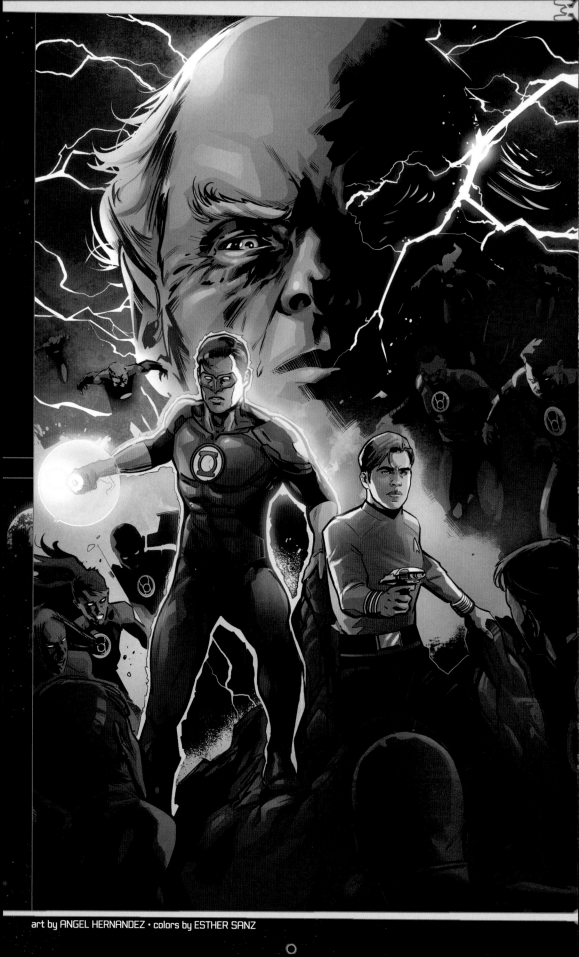

art by ANGEL HERNANDEZ • colors by ESTHER SANZ

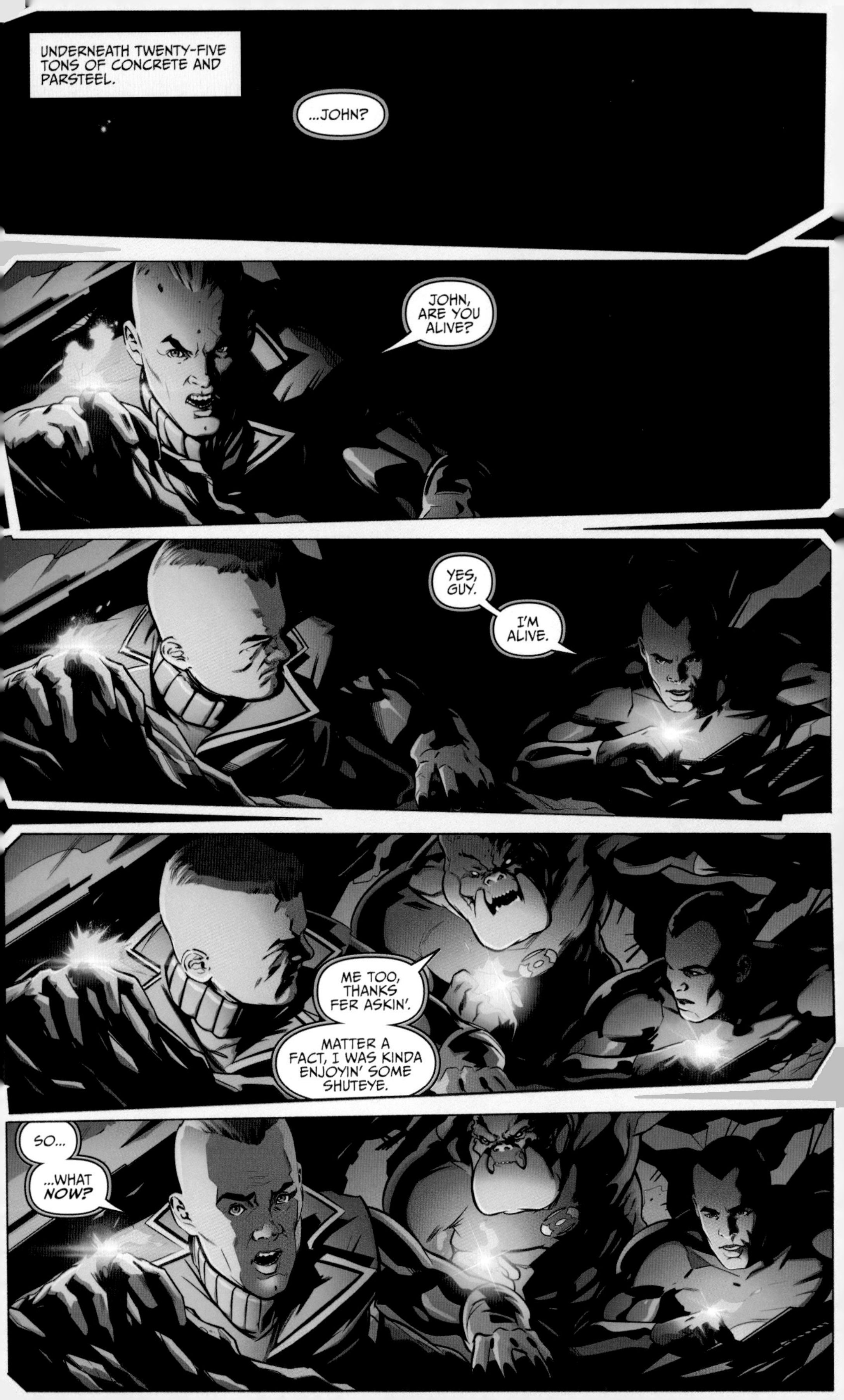

UNDERNEATH TWENTY-FIVE TONS OF CONCRETE AND PARSTEEL.
...JOHN?
JOHN, ARE YOU ALIVE?
YES, GUY.
I'M ALIVE.
ME TOO, THANKS FER ASKIN'.
MATTER A FACT, I WAS KINDA ENJOYIN' SOME SHUTEYE.
SO...
...WHAT NOW?

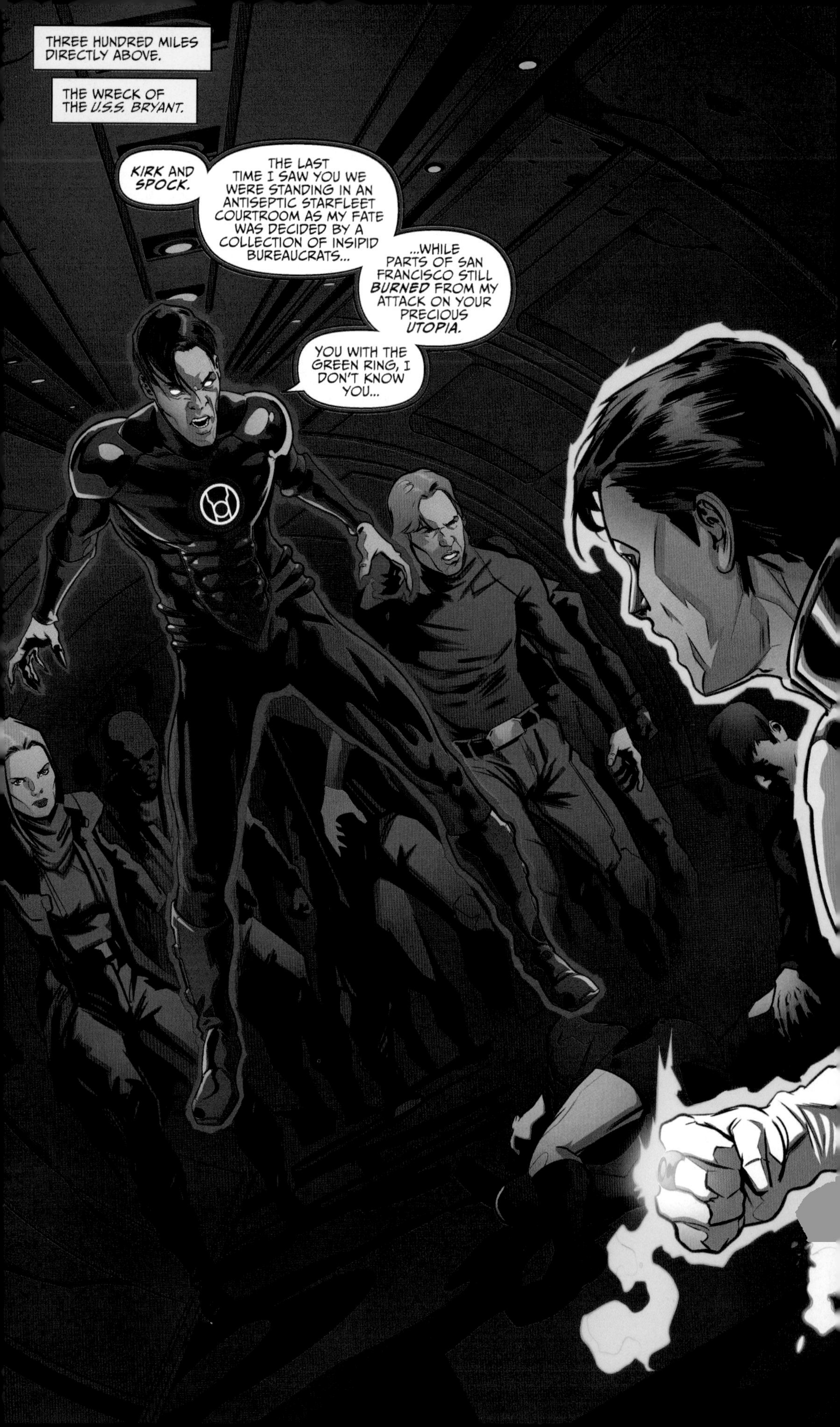
THREE HUNDRED MILES DIRECTLY ABOVE.
THE WRECK OF THE *U.S.S. BRYANT.*
KIRK AND ***SPOCK.***
THE LAST TIME I SAW YOU WE WERE STANDING IN AN ANTISEPTIC STARFLEET COURTROOM AS MY FATE WAS DECIDED BY A COLLECTION OF INSIPID BUREAUCRATS...
...WHILE PARTS OF SAN FRANCISCO STILL ***BURNED*** FROM MY ATTACK ON YOUR PRECIOUS ***UTOPIA.***
YOU WITH THE GREEN RING, I DON'T KNOW YOU...

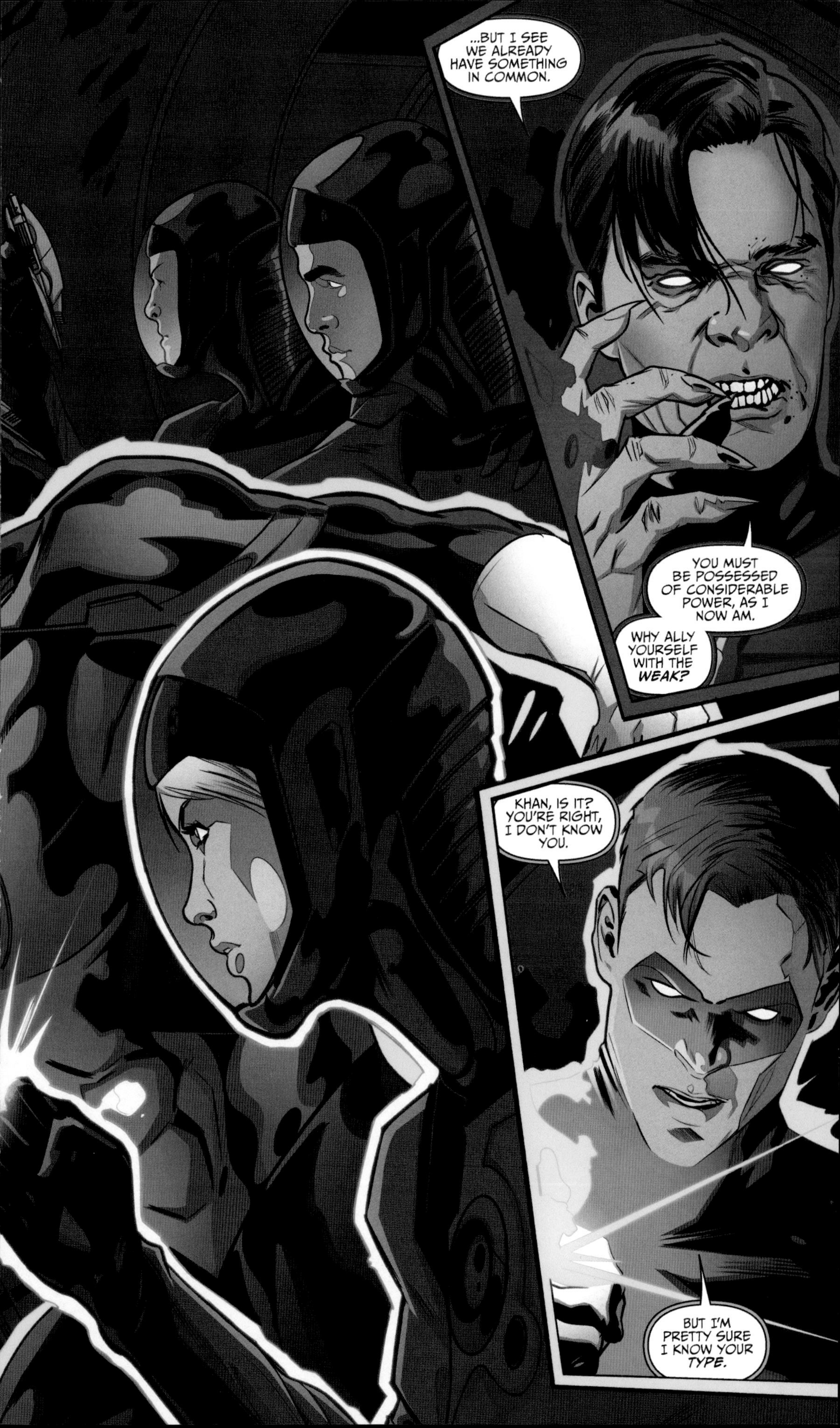
...BUT I SEE WE ALREADY HAVE SOMETHING IN COMMON.
YOU MUST BE POSSESSED OF CONSIDERABLE POWER, AS I NOW AM.
WHY ALLY YOURSELF WITH THE *WEAK?*
KHAN, IS IT? YOU'RE RIGHT, I DON'T KNOW YOU.
BUT I'M PRETTY SURE I KNOW YOUR *TYPE.*

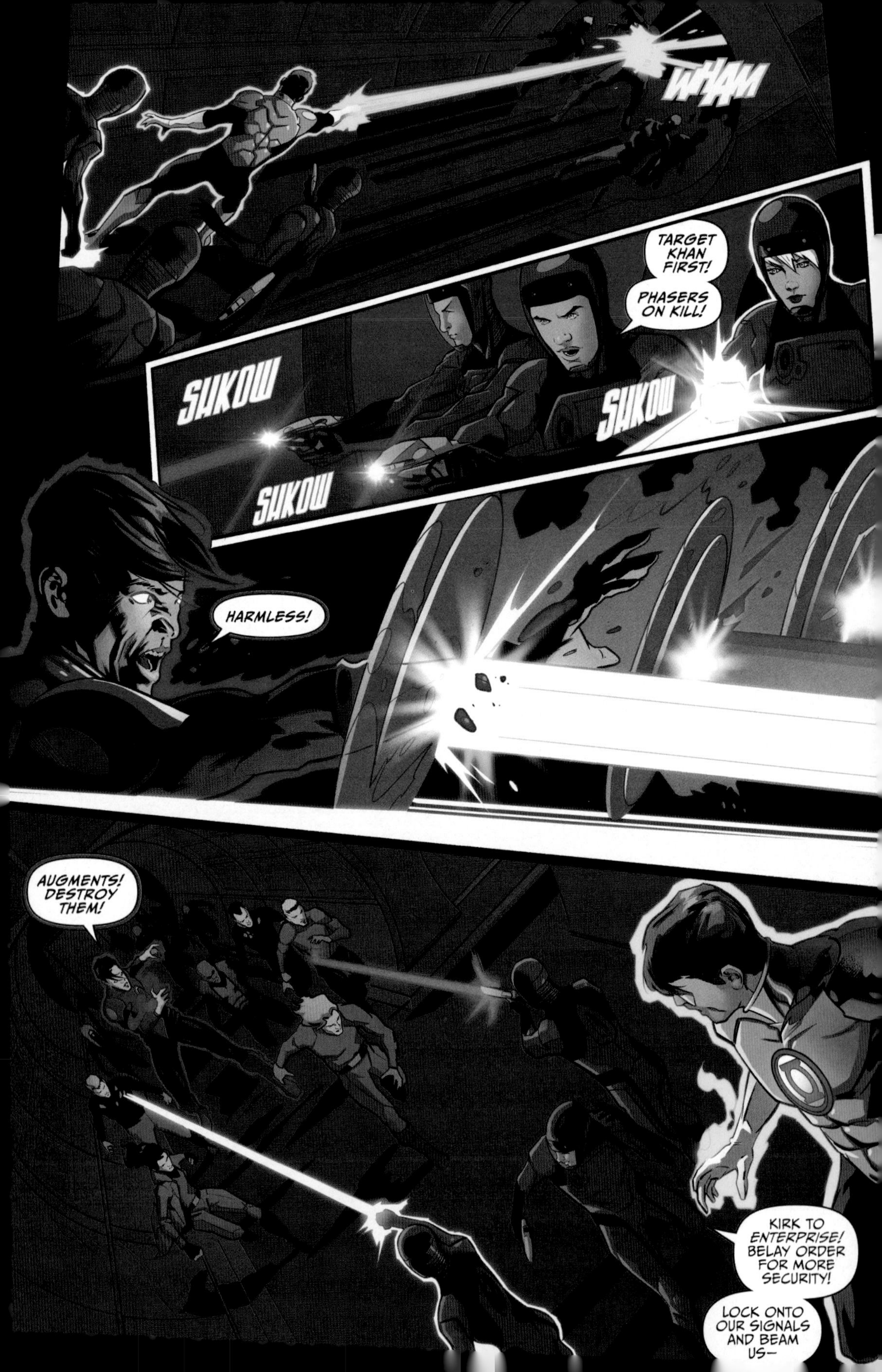
WHAM
TARGET KHAN FIRST!
PHASERS ON KILL!
SUKOW
SUKOW
SUKOW
HARMLESS!
AUGMENTS! DESTROY THEM!
KIRK TO *ENTERPRISE!* BELAY ORDER FOR MORE SECURITY!
LOCK ONTO OUR SIGNALS AND BEAM US—

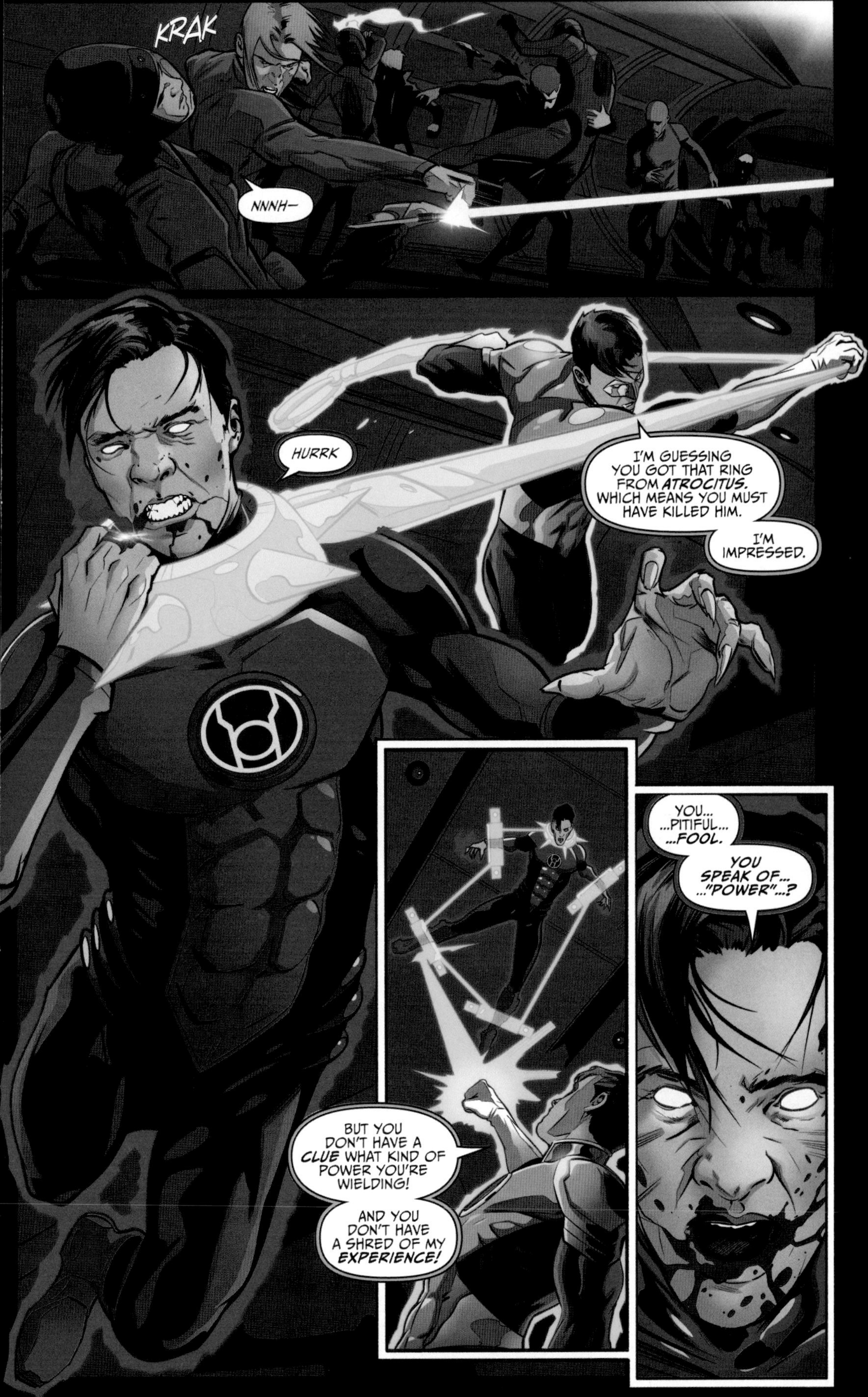
KRAK
NNNH—
HURRK
I'M GUESSING YOU GOT THAT RING FROM ATROCITUS. WHICH MEANS YOU MUST HAVE KILLED HIM.
I'M IMPRESSED.
YOU... ...PITIFUL... ...FOOL.
YOU SPEAK OF... ..."POWER"...?
BUT YOU DON'T HAVE A CLUE WHAT KIND OF POWER YOU'RE WIELDING!
AND YOU DON'T HAVE A SHRED OF MY EXPERIENCE!

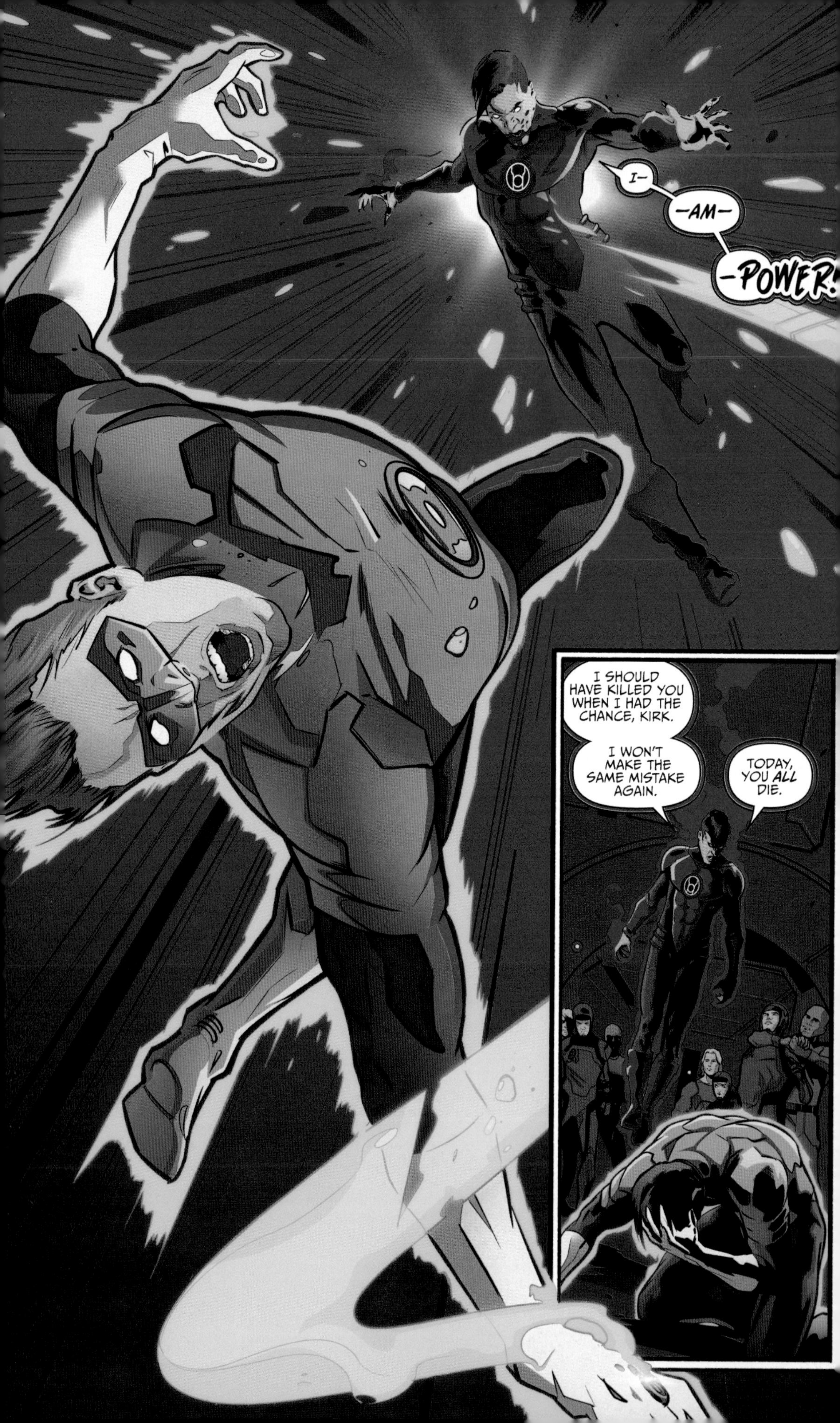
I—
—AM—
—POWER!
I SHOULD HAVE KILLED YOU WHEN I HAD THE CHANCE, KIRK.
I WON'T MAKE THE SAME MISTAKE AGAIN.
TODAY, YOU ALL DIE.

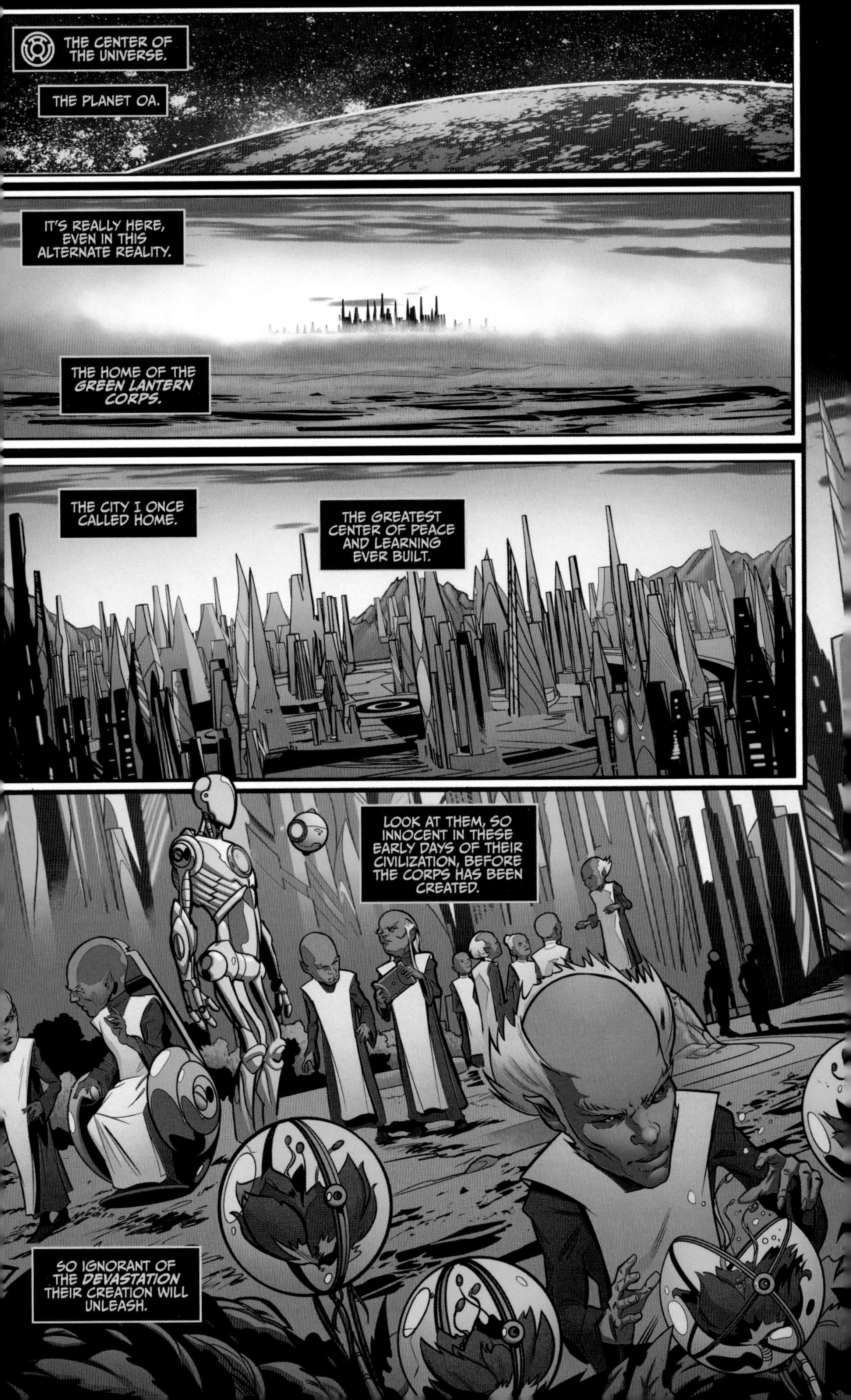
THE CENTER OF THE UNIVERSE.
THE PLANET OA.
IT'S REALLY HERE, EVEN IN THIS ALTERNATE REALITY.
THE HOME OF THE *GREEN LANTERN CORPS.*
THE CITY I ONCE CALLED HOME.
THE GREATEST CENTER OF PEACE AND LEARNING EVER BUILT.
LOOK AT THEM, SO INNOCENT IN THESE EARLY DAYS OF THEIR CIVILIZATION, BEFORE THE CORPS HAS BEEN CREATED.
SO IGNORANT OF THE *DEVASTATION* THEIR CREATION WILL UNLEASH.

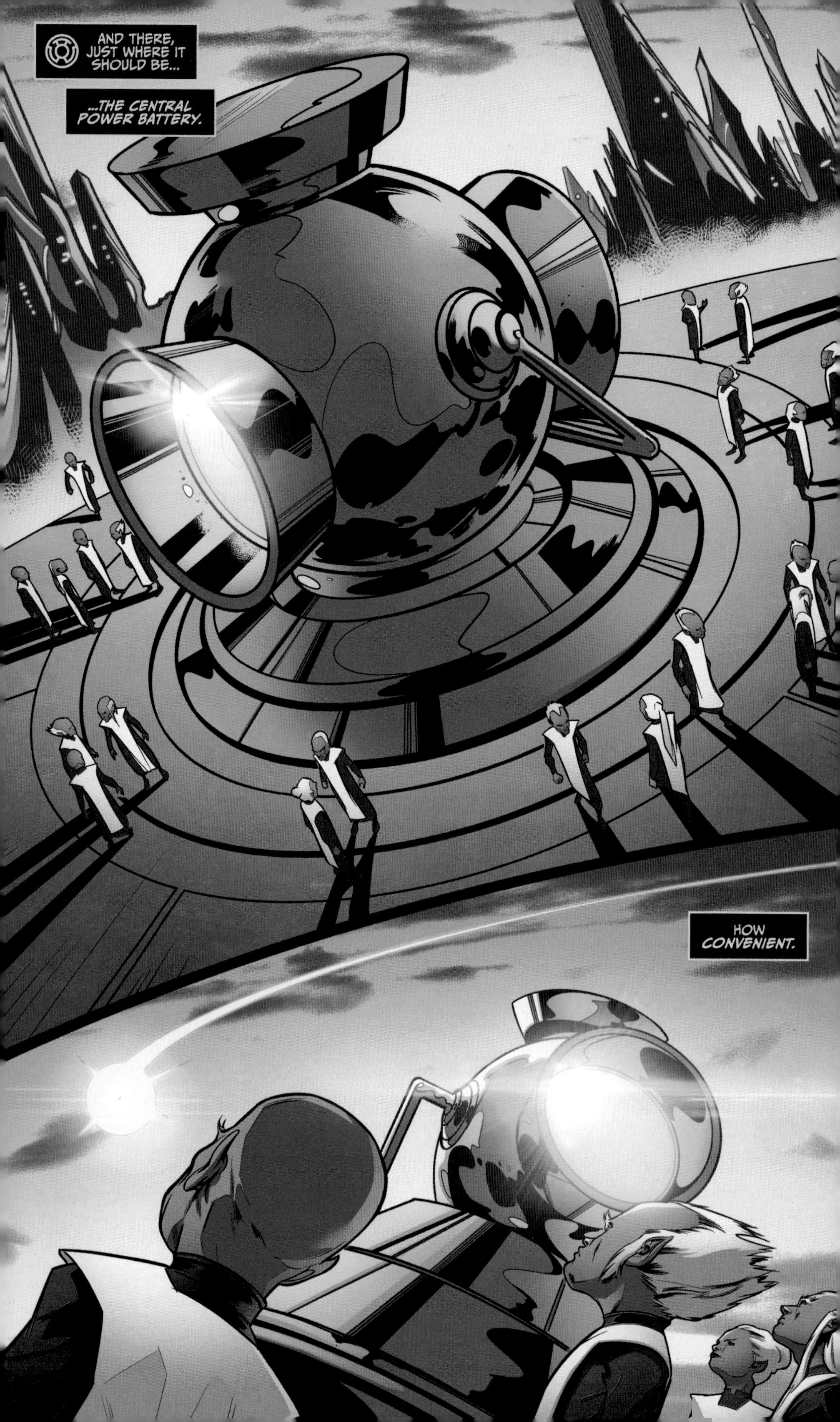
AND THERE, JUST WHERE IT SHOULD BE...
...THE CENTRAL POWER BATTERY.
HOW CONVENIENT.

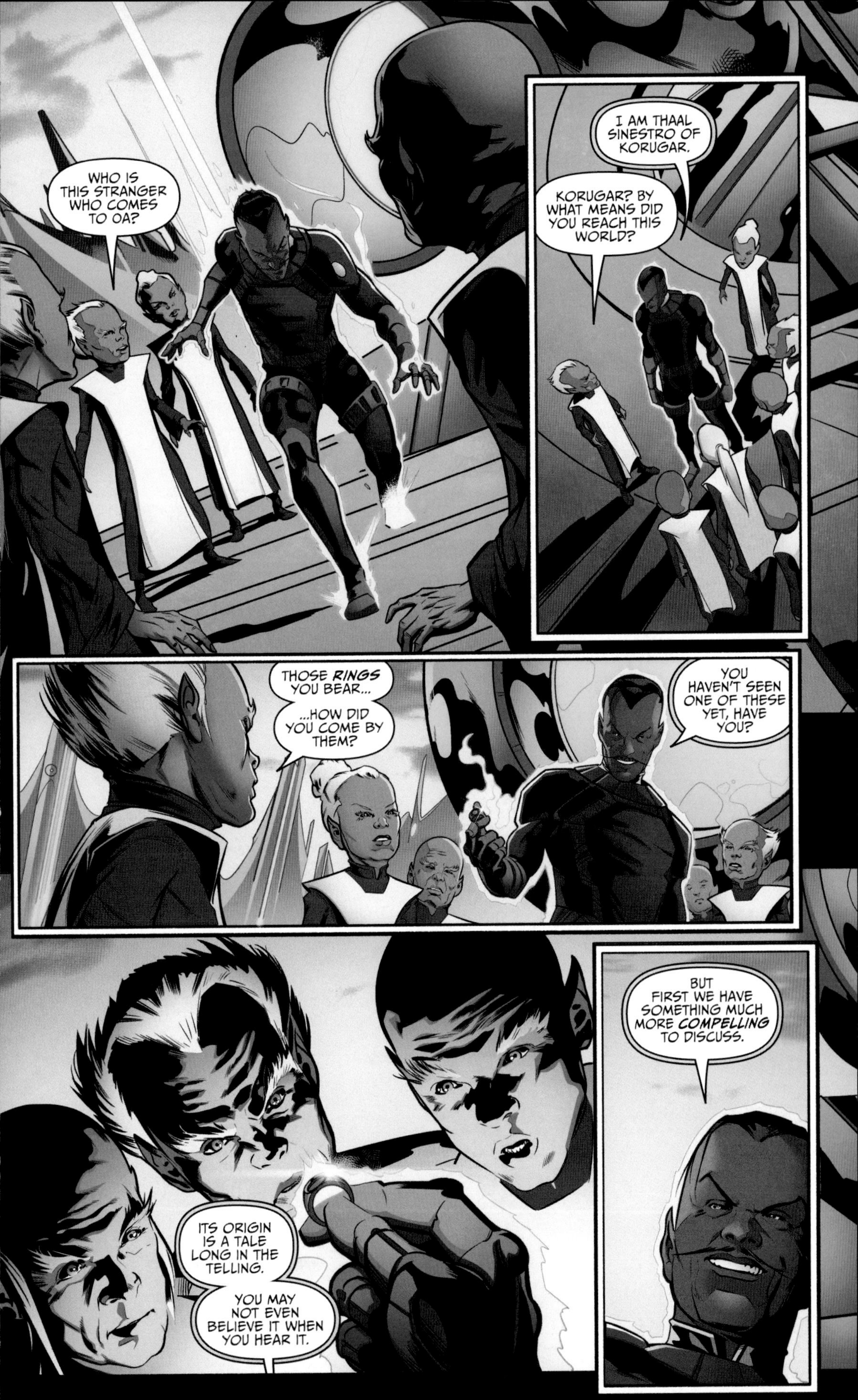
WHO IS THIS STRANGER WHO COMES TO OA?
I AM THAAL SINESTRO OF KORUGAR.
KORUGAR? BY WHAT MEANS DID YOU REACH THIS WORLD?
THOSE RINGS YOU BEAR...
...HOW DID YOU COME BY THEM?
YOU HAVEN'T SEEN ONE OF THESE YET, HAVE YOU?
ITS ORIGIN IS A TALE LONG IN THE TELLING.
YOU MAY NOT EVEN BELIEVE IT WHEN YOU HEAR IT.
BUT FIRST WE HAVE SOMETHING MUCH MORE COMPELLING TO DISCUSS.

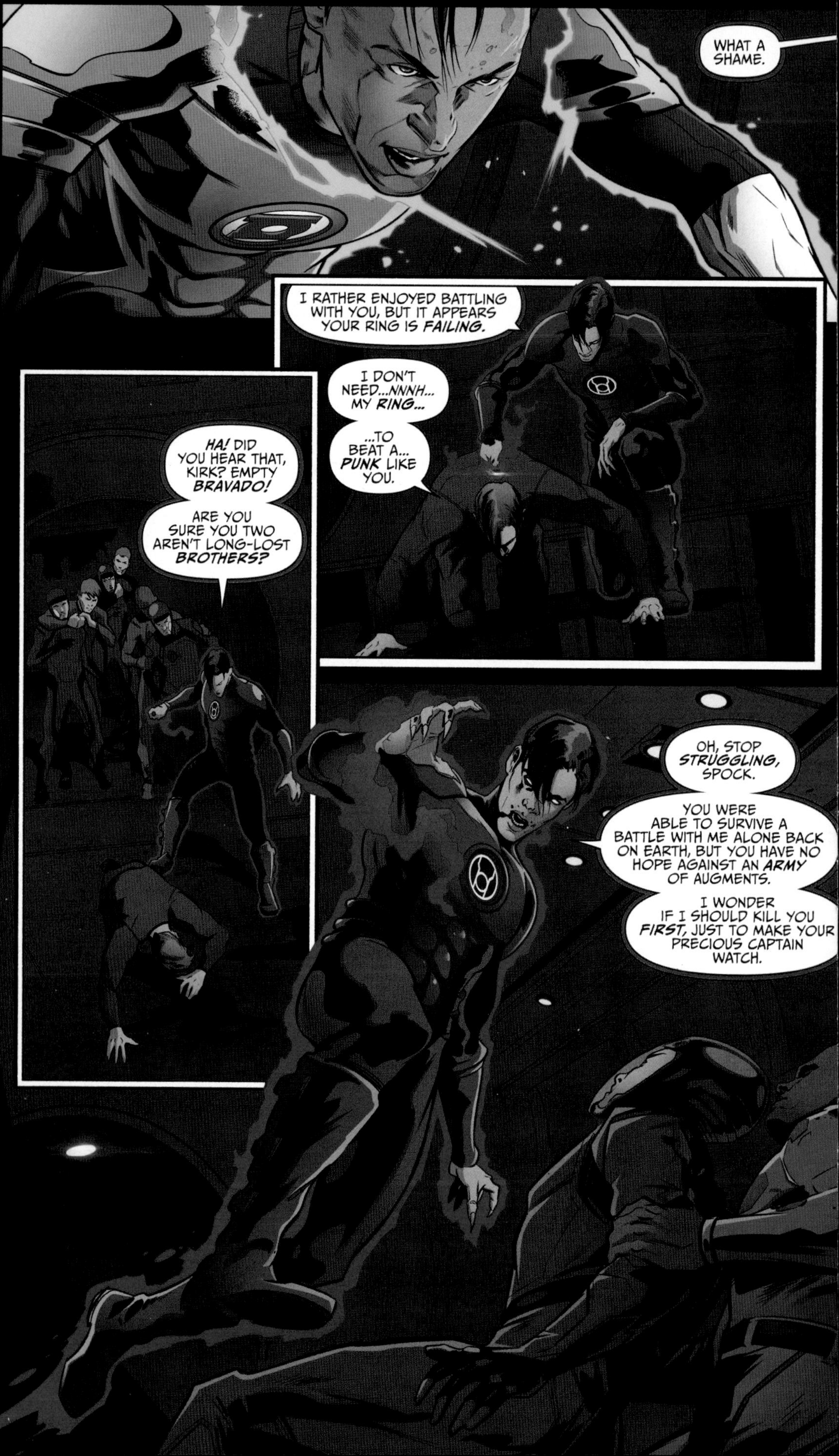
WHAT A SHAME.
I RATHER ENJOYED BATTLING WITH YOU, BUT IT APPEARS YOUR RING IS FAILING.
I DON'T NEED...NNNH... MY RING...
...TO BEAT A... PUNK LIKE YOU.
HA! DID YOU HEAR THAT, KIRK? EMPTY BRAVADO!
ARE YOU SURE YOU TWO AREN'T LONG-LOST BROTHERS?
OH, STOP STRUGGLING, SPOCK.
YOU WERE ABLE TO SURVIVE A BATTLE WITH ME ALONE BACK ON EARTH, BUT YOU HAVE NO HOPE AGAINST AN ARMY OF AUGMENTS.
I WONDER IF I SHOULD KILL YOU FIRST, JUST TO MAKE YOUR PRECIOUS CAPTAIN WATCH.

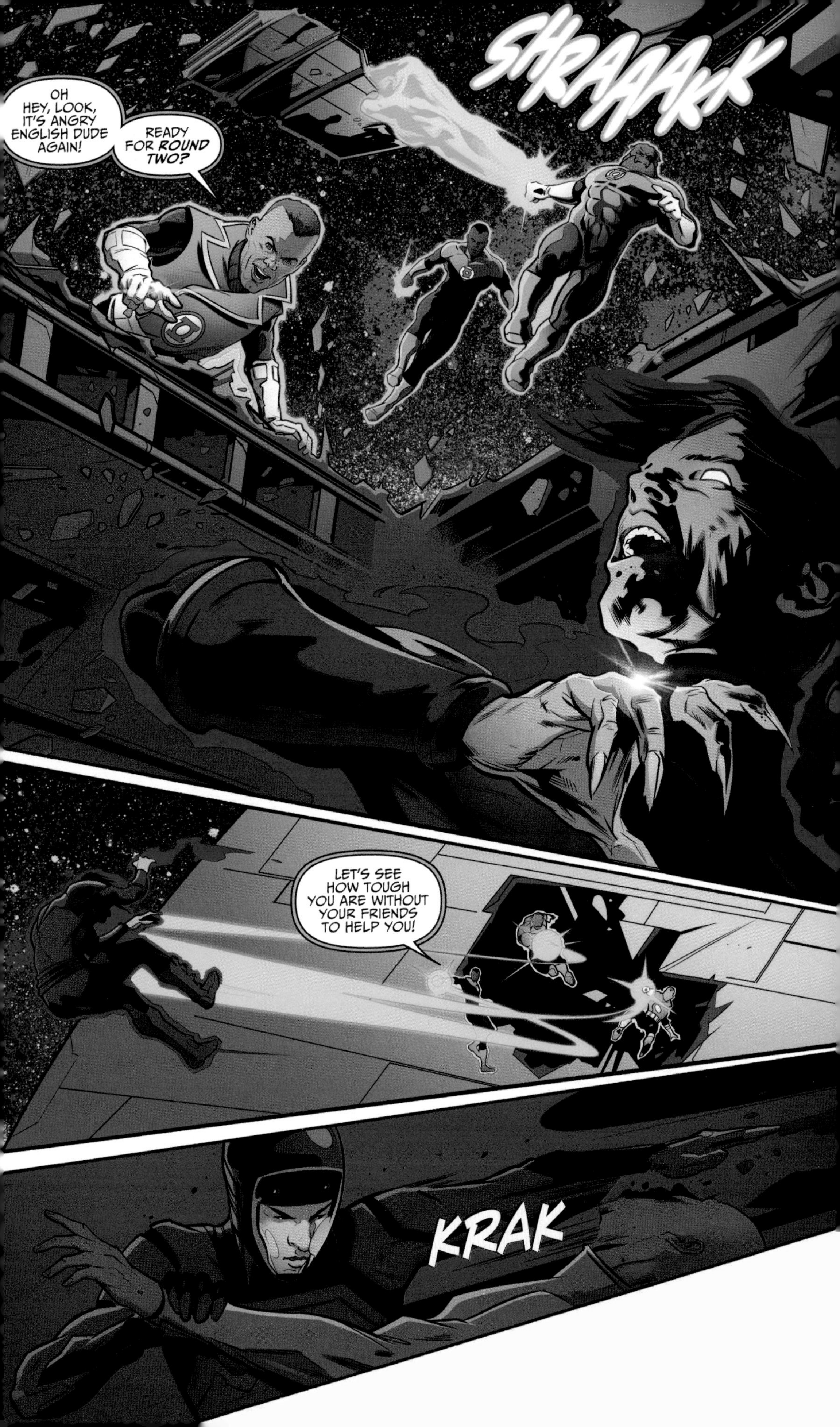
SHRAAAKK
OH HEY, LOOK, IT'S ANGRY ENGLISH DUDE AGAIN!
READY FOR ROUND TWO?
LET'S SEE HOW TOUGH YOU ARE WITHOUT YOUR FRIENDS TO HELP YOU!
KRAK

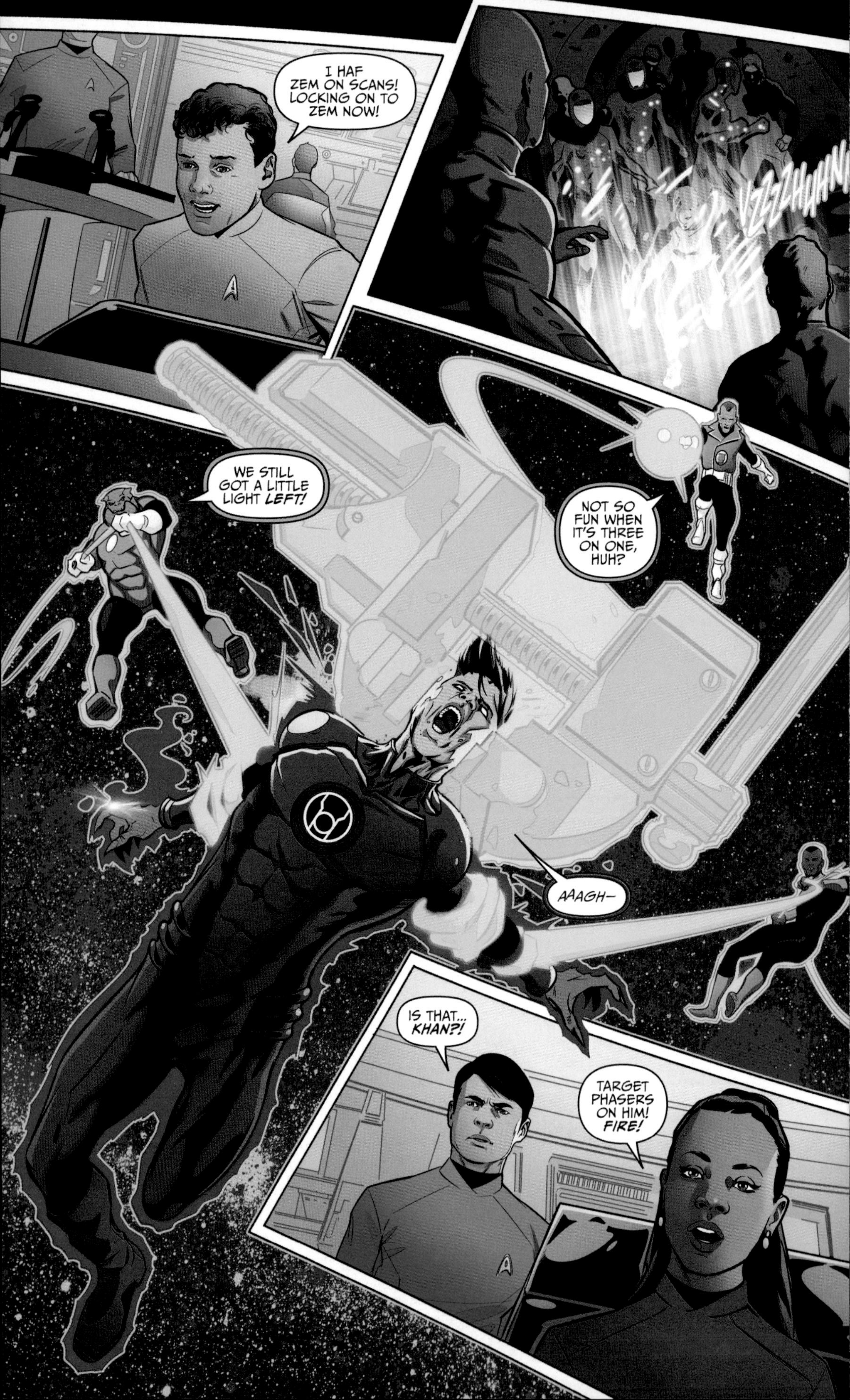
I HAF ZEM ON SCANS! LOCKING ON TO ZEM NOW!
VZZZZHUHN
WE STILL GOT A LITTLE LIGHT LEFT!
NOT SO FUN WHEN IT'S THREE ON ONE, HUH?
AAAGH—
IS THAT... KHAN?!
TARGET PHASERS ON HIM! FIRE!

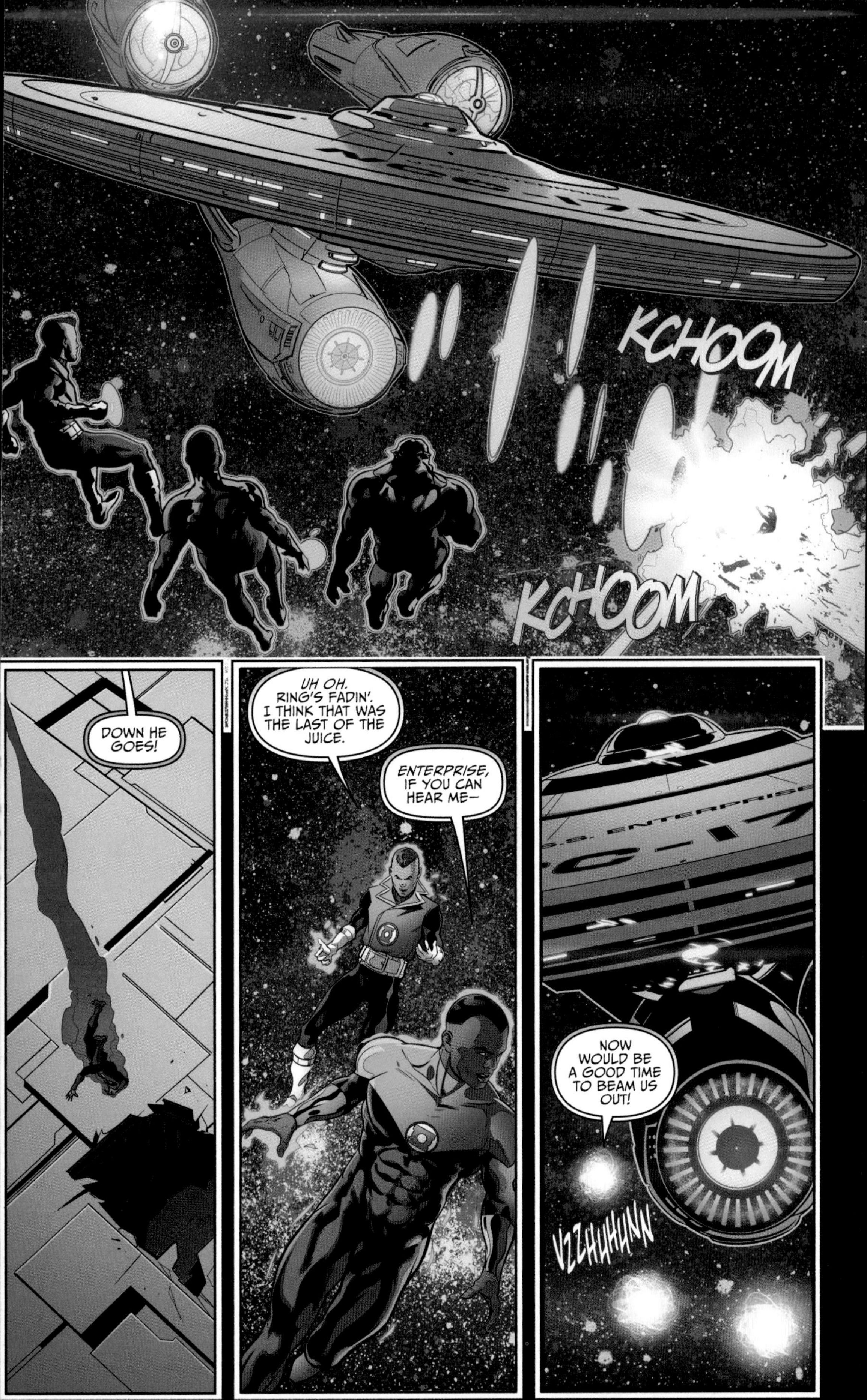
KCHOOM
KCHOOM
DOWN HE GOES!
UH OH. RING'S FADIN'. I THINK THAT WAS THE LAST OF THE JUICE.
ENTERPRISE, IF YOU CAN HEAR ME—
NOW WOULD BE A GOOD TIME TO BEAM US OUT!
VZZHUHUNN

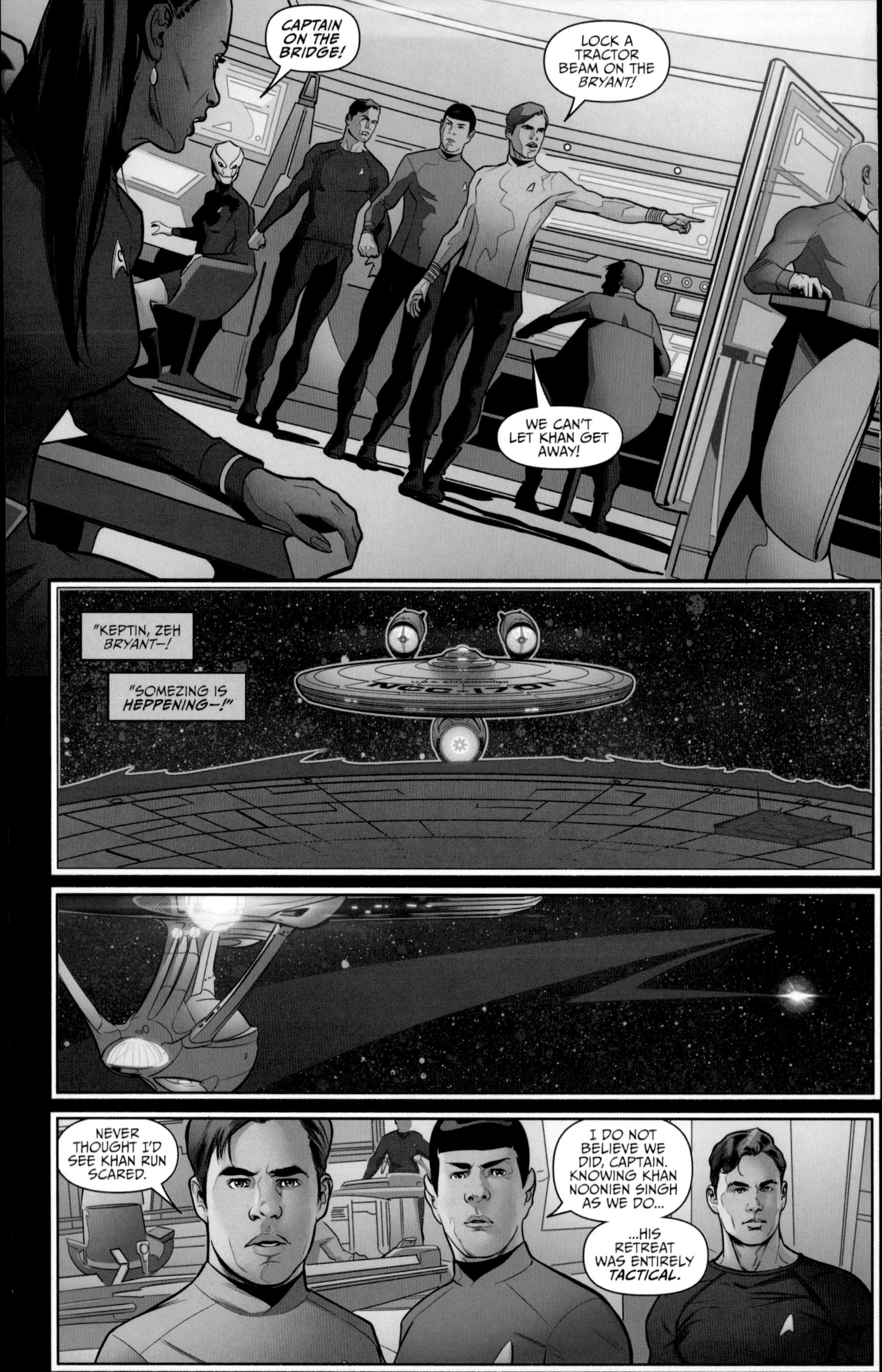
CAPTAIN ON THE BRIDGE!
LOCK A TRACTOR BEAM ON THE *BRYANT!*
WE CAN'T LET KHAN GET AWAY!
"KEPTIN, ZEH *BRYANT*–!
"SOMEZING IS *HEPPENING*–!"
NCC-1701
NEVER THOUGHT I'D SEE KHAN RUN SCARED.
I DO NOT BELIEVE WE DID, CAPTAIN. KNOWING KHAN NOONIEN SINGH AS WE DO...
...HIS RETREAT WAS ENTIRELY *TACTICAL.*

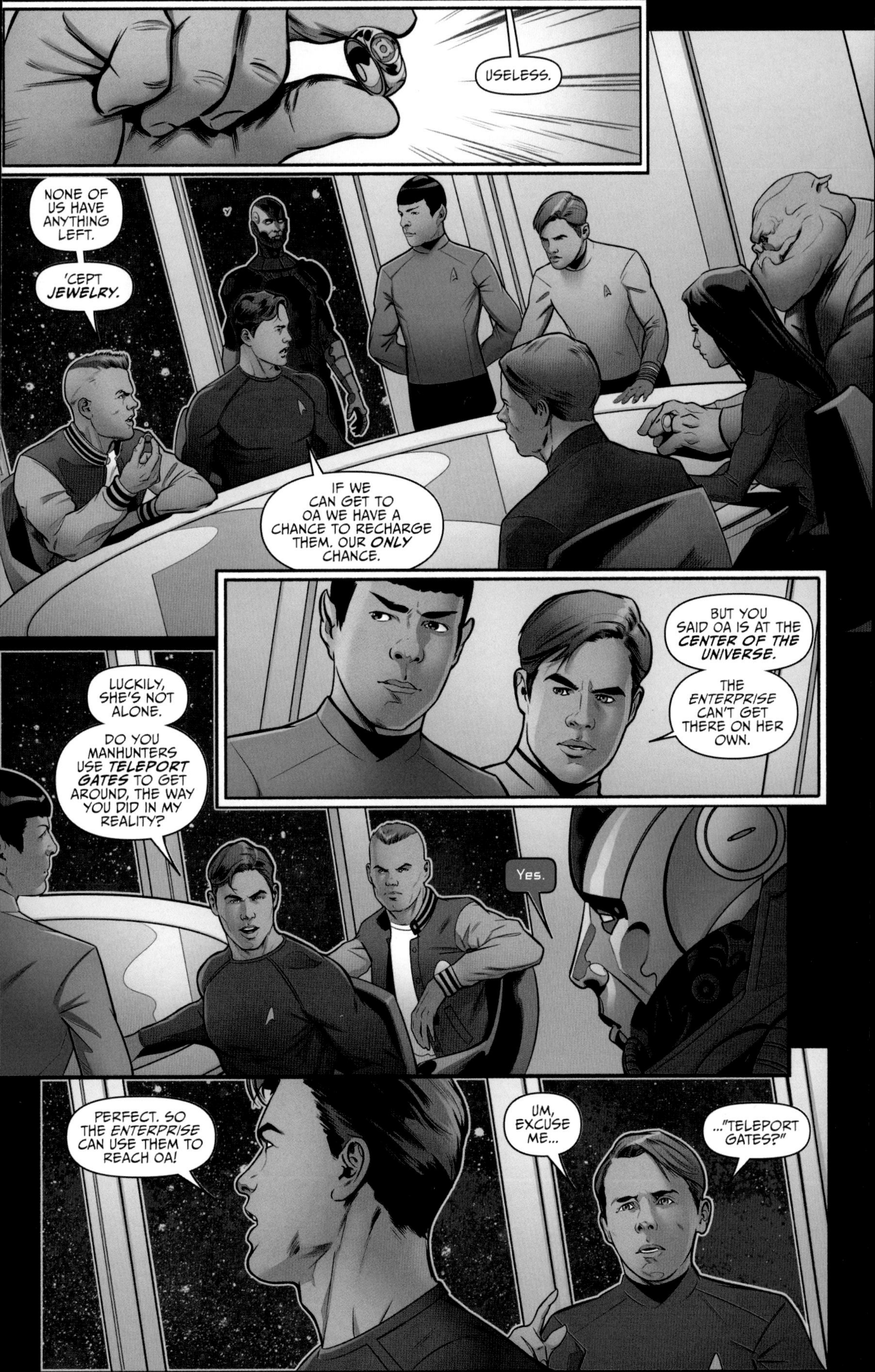

USELESS.
NONE OF US HAVE ANYTHING LEFT.
'CEPT *JEWELRY.*
IF WE CAN GET TO OA WE HAVE A CHANCE TO RECHARGE THEM. OUR *ONLY* CHANCE.
BUT YOU SAID OA IS AT THE ***CENTER OF THE UNIVERSE.***
THE *ENTERPRISE* CAN'T GET THERE ON HER OWN.
LUCKILY, SHE'S NOT ALONE.
DO YOU MANHUNTERS USE ***TELEPORT GATES*** TO GET AROUND, THE WAY YOU DID IN MY REALITY?
Yes.
PERFECT. SO THE *ENTERPRISE* CAN USE THEM TO REACH OA!
UM, EXCUSE ME...
..."TELEPORT GATES?"

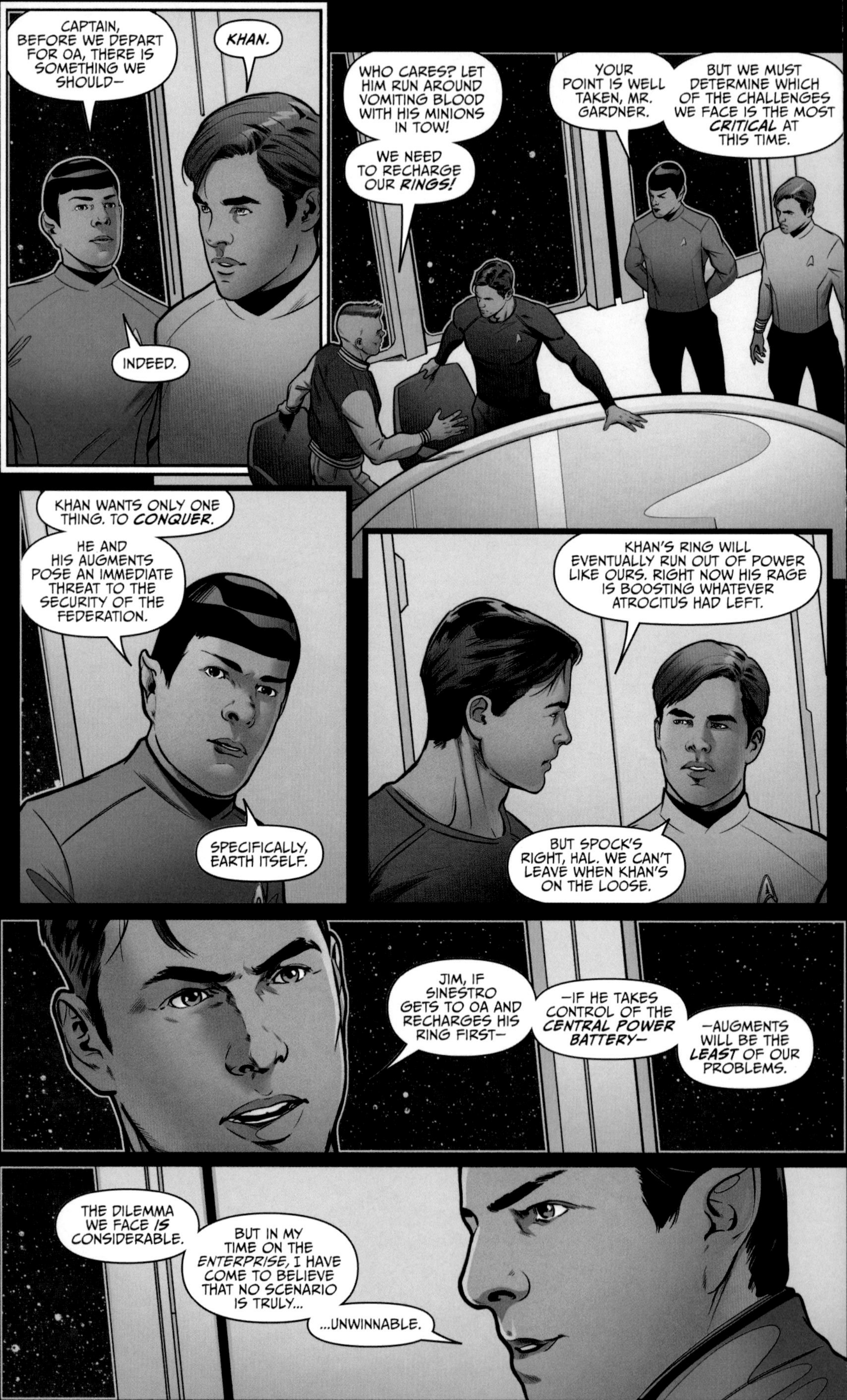
CAPTAIN, BEFORE WE DEPART FOR OA, THERE IS SOMETHING WE SHOULD—
KHAN.
INDEED.
WHO CARES? LET HIM RUN AROUND VOMITING BLOOD WITH HIS MINIONS IN TOW!
WE NEED TO RECHARGE OUR RINGS!
YOUR POINT IS WELL TAKEN, MR. GARDNER.
BUT WE MUST DETERMINE WHICH OF THE CHALLENGES WE FACE IS THE MOST CRITICAL AT THIS TIME.
KHAN WANTS ONLY ONE THING. TO CONQUER.
HE AND HIS AUGMENTS POSE AN IMMEDIATE THREAT TO THE SECURITY OF THE FEDERATION.
SPECIFICALLY, EARTH ITSELF.
KHAN'S RING WILL EVENTUALLY RUN OUT OF POWER LIKE OURS. RIGHT NOW HIS RAGE IS BOOSTING WHATEVER ATROCITUS HAD LEFT.
BUT SPOCK'S RIGHT, HAL. WE CAN'T LEAVE WHEN KHAN'S ON THE LOOSE.
JIM, IF SINESTRO GETS TO OA AND RECHARGES HIS RING FIRST—
—IF HE TAKES CONTROL OF THE CENTRAL POWER BATTERY—
—AUGMENTS WILL BE THE LEAST OF OUR PROBLEMS.
THE DILEMMA WE FACE IS CONSIDERABLE.
BUT IN MY TIME ON THE ENTERPRISE, I HAVE COME TO BELIEVE THAT NO SCENARIO IS TRULY...
...UNWINNABLE.

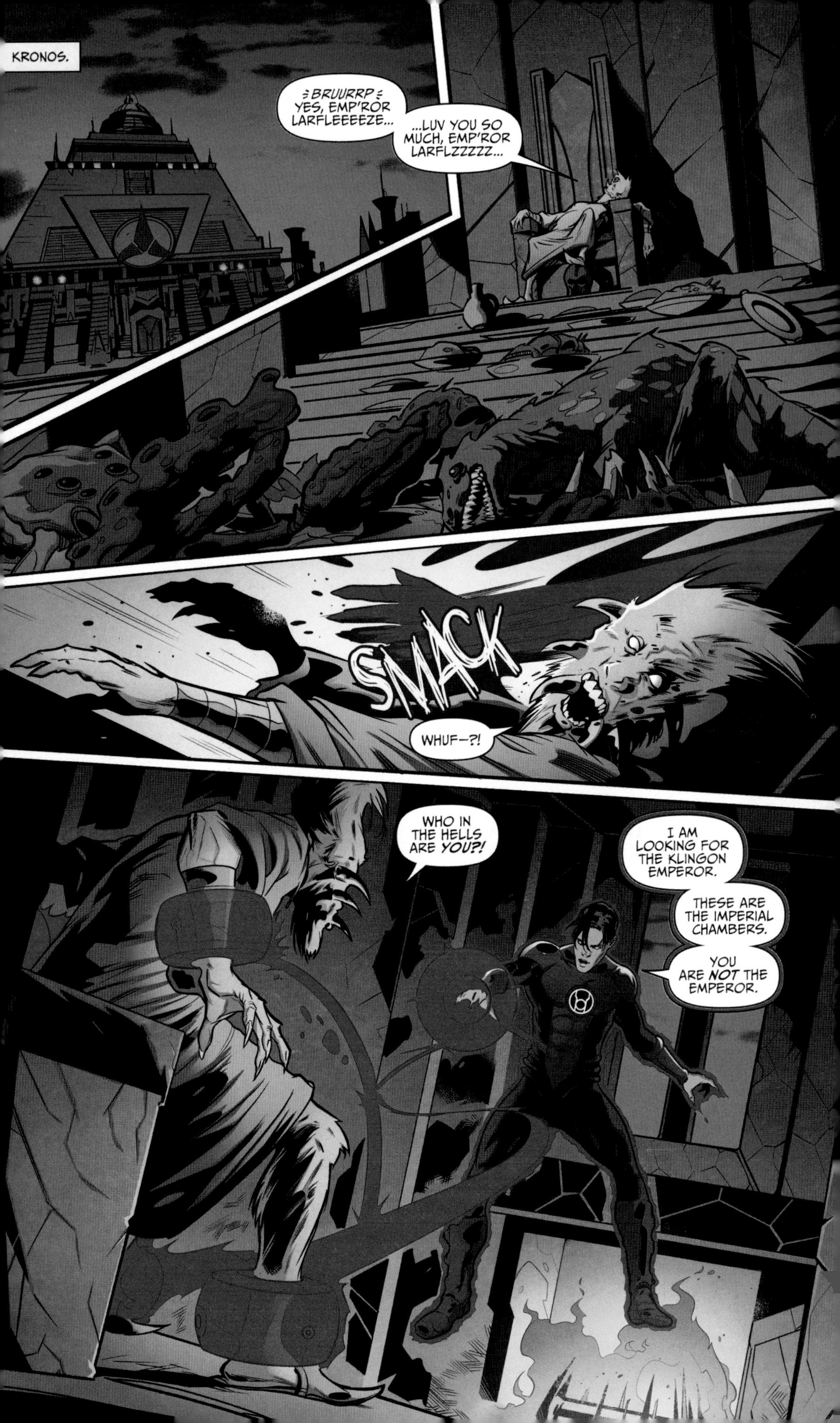
KRONOS.
BRUURRP YES, EMP'ROR LARFLEEEEZE...
...LUV YOU SO MUCH, EMP'ROR LARFLZZZZZ...
SMACK
WHUF--?!
WHO IN THE HELLS ARE YOU?!
I AM LOOKING FOR THE KLINGON EMPEROR.
THESE ARE THE IMPERIAL CHAMBERS.
YOU ARE NOT THE EMPEROR.

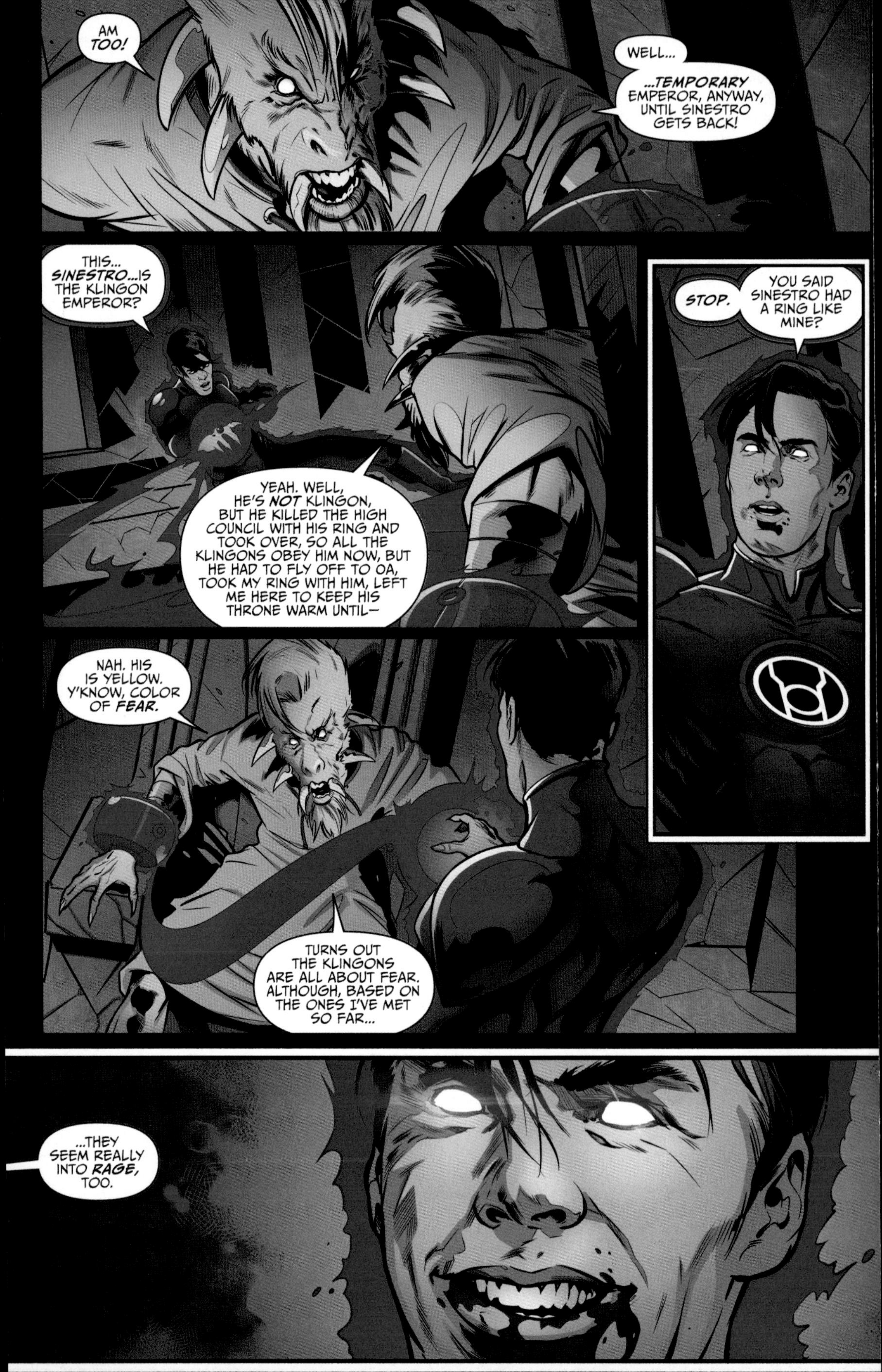
AM TOO!
WELL...
...TEMPORARY EMPEROR, ANYWAY, UNTIL SINESTRO GETS BACK!
THIS... SINESTRO...IS THE KLINGON EMPEROR?
YEAH. WELL, HE'S NOT KLINGON, BUT HE KILLED THE HIGH COUNCIL WITH HIS RING AND TOOK OVER, SO ALL THE KLINGONS OBEY HIM NOW, BUT HE HAD TO FLY OFF TO OA, TOOK MY RING WITH HIM, LEFT ME HERE TO KEEP HIS THRONE WARM UNTIL—
STOP.
YOU SAID SINESTRO HAD A RING LIKE MINE?
NAH. HIS IS YELLOW. Y'KNOW, COLOR OF FEAR.
TURNS OUT THE KLINGONS ARE ALL ABOUT FEAR. ALTHOUGH, BASED ON THE ONES I'VE MET SO FAR...
...THEY SEEM REALLY INTO RAGE, TOO.

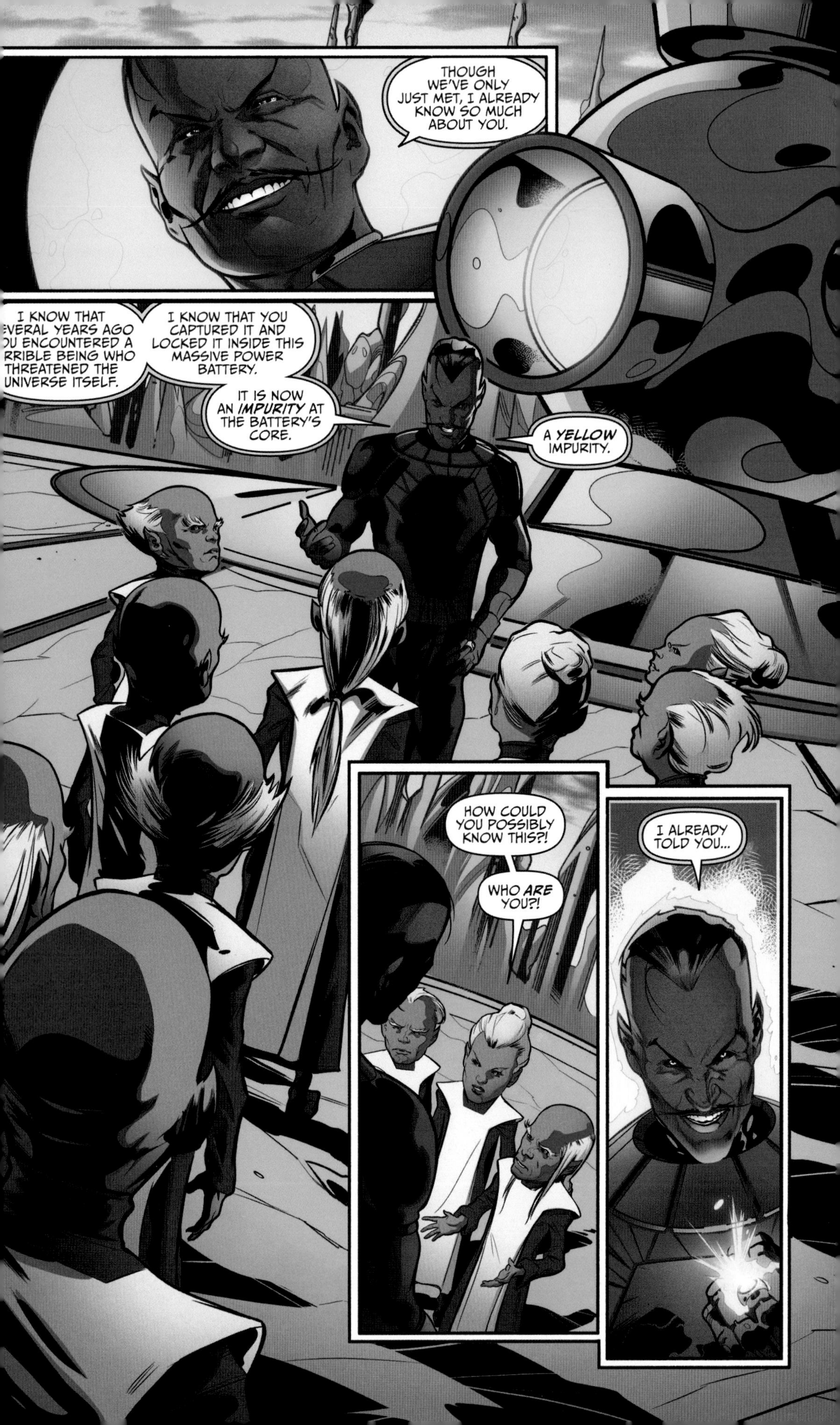
THOUGH WE'VE ONLY JUST MET, I ALREADY KNOW SO MUCH ABOUT YOU.
I KNOW THAT EVERAL YEARS AGO OU ENCOUNTERED A RRIBLE BEING WHO THREATENED THE UNIVERSE ITSELF.
I KNOW THAT YOU CAPTURED IT AND LOCKED IT INSIDE THIS MASSIVE POWER BATTERY.
IT IS NOW AN *IMPURITY* AT THE BATTERY'S CORE.
A *YELLOW* IMPURITY.
HOW COULD YOU POSSIBLY KNOW THIS?!
WHO *ARE* YOU?!
I ALREADY TOLD YOU...

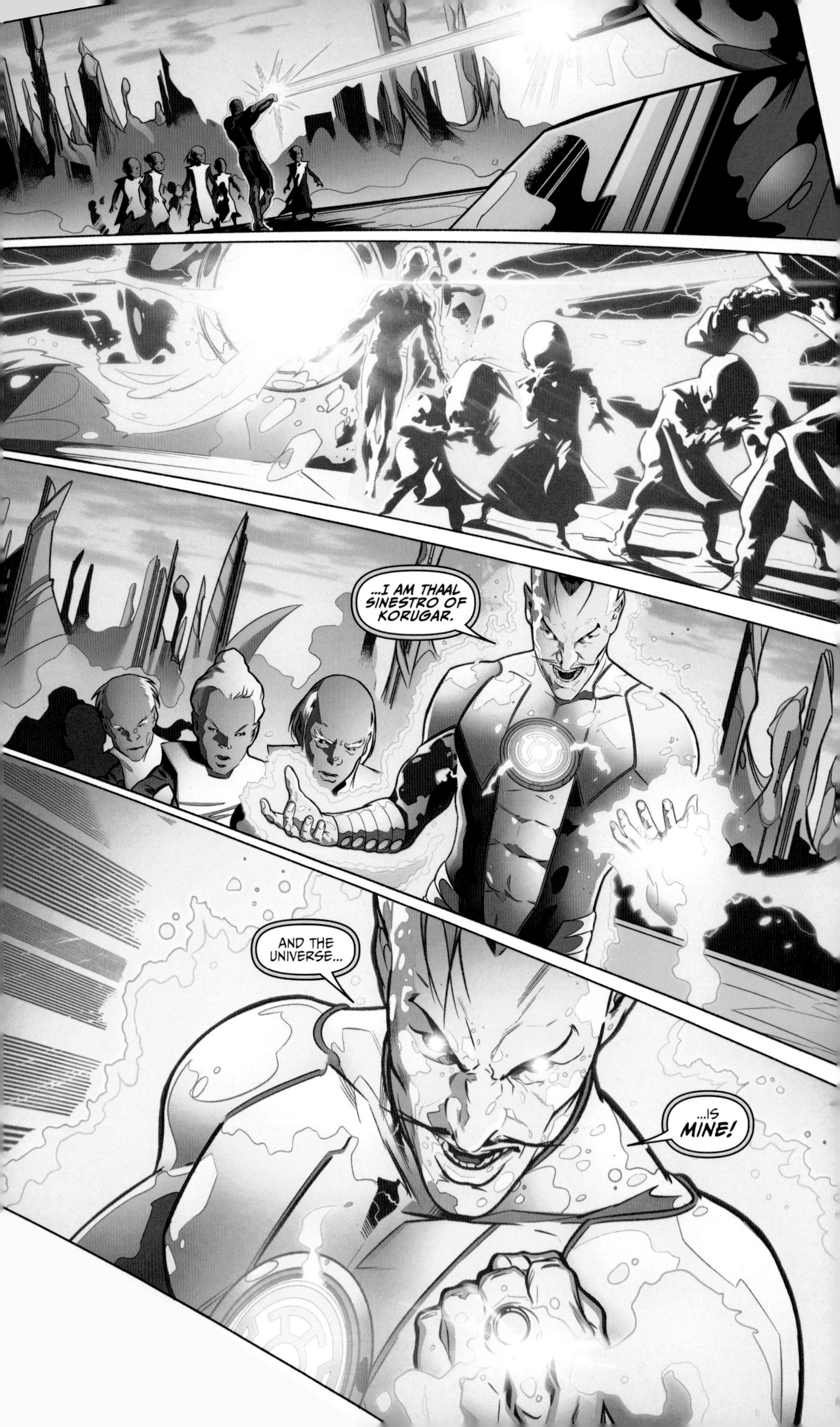
...I AM THAAL SINESTRO OF KORUGAR.
AND THE UNIVERSE...
...IS MINE!

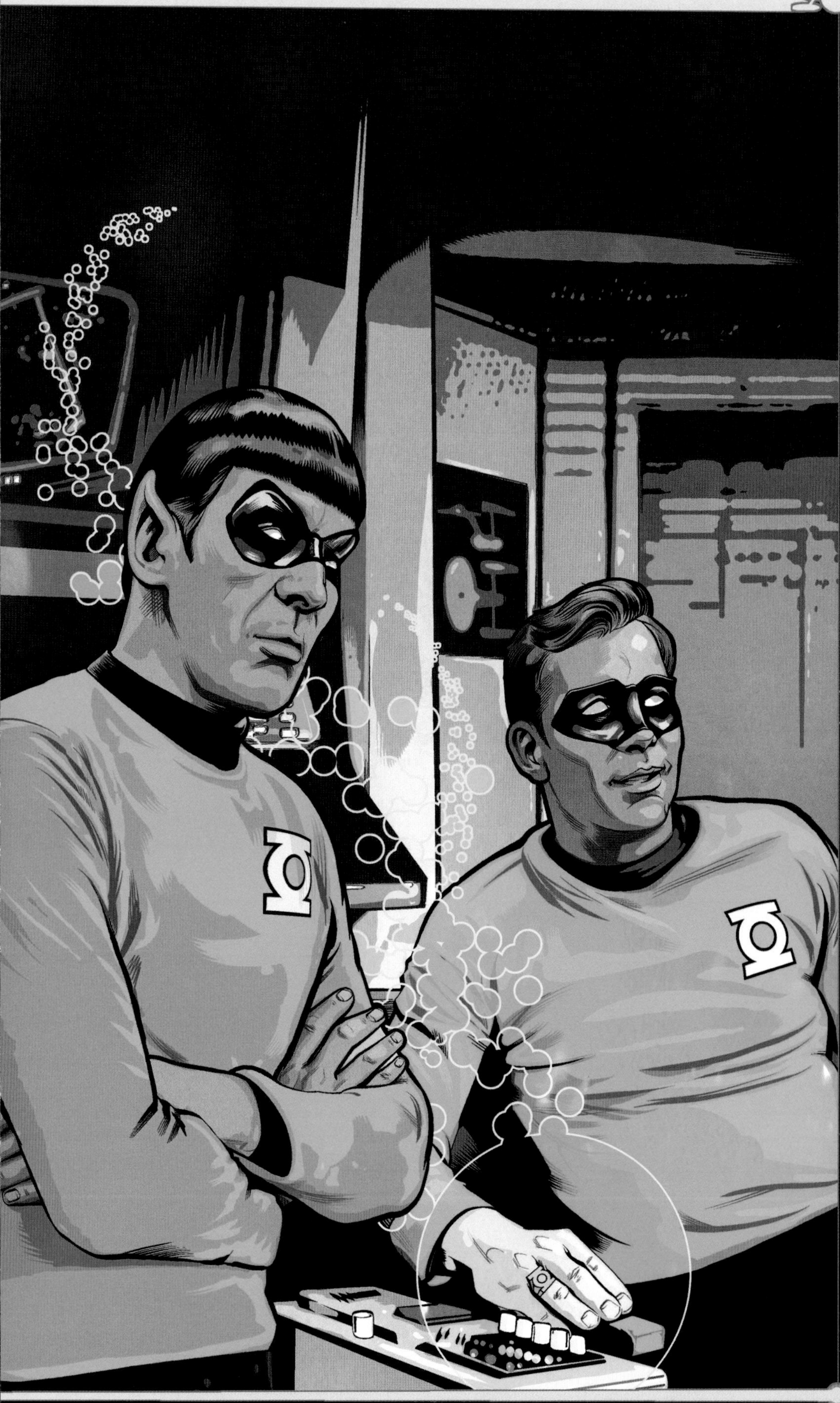

rt by TONY SHASTEEN

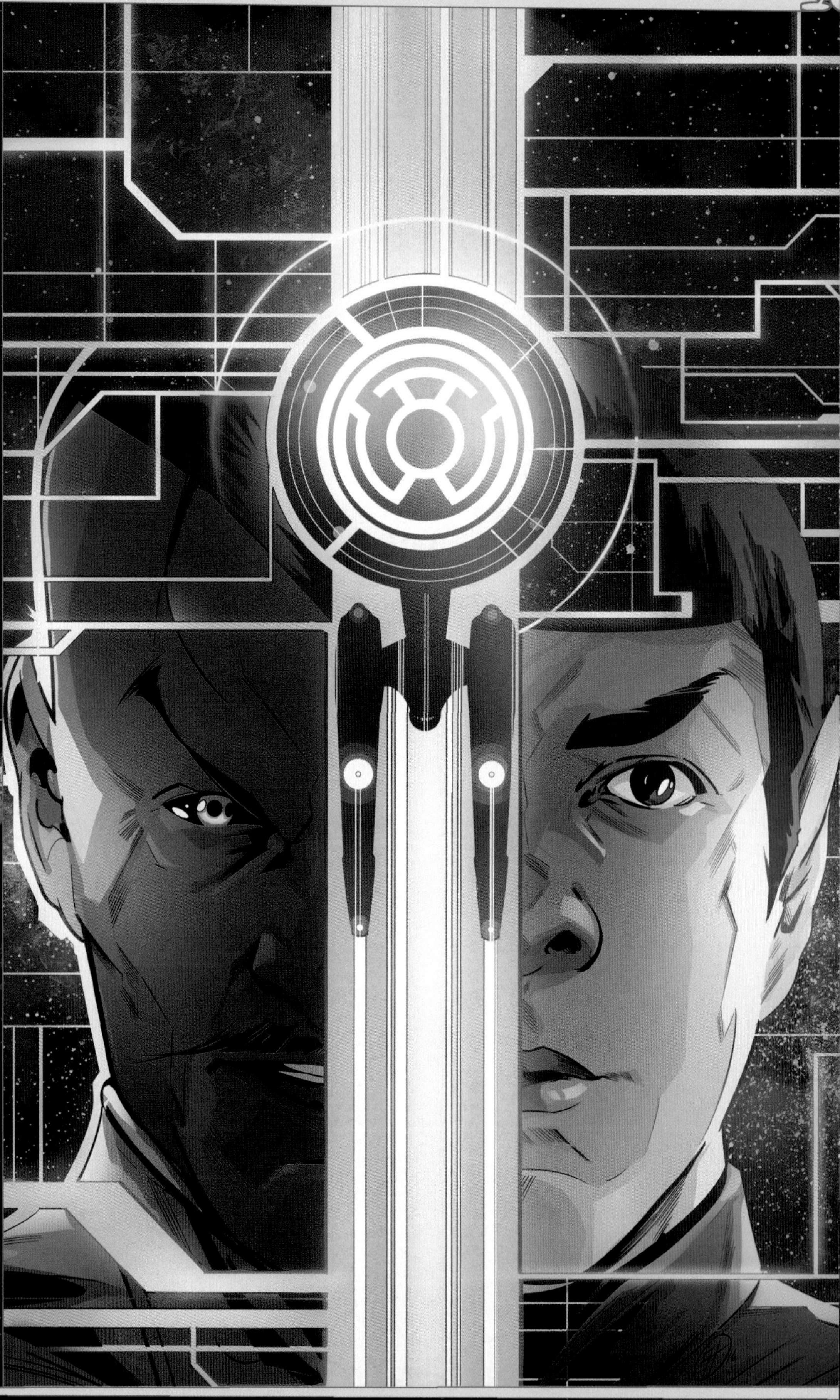

art by ANGEL HERNANDEZ • colors by ESTHER SANZ

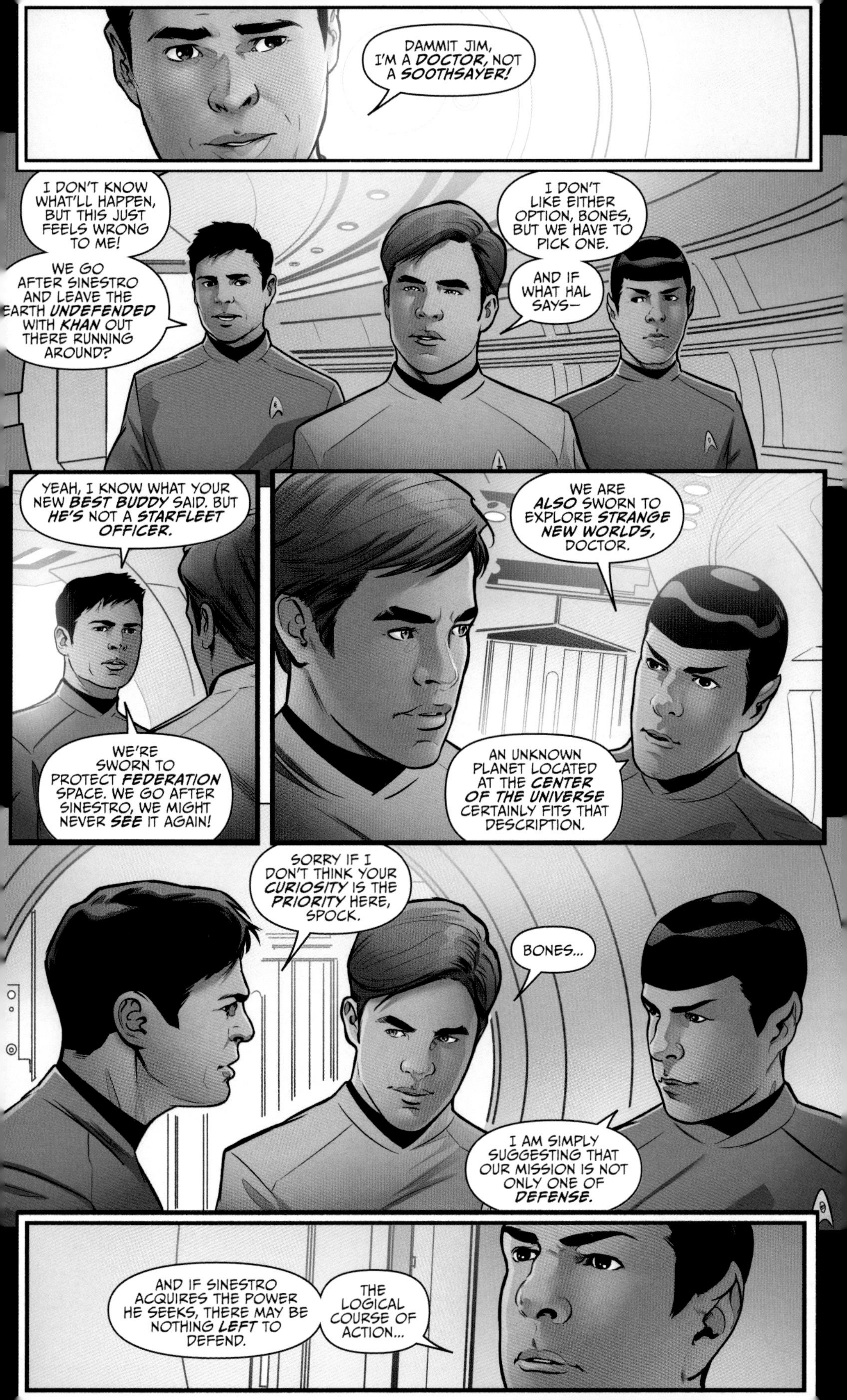
DAMMIT JIM, I'M A DOCTOR, NOT A SOOTHSAYER!
I DON'T KNOW WHAT'LL HAPPEN, BUT THIS JUST FEELS WRONG TO ME!
WE GO AFTER SINESTRO AND LEAVE THE EARTH UNDEFENDED WITH KHAN OUT THERE RUNNING AROUND?
I DON'T LIKE EITHER OPTION, BONES, BUT WE HAVE TO PICK ONE.
AND IF WHAT HAL SAYS—
YEAH, I KNOW WHAT YOUR NEW BEST BUDDY SAID. BUT HE'S NOT A STARFLEET OFFICER.
WE'RE SWORN TO PROTECT FEDERATION SPACE. WE GO AFTER SINESTRO, WE MIGHT NEVER SEE IT AGAIN!
WE ARE ALSO SWORN TO EXPLORE STRANGE NEW WORLDS, DOCTOR.
AN UNKNOWN PLANET LOCATED AT THE CENTER OF THE UNIVERSE CERTAINLY FITS THAT DESCRIPTION.
SORRY IF I DON'T THINK YOUR CURIOSITY IS THE PRIORITY HERE, SPOCK.
BONES...
I AM SIMPLY SUGGESTING THAT OUR MISSION IS NOT ONLY ONE OF DEFENSE.
THE LOGICAL COURSE OF ACTION...
AND IF SINESTRO ACQUIRES THE POWER HE SEEKS, THERE MAY BE NOTHING LEFT TO DEFEND.

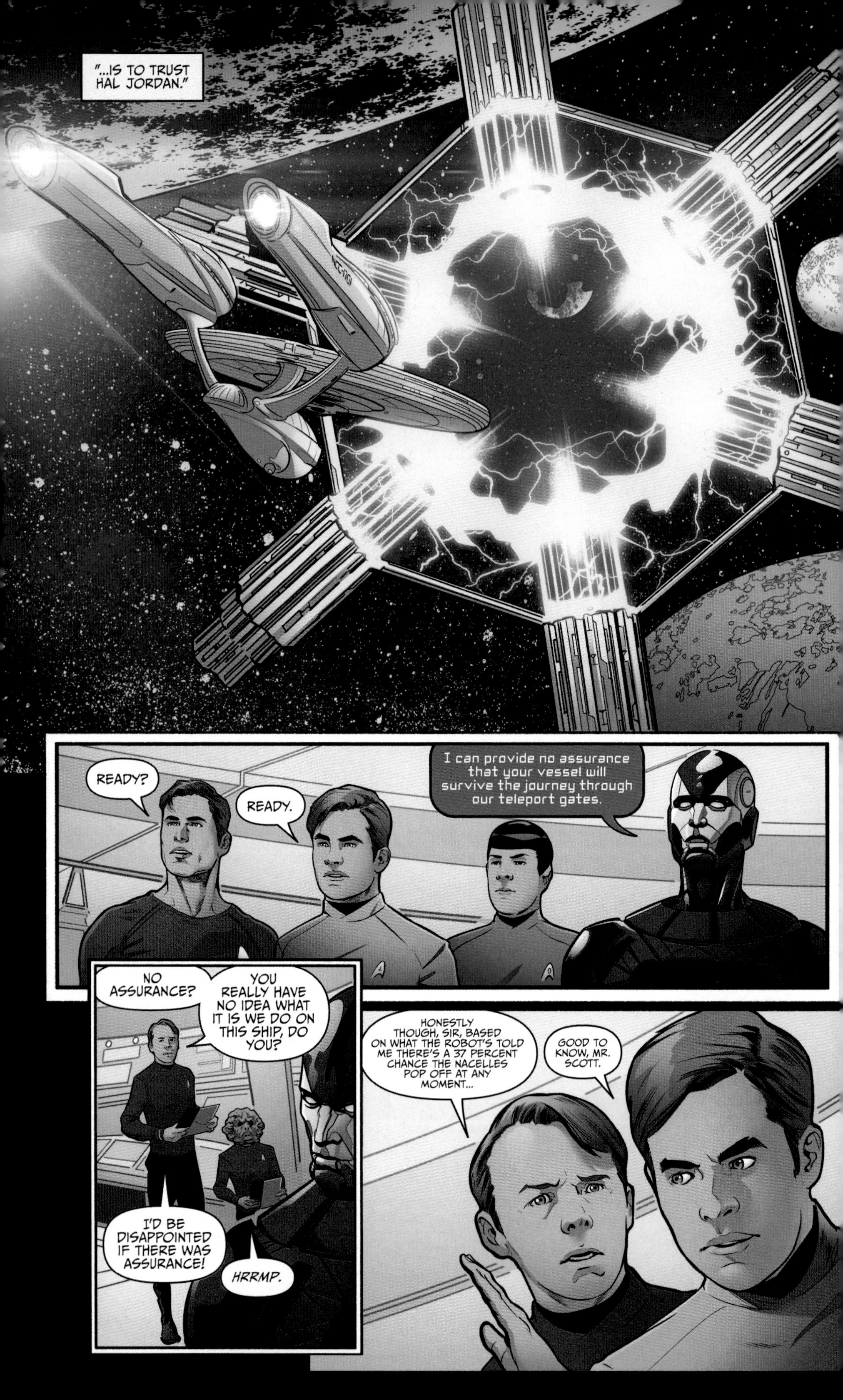
"...IS TO TRUST HAL JORDAN."
NCC-1701
READY?
READY.
I can provide no assurance that your vessel will survive the journey through our teleport gates.
NO ASSURANCE?
YOU REALLY HAVE NO IDEA WHAT IT IS WE DO ON THIS SHIP, DO YOU?
I'D BE DISAPPOINTED IF THERE WAS ASSURANCE!
HRRMP.
HONESTLY THOUGH, SIR, BASED ON WHAT THE ROBOT'S TOLD ME THERE'S A 37 PERCENT CHANCE THE NACELLES POP OFF AT ANY MOMENT...
GOOD TO KNOW, MR. SCOTT.

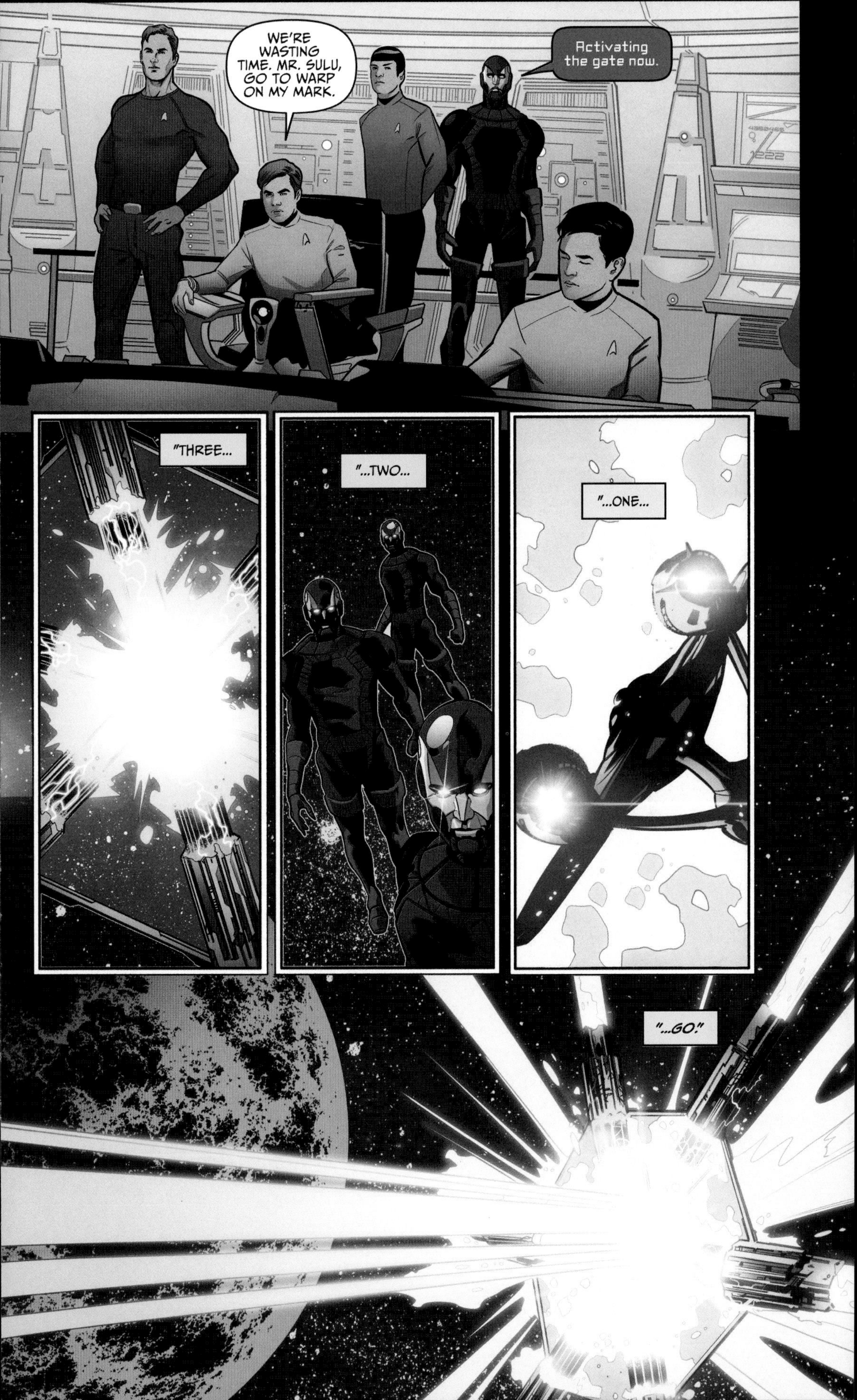
WE'RE WASTING TIME. MR. SULU, GO TO WARP ON MY MARK.
Activating the gate now.
"THREE...
"...TWO...
"...ONE...
"...GO."

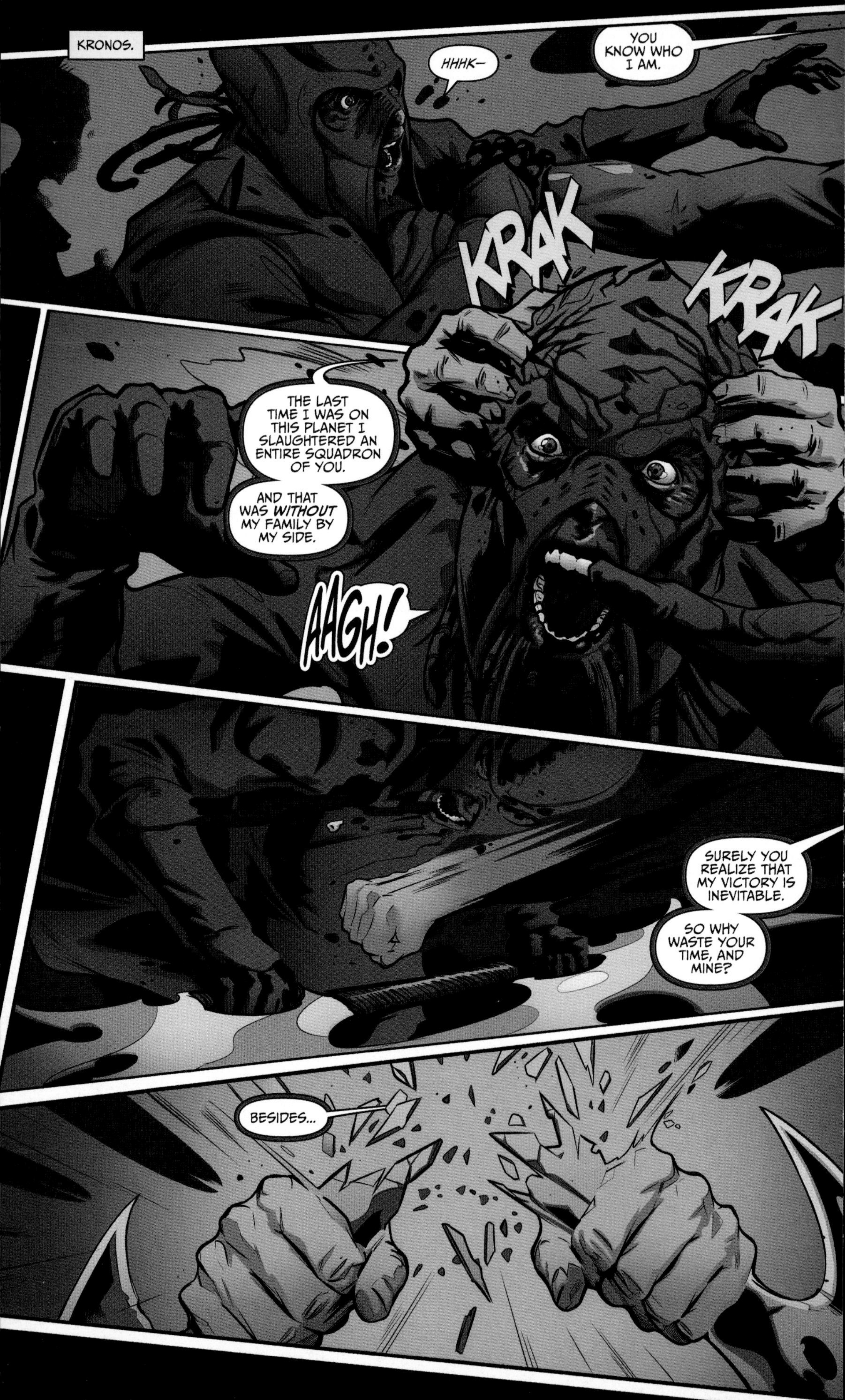
KRONOS.
HHHK—
YOU KNOW WHO I AM.
KRAK
KRAK
THE LAST TIME I WAS ON THIS PLANET I SLAUGHTERED AN ENTIRE SQUADRON OF YOU.
AND THAT WAS *WITHOUT* MY FAMILY BY MY SIDE.
AAGH!
SURELY YOU REALIZE THAT MY VICTORY IS INEVITABLE.
SO WHY WASTE YOUR TIME, AND MINE?
BESIDES...

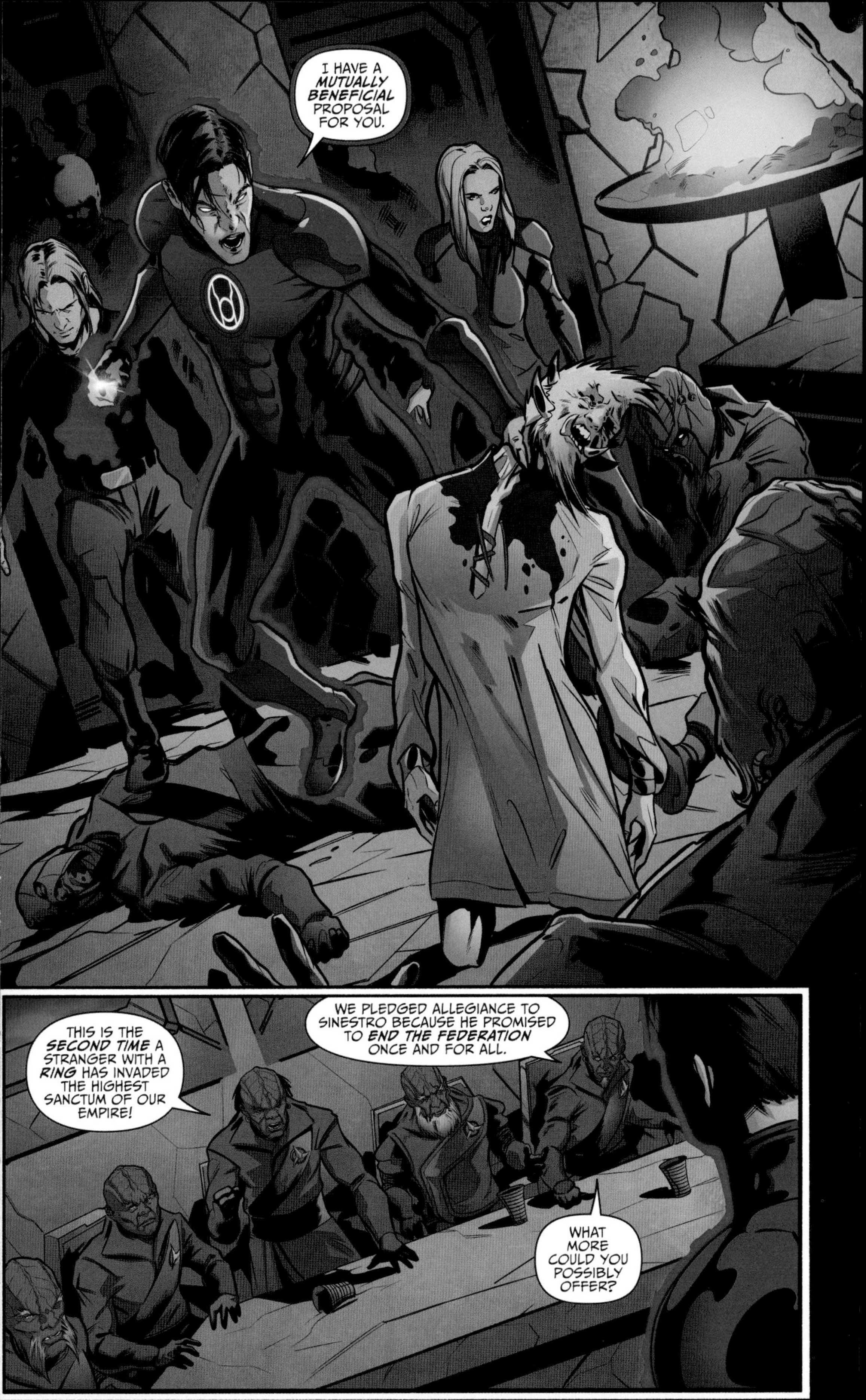
I HAVE A MUTUALLY BENEFICIAL PROPOSAL FOR YOU.
THIS IS THE SECOND TIME A STRANGER WITH A RING HAS INVADED THE HIGHEST SANCTUM OF OUR EMPIRE!
WE PLEDGED ALLEGIANCE TO SINESTRO BECAUSE HE PROMISED TO END THE FEDERATION ONCE AND FOR ALL.
WHAT MORE COULD YOU POSSIBLY OFFER?

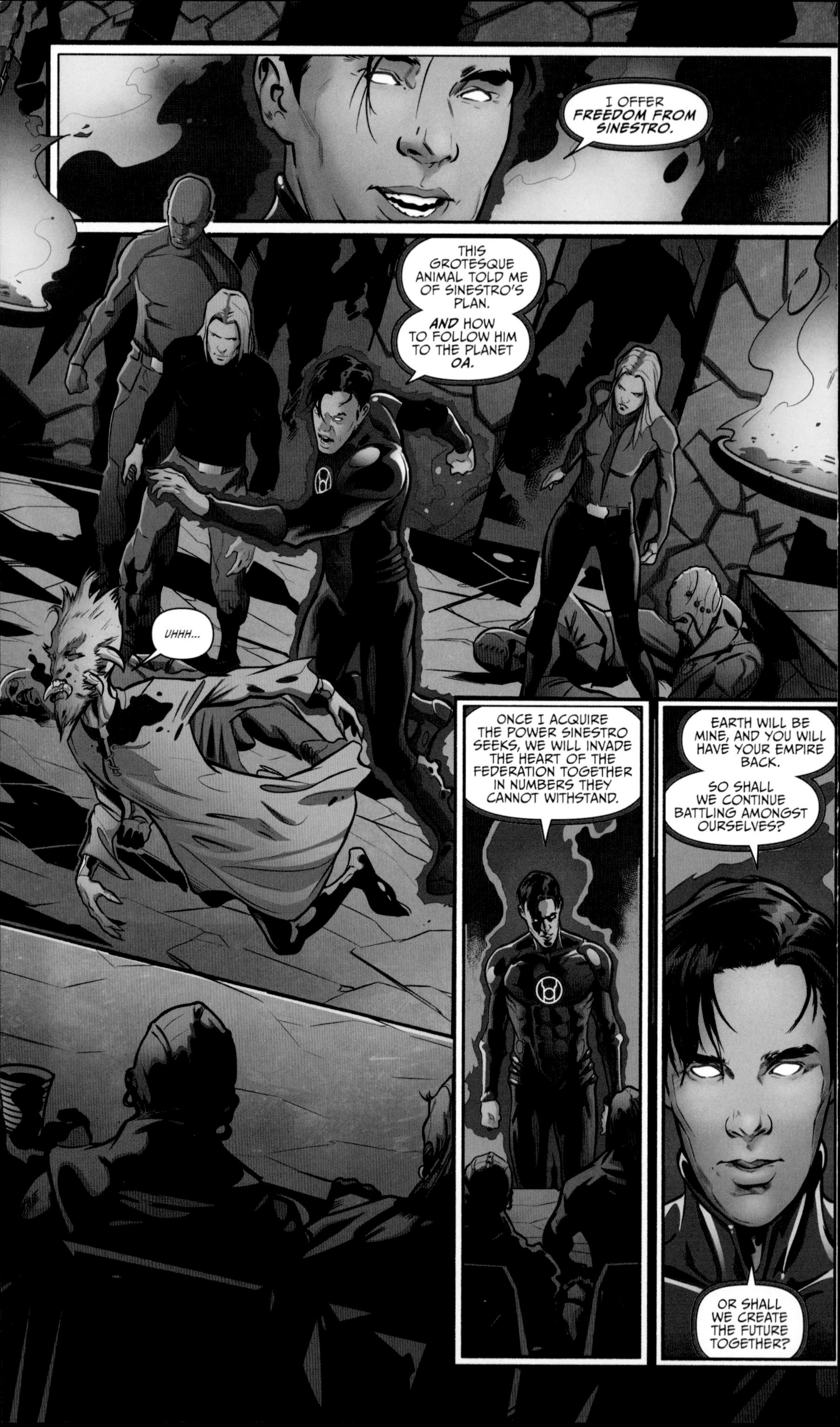
I OFFER FREEDOM FROM SINESTRO.
THIS GROTESQUE ANIMAL TOLD ME OF SINESTRO'S PLAN.
AND HOW TO FOLLOW HIM TO THE PLANET OA.
UHHH...
ONCE I ACQUIRE THE POWER SINESTRO SEEKS, WE WILL INVADE THE HEART OF THE FEDERATION TOGETHER IN NUMBERS THEY CANNOT WITHSTAND.
EARTH WILL BE MINE, AND YOU WILL HAVE YOUR EMPIRE BACK.
SO SHALL WE CONTINUE BATTLING AMONGST OURSELVES?
OR SHALL WE CREATE THE FUTURE TOGETHER?

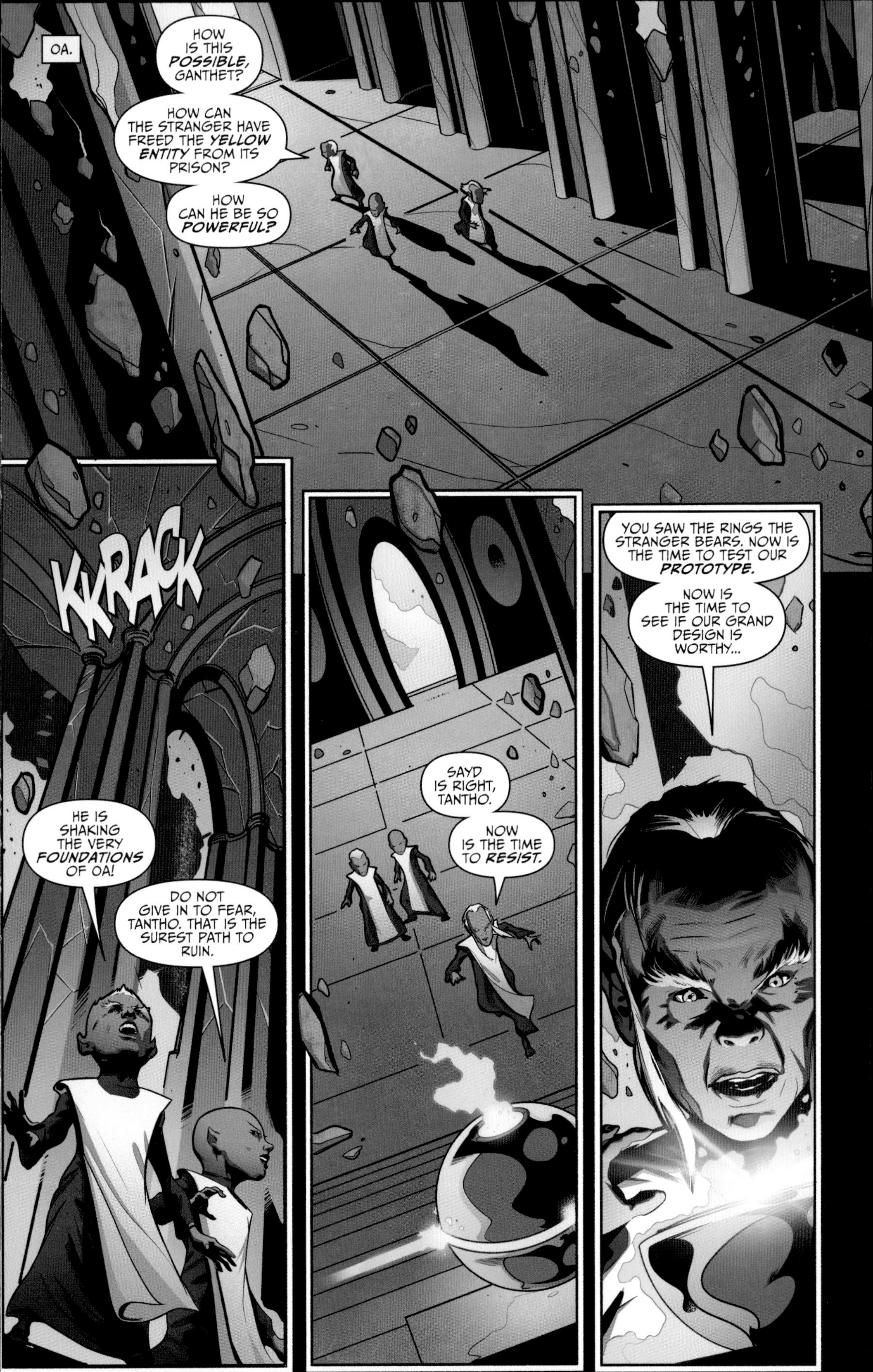
OA.
HOW IS THIS POSSIBLE, GANTHET?
HOW CAN THE STRANGER HAVE FREED THE YELLOW ENTITY FROM ITS PRISON?
HOW CAN HE BE SO POWERFUL?
KKRACK
HE IS SHAKING THE VERY FOUNDATIONS OF OA!
DO NOT GIVE IN TO FEAR, TANTHO. THAT IS THE SUREST PATH TO RUIN.
SAYD IS RIGHT, TANTHO.
NOW IS THE TIME TO RESIST.
YOU SAW THE RINGS THE STRANGER BEARS. NOW IS THE TIME TO TEST OUR PROTOTYPE.
NOW IS THE TIME TO SEE IF OUR GRAND DESIGN IS WORTHY...

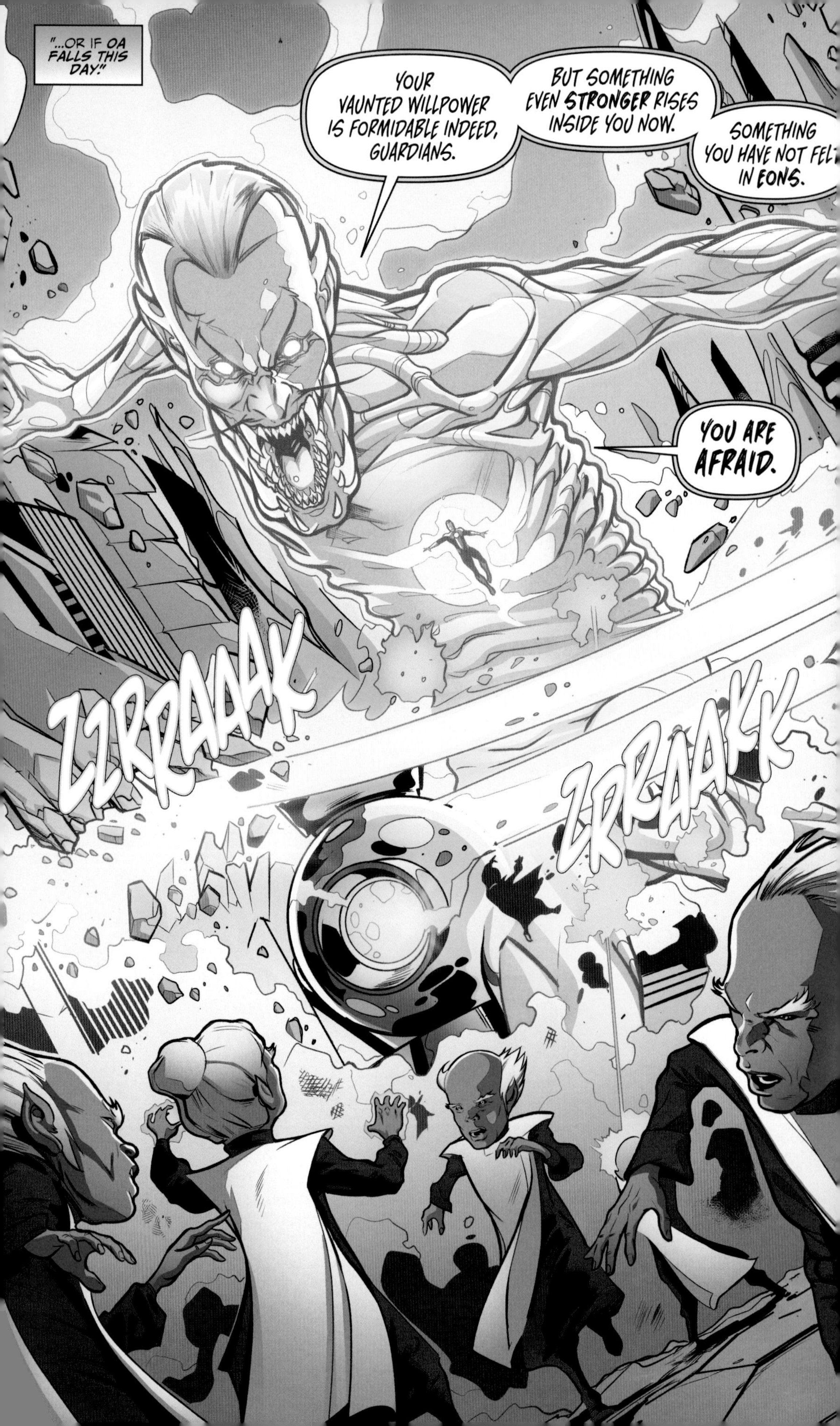
"...OR IF OA FALLS THIS DAY."
YOUR VAUNTED WILLPOWER IS FORMIDABLE INDEED, GUARDIANS.
BUT SOMETHING EVEN STRONGER RISES INSIDE YOU NOW.
SOMETHING YOU HAVE NOT FEL IN EONS.
YOU ARE AFRAID.
ZZRRAAAK
ZZRRAAKK

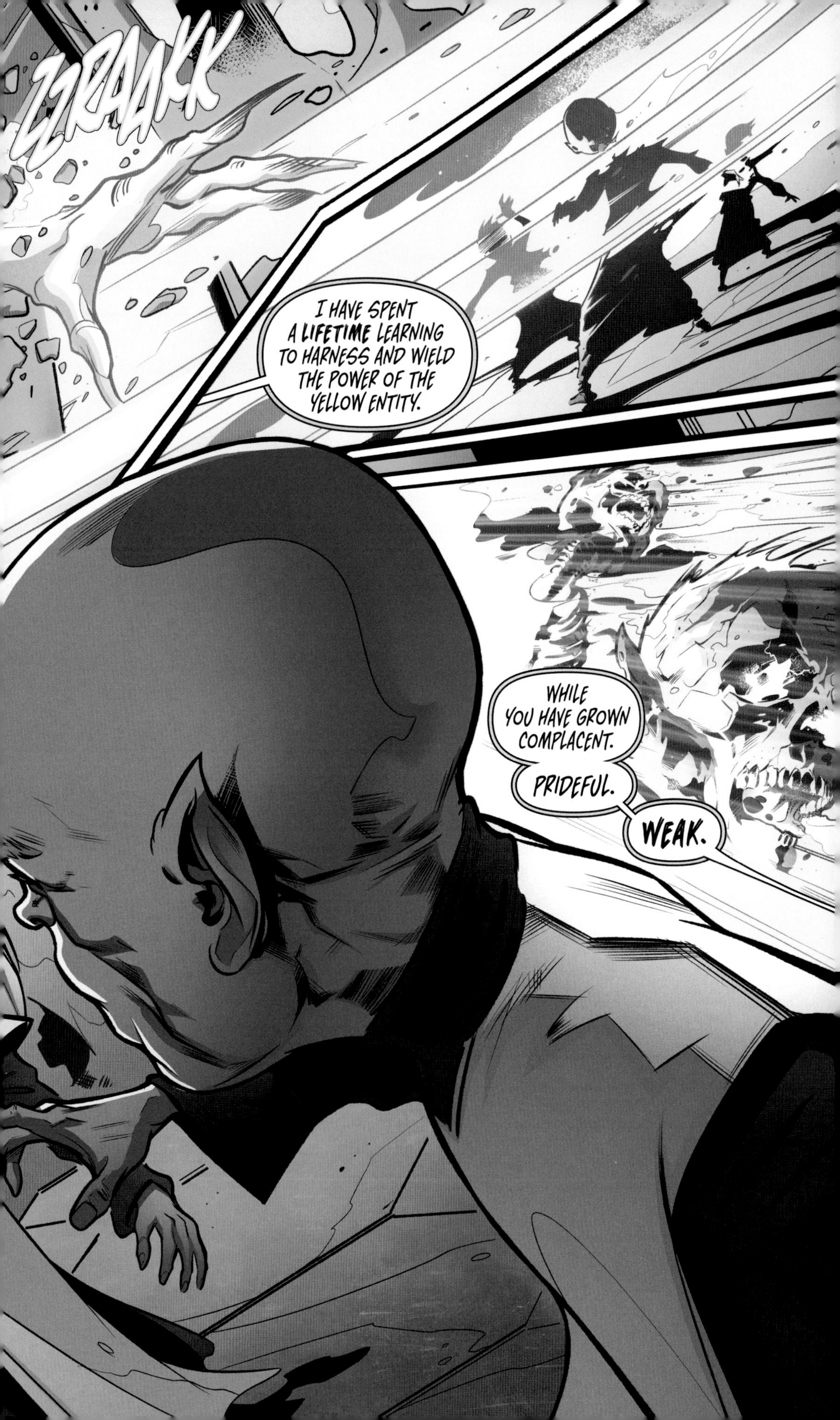
ZZRAAKK
I HAVE SPENT A LIFETIME LEARNING TO HARNESS AND WIELD THE POWER OF THE YELLOW ENTITY.
WHILE YOU HAVE GROWN COMPLACENT.
PRIDEFUL.
WEAK.

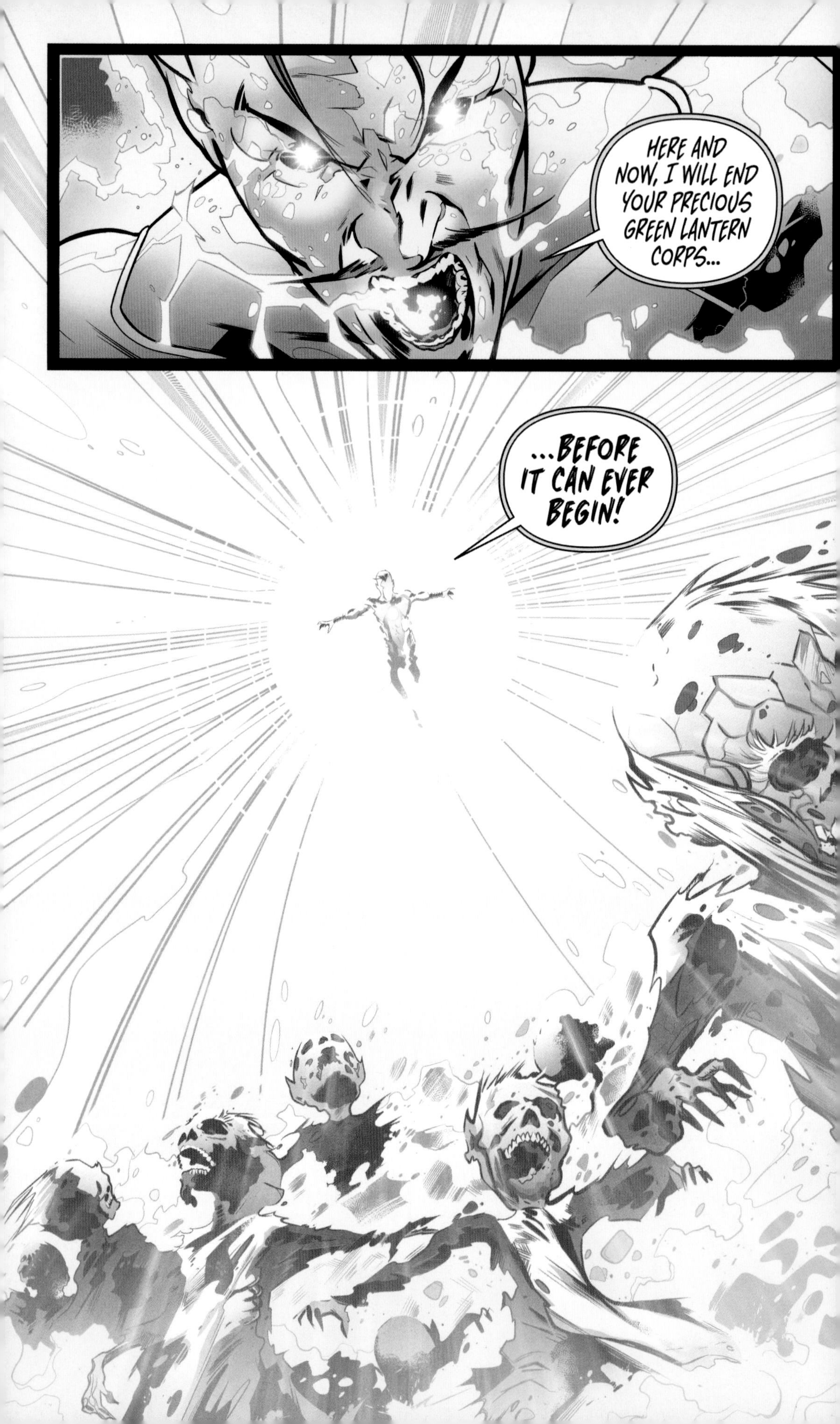
HERE AND NOW, I WILL END YOUR PRECIOUS GREEN LANTERN CORPS...
...BEFORE IT CAN EVER BEGIN!

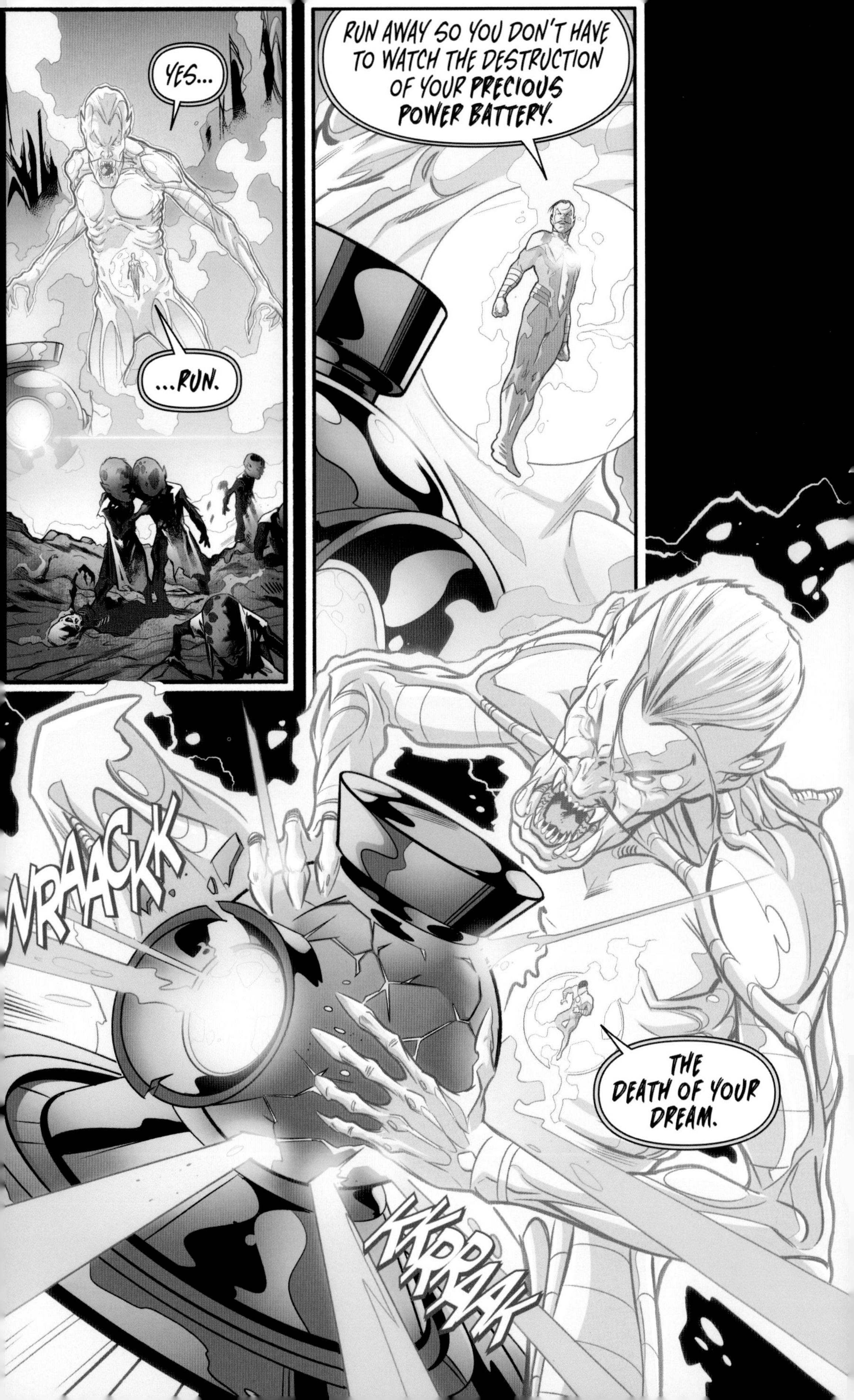
YES...
...RUN.
RUN AWAY SO YOU DON'T HAVE TO WATCH THE DESTRUCTION OF YOUR PRECIOUS POWER BATTERY.
NRAACKK
THE DEATH OF YOUR DREAM.
KKKRRAAK

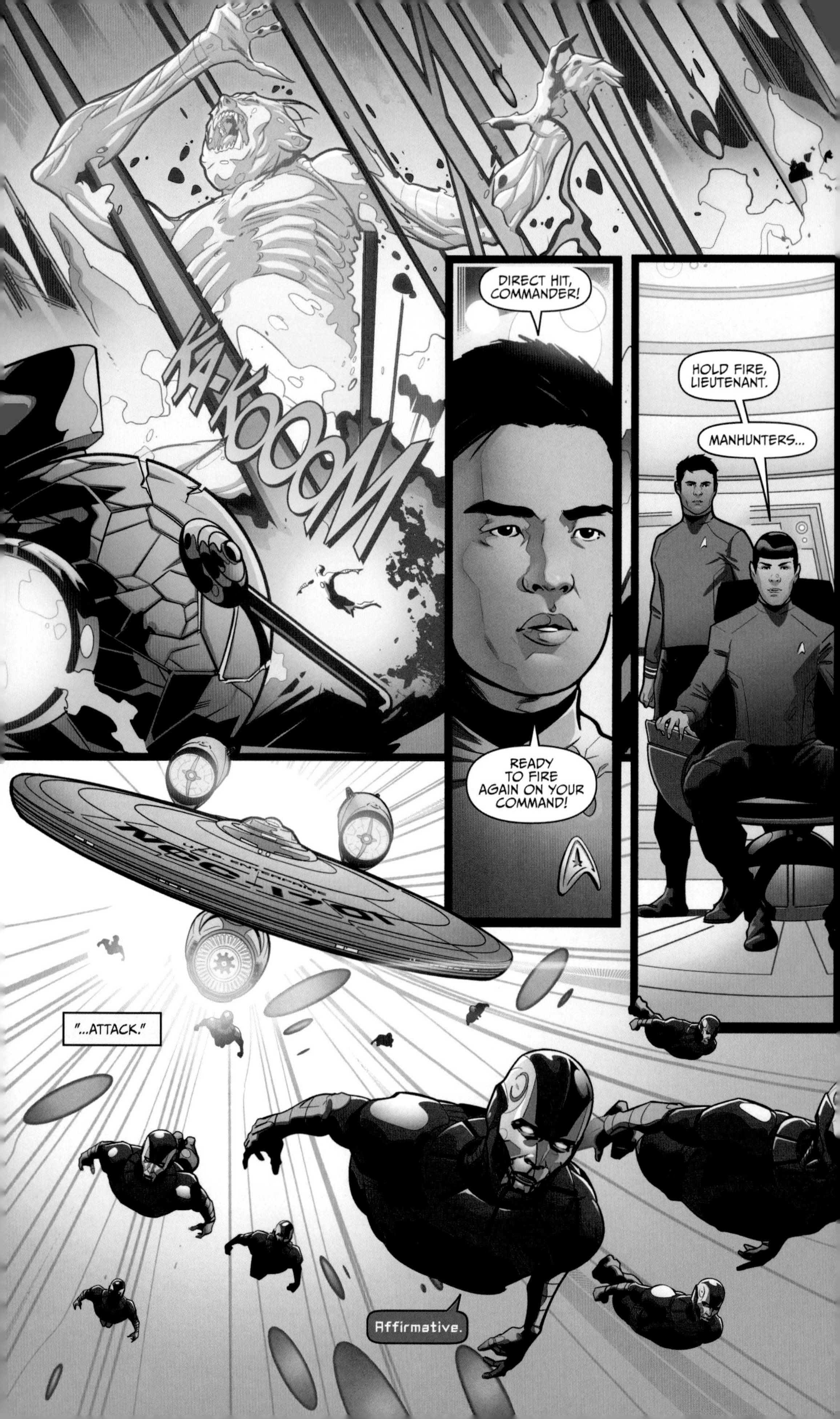
KA-KOOOM
DIRECT HIT, COMMANDER!
READY TO FIRE AGAIN ON YOUR COMMAND!
HOLD FIRE, LIEUTENANT.
MANHUNTERS...
"...ATTACK."
Affirmative.

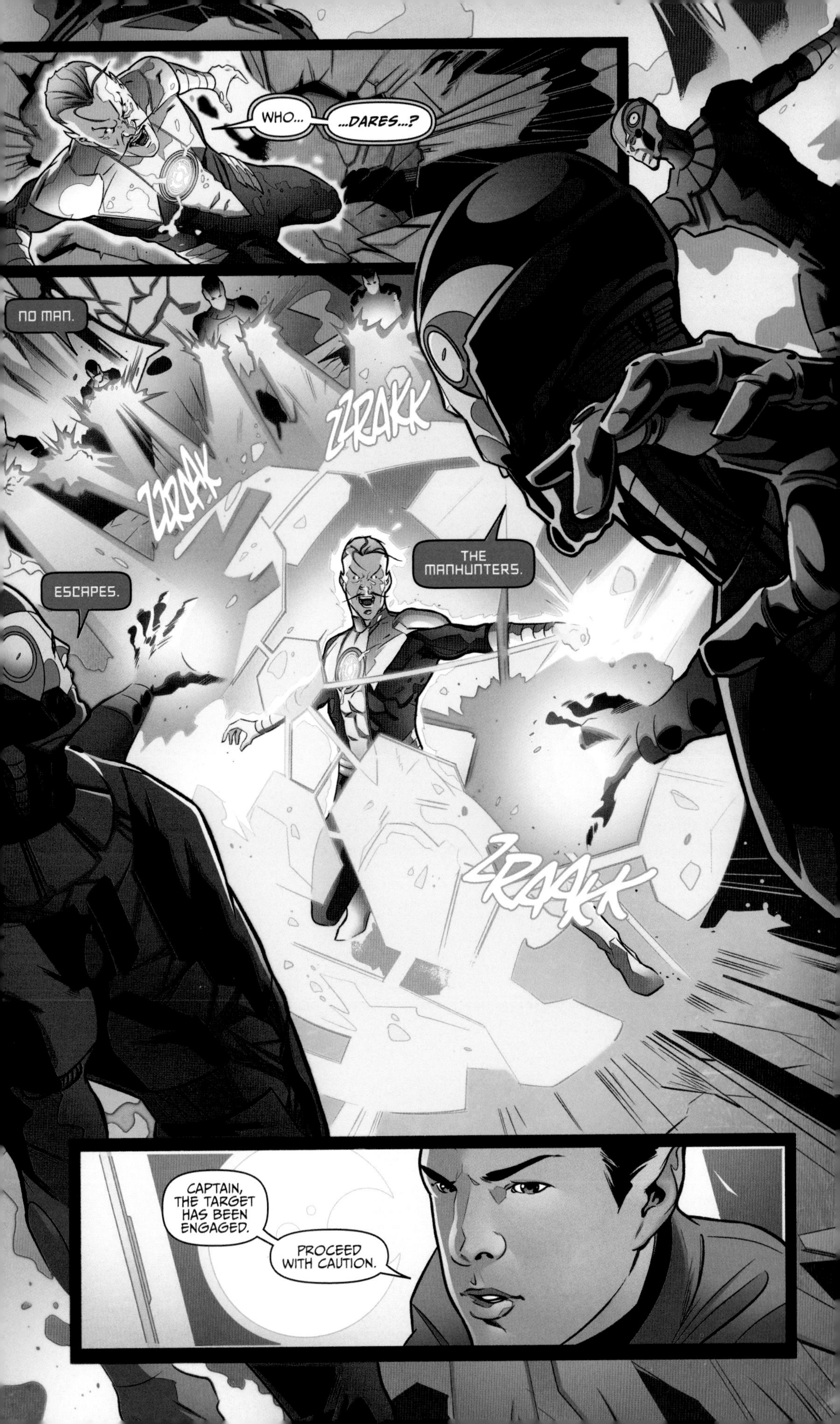
WHO...
...DARES...?
NO MAN.
ZZRAKK
ZZRAKK
ESCAPES.
THE MANHUNTERS.
ZRAKKK
CAPTAIN, THE TARGET HAS BEEN ENGAGED.
PROCEED WITH CAUTION.

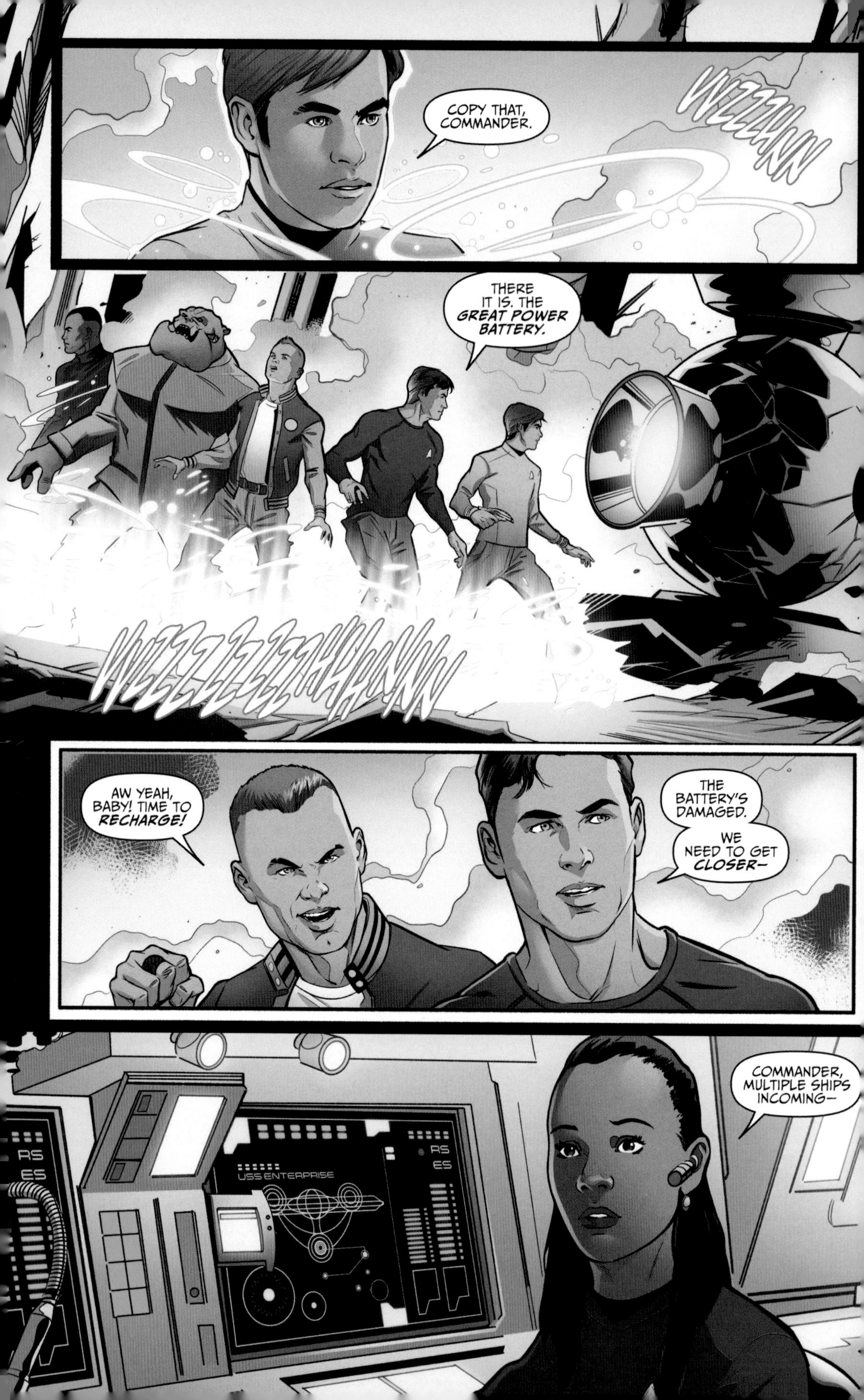
COPY THAT, COMMANDER.
VWZZZHNN
THERE IT IS. THE GREAT POWER BATTERY.
VWZZZZZZZHHNNN
AW YEAH, BABY! TIME TO RECHARGE!
THE BATTERY'S DAMAGED.
WE NEED TO GET CLOSER—
USS ENTERPRISE
RS
ES
COMMANDER, MULTIPLE SHIPS INCOMING—

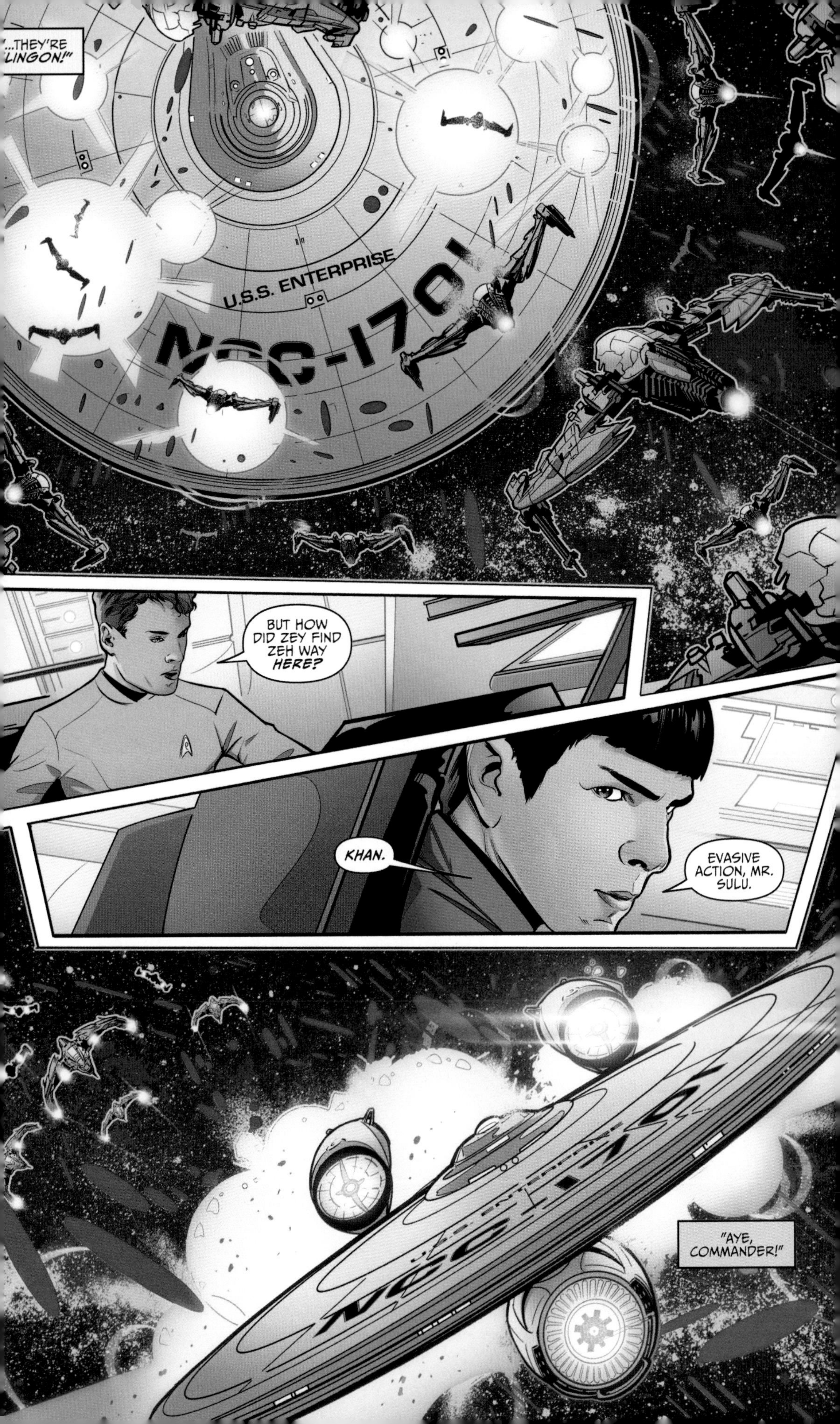
"...THEY'RE
LINGON!"
U.S.S. ENTERPRISE
BUT HOW DID ZEY FIND ZEH WAY HERE?
KHAN.
EVASIVE ACTION, MR. SULU.
"AYE, COMMANDER!"

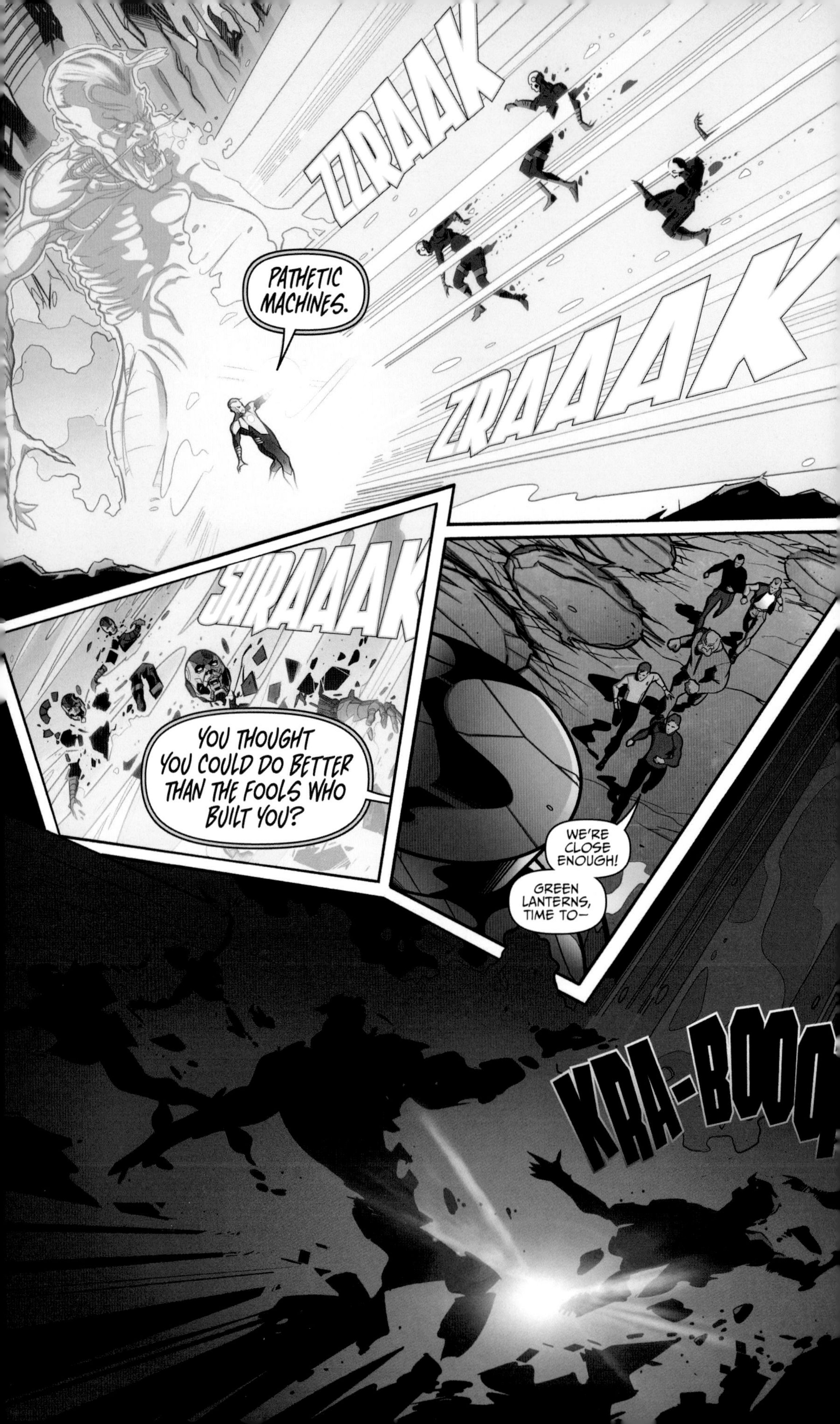
ZZRAAK
PATHETIC MACHINES.
ZRAAAAK
SKRAAAK
YOU THOUGHT YOU COULD DO BETTER THAN THE FOOLS WHO BUILT YOU?
WE'RE CLOSE ENOUGH!
GREEN LANTERNS, TIME TO—
KRA-BOOO

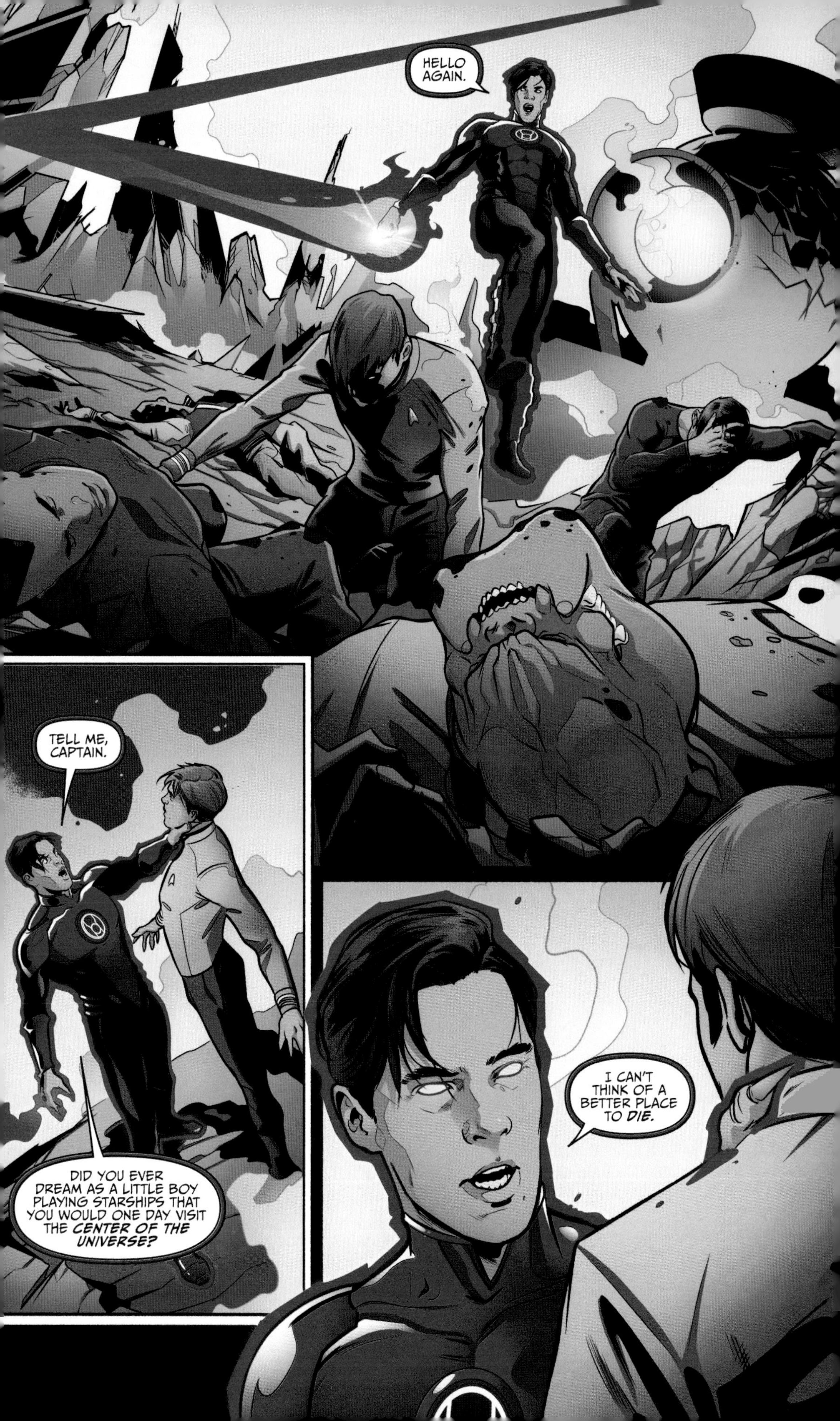
HELLO AGAIN.
TELL ME, CAPTAIN.
DID YOU EVER DREAM AS A LITTLE BOY PLAYING STARSHIPS THAT YOU WOULD ONE DAY VISIT THE *CENTER OF THE UNIVERSE?*
I CAN'T THINK OF A BETTER PLACE TO *DIE.*

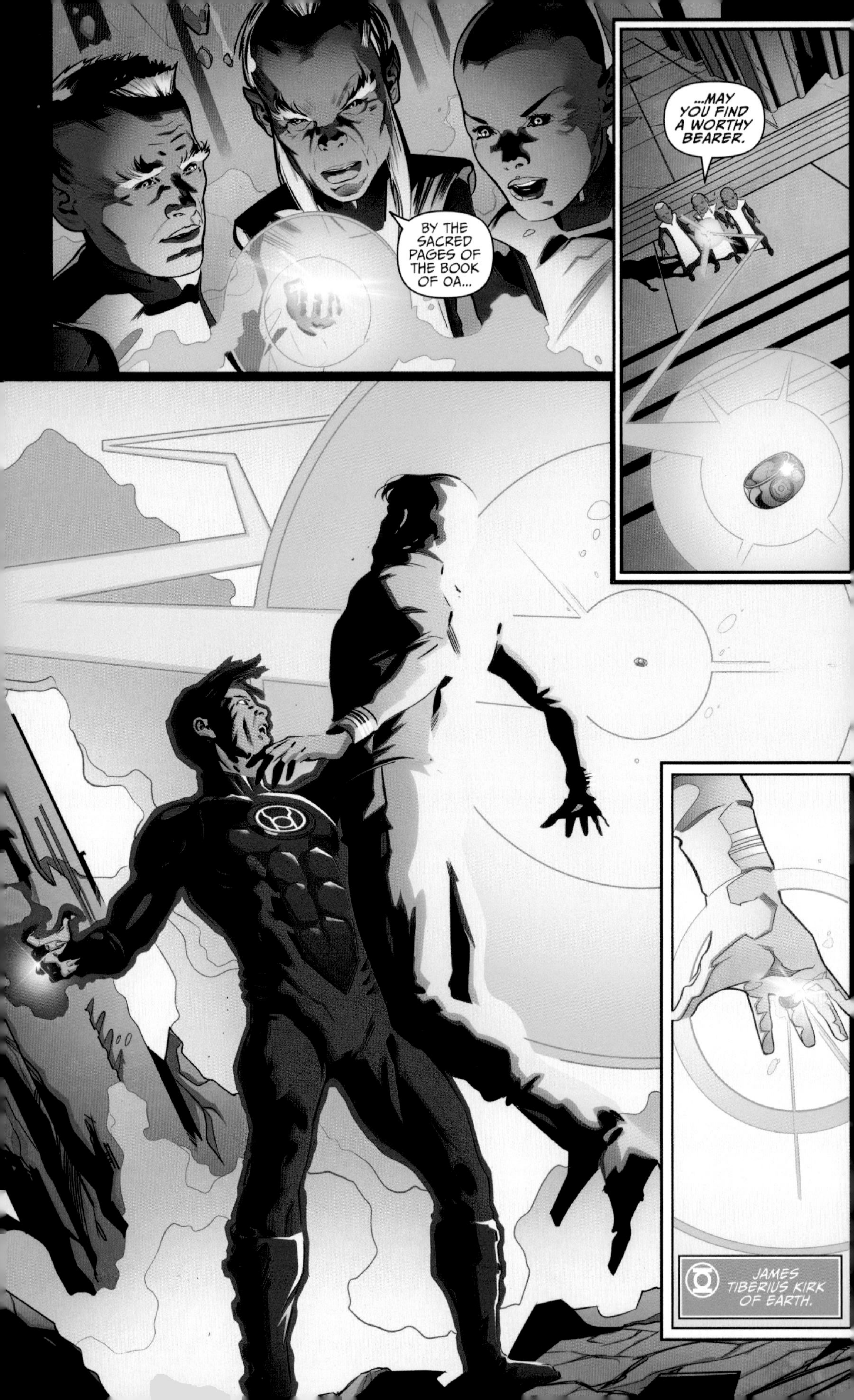
BY THE SACRED PAGES OF THE BOOK OF OA...
...MAY YOU FIND A WORTHY BEARER.
JAMES TIBERIUS KIRK OF EARTH.

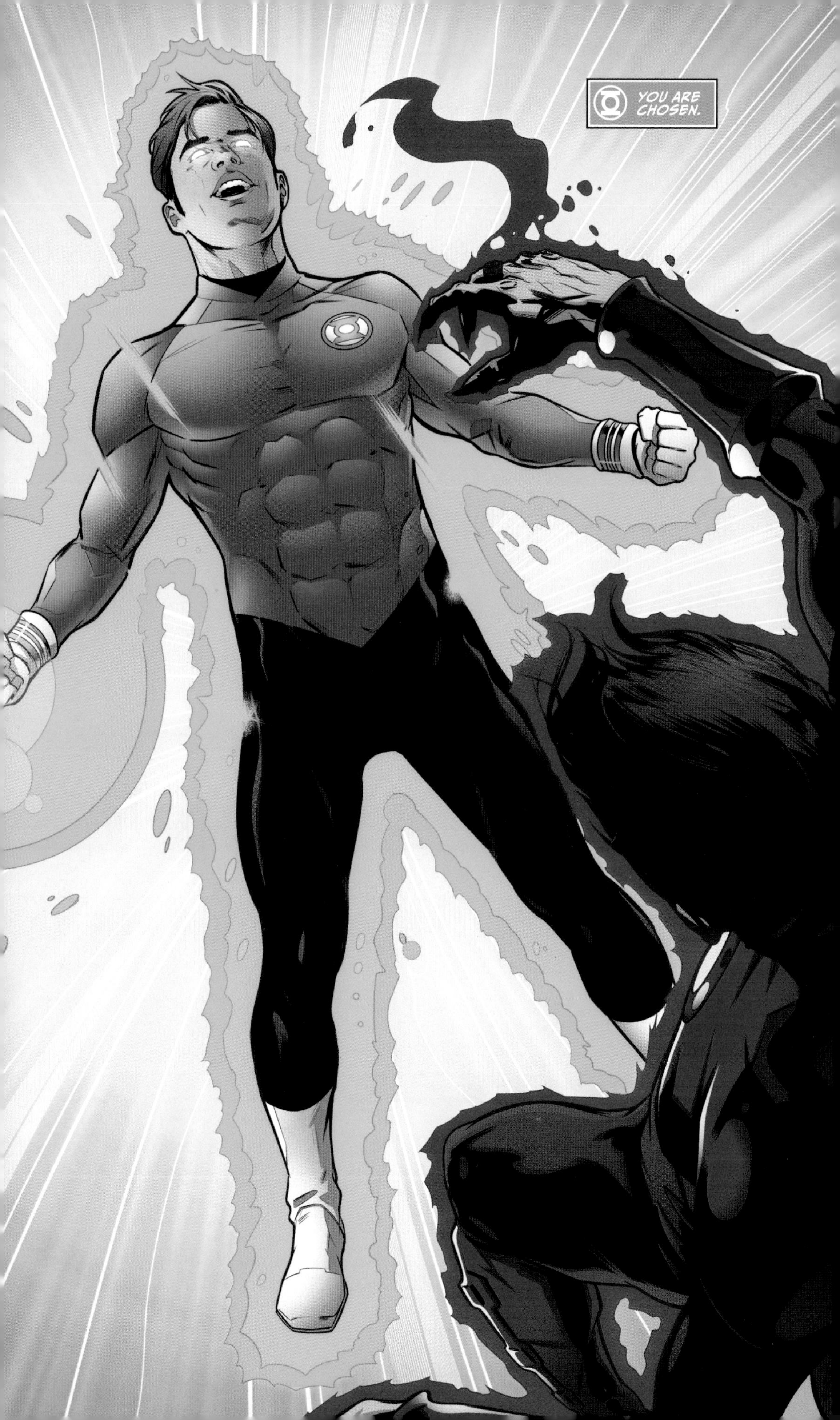
YOU ARE CHOSEN.

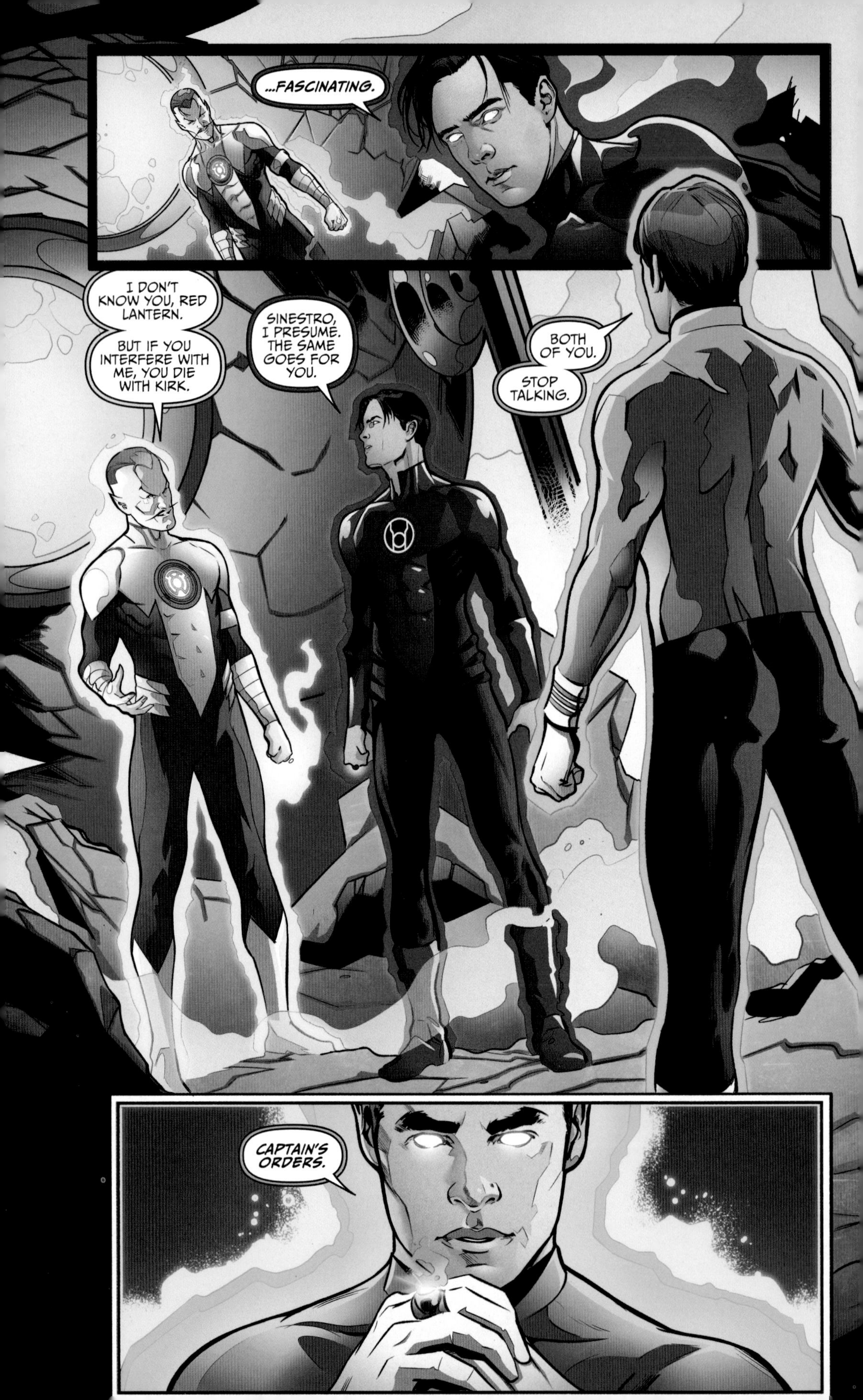
...FASCINATING.
I DON'T KNOW YOU, RED LANTERN.
BUT IF YOU INTERFERE WITH ME, YOU DIE WITH KIRK.
SINESTRO, I PRESUME. THE SAME GOES FOR YOU.
BOTH OF YOU.
STOP TALKING.
CAPTAIN'S ORDERS.

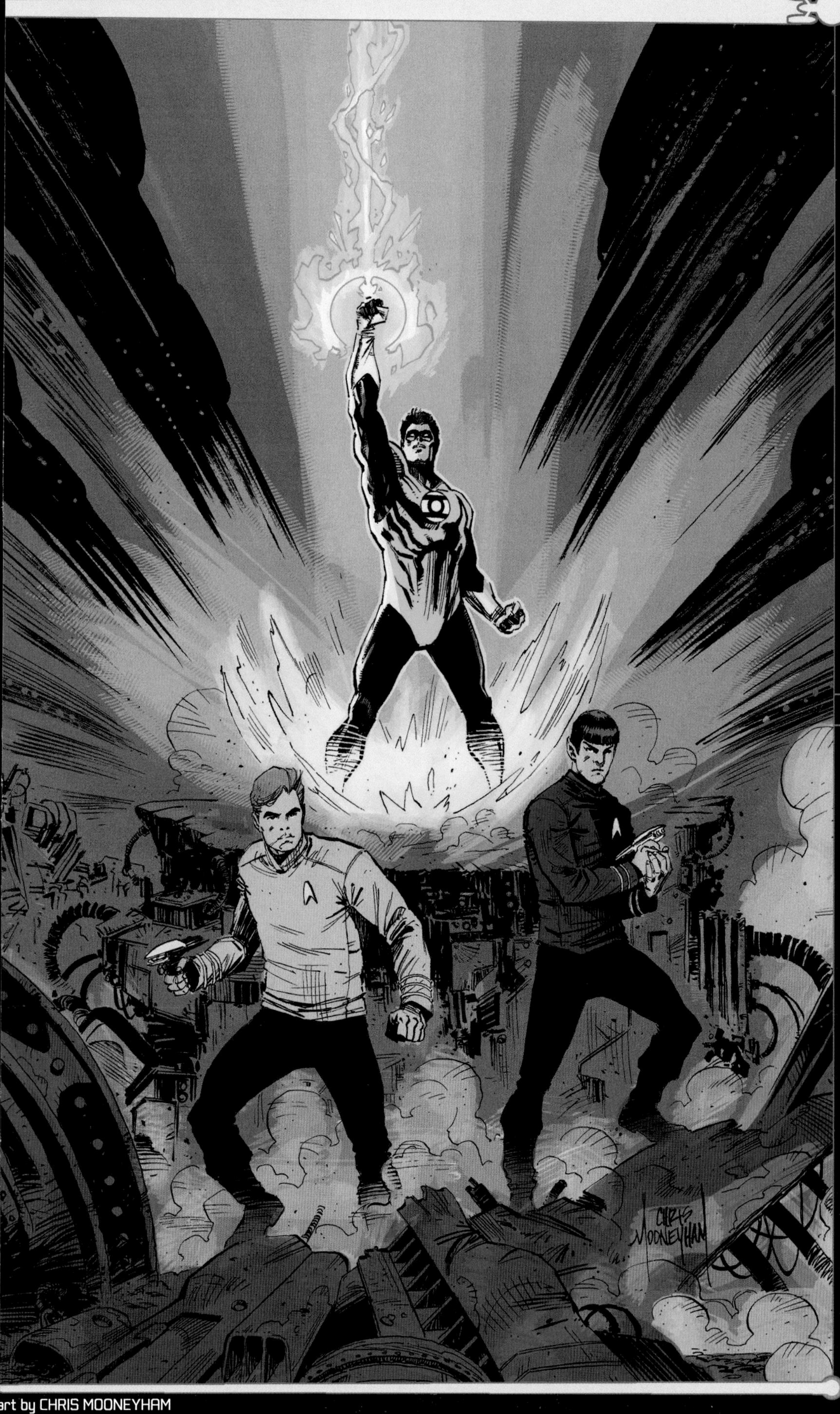
CHRIS MOONEYHAM

art by CHRIS MOONEYHAM

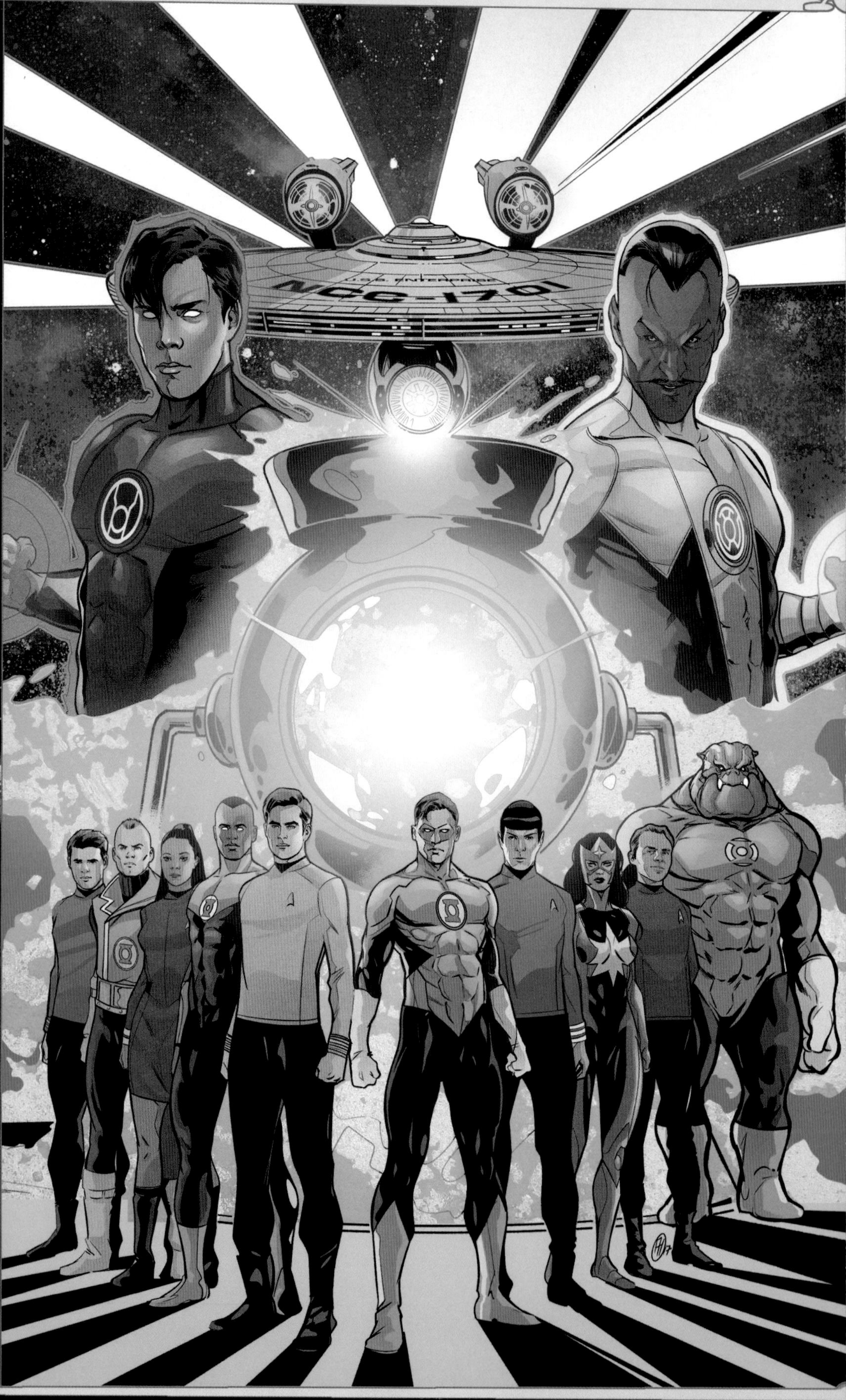

U.S.S. ENTERPRISE
NCC-1701

art by ANGEL HERNANDEZ • colors by ESTHER SANZ

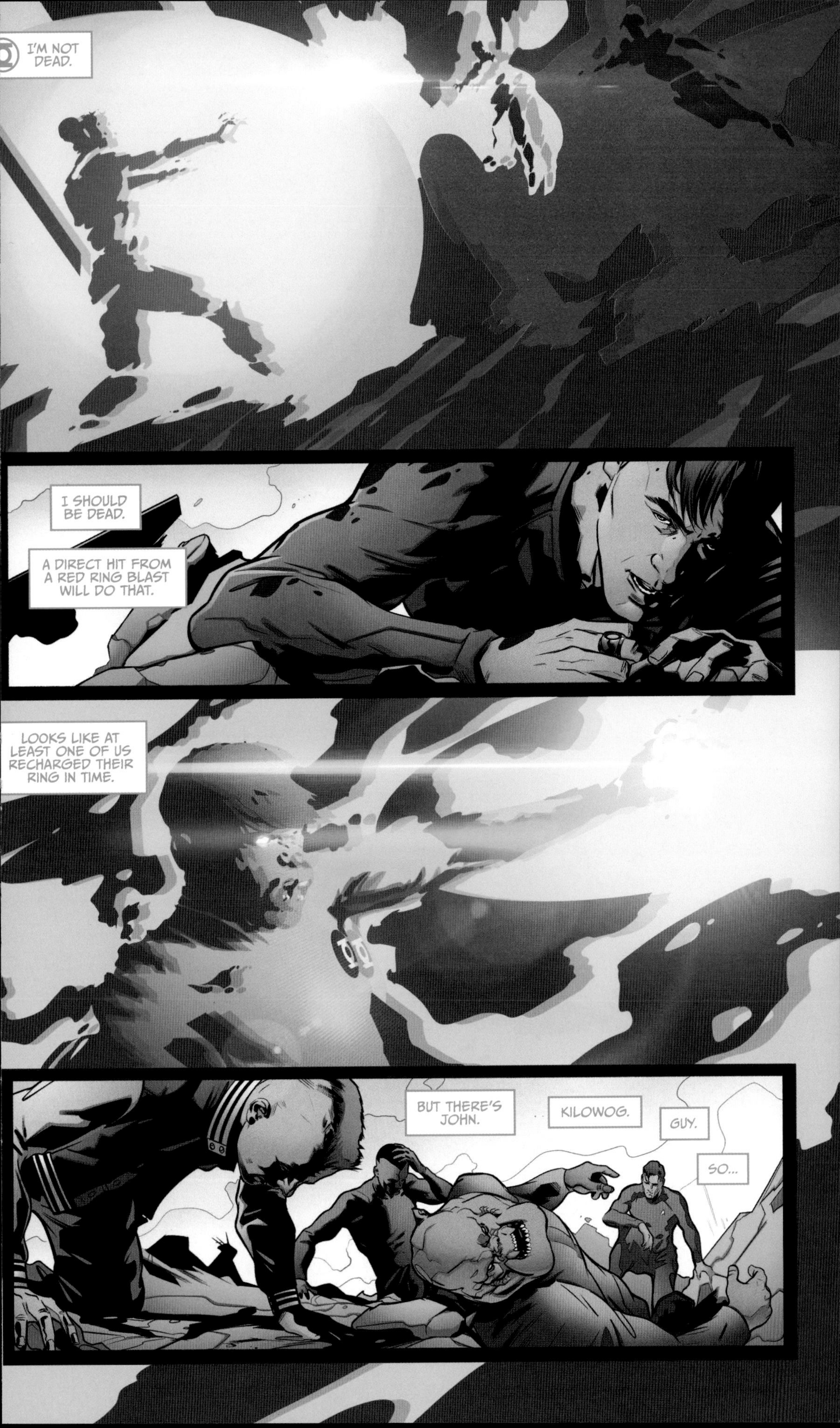
I'M NOT DEAD.
I SHOULD BE DEAD.
A DIRECT HIT FROM A RED RING BLAST WILL DO THAT.
LOOKS LIKE AT LEAST ONE OF US RECHARGED THEIR RING IN TIME.
BUT THERE'S JOHN.
KILOWOG.
GUY.
SO...

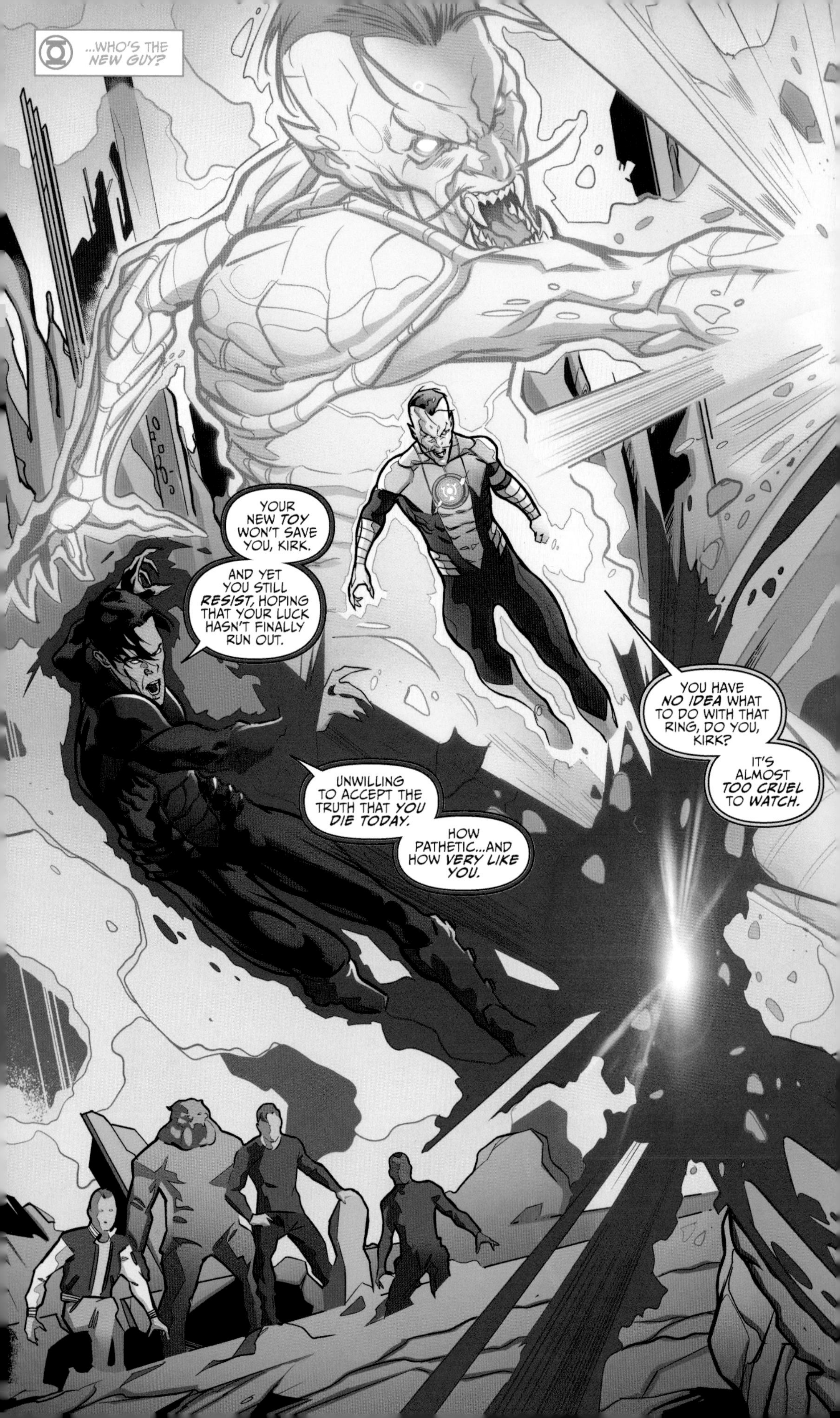
...WHO'S THE NEW GUY?
YOUR NEW TOY WON'T SAVE YOU, KIRK.
AND YET YOU STILL RESIST, HOPING THAT YOUR LUCK HASN'T FINALLY RUN OUT.
YOU HAVE NO IDEA WHAT TO DO WITH THAT RING, DO YOU, KIRK?
IT'S ALMOST TOO CRUEL TO WATCH.
UNWILLING TO ACCEPT THE TRUTH THAT YOU DIE TODAY.
HOW PATHETIC...AND HOW VERY LIKE YOU.

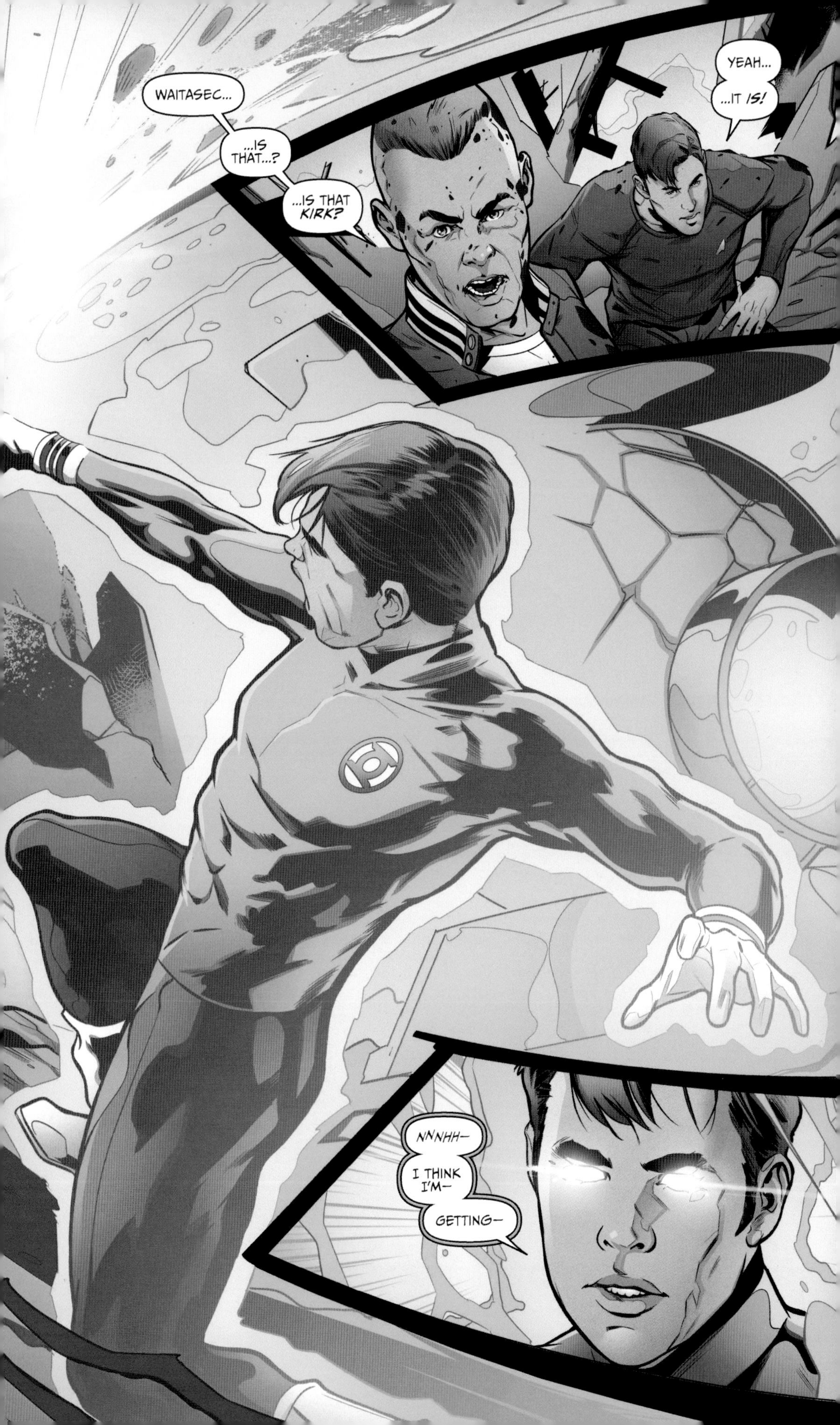
WAITASEC...
...IS THAT...?
...IS THAT KIRK?
YEAH...
...IT IS!
NNNHH—
I THINK I'M—
GETTING—

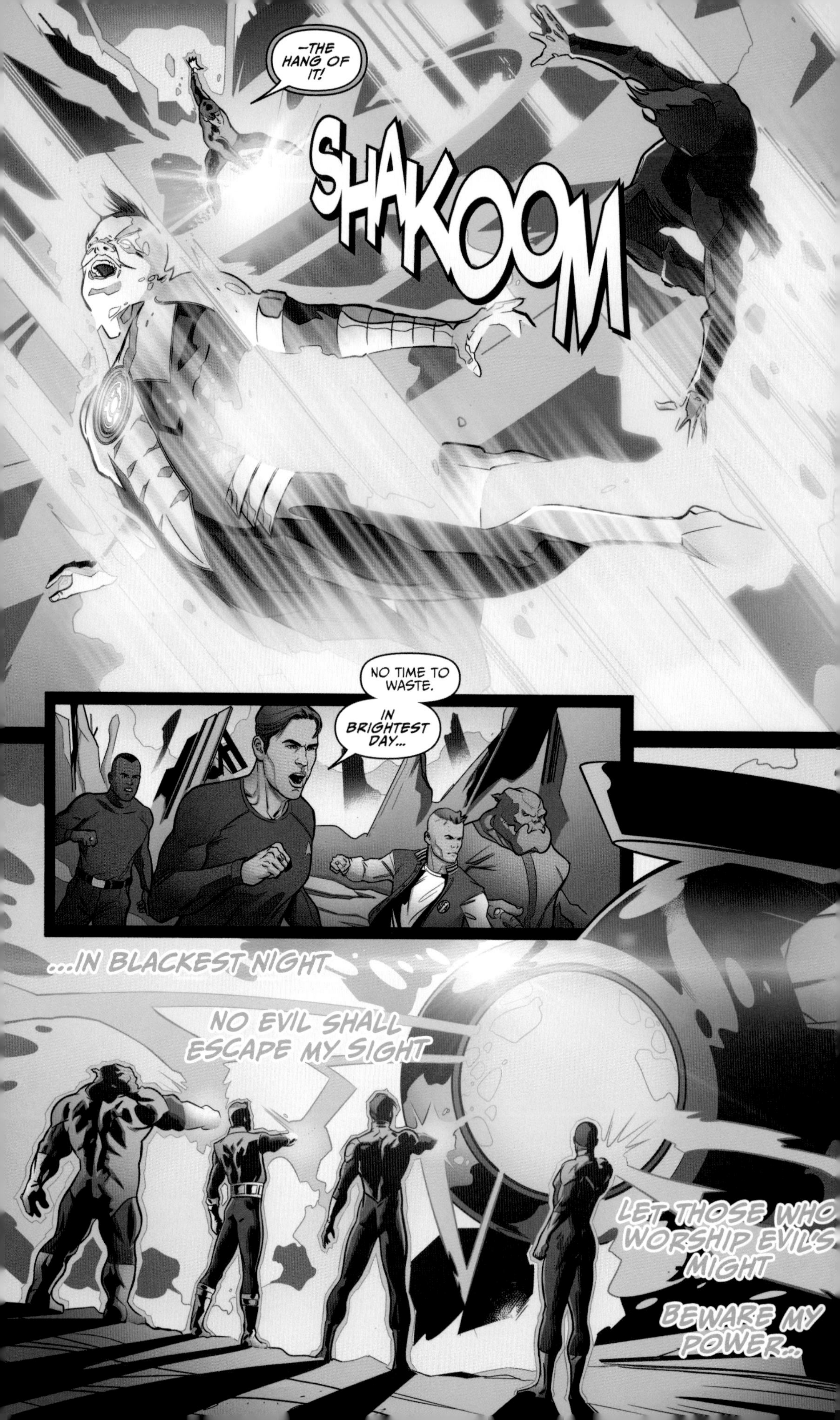
—THE HANG OF IT!
SHAKOOM
NO TIME TO WASTE.
IN BRIGHTEST DAY...
...IN BLACKEST NIGHT
NO EVIL SHALL ESCAPE MY SIGHT
LET THOSE WHO WORSHIP EVIL'S MIGHT
BEWARE MY POWER...

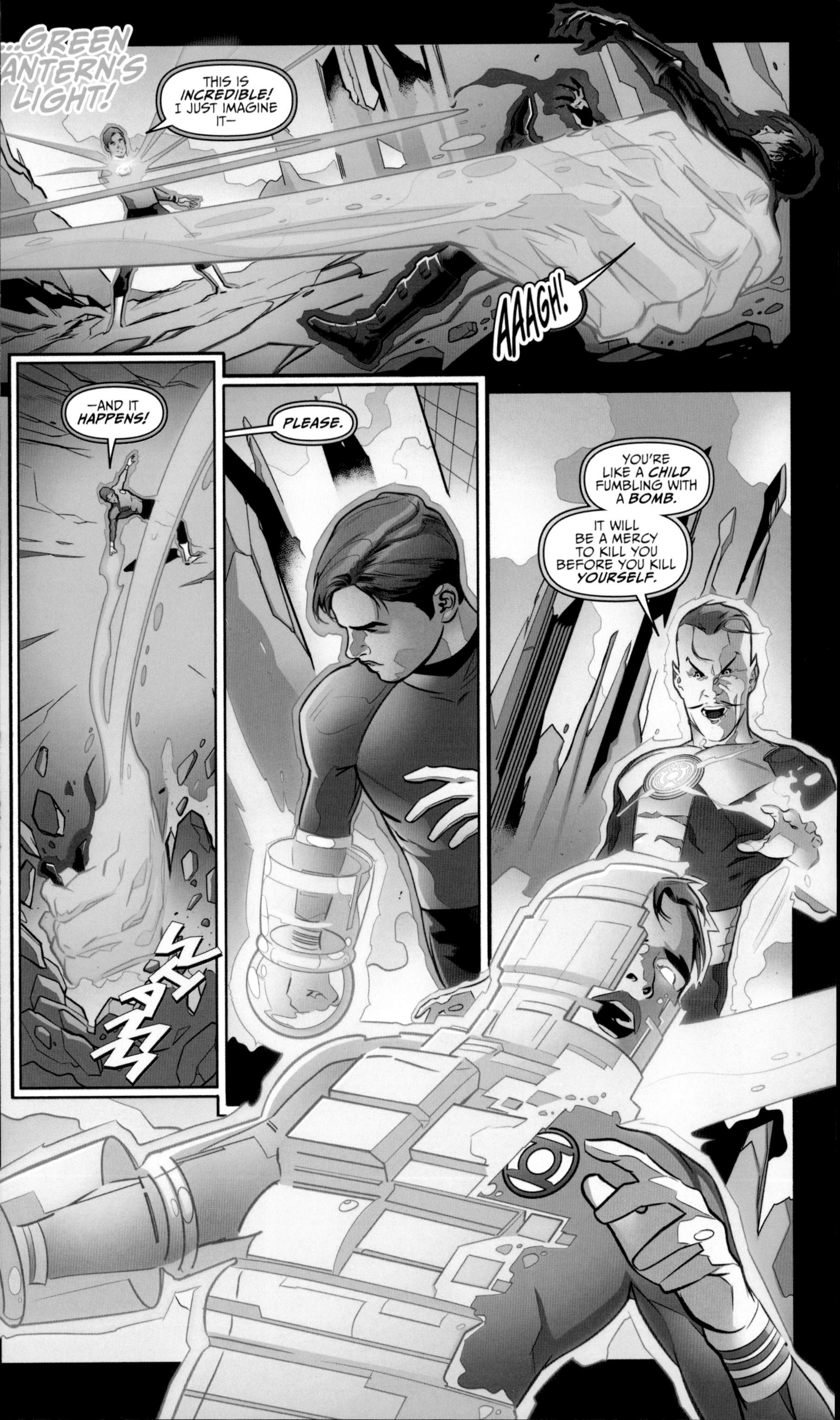
...GREEN LANTERN'S LIGHT!
THIS IS INCREDIBLE! I JUST IMAGINE IT—
AAAGH!
—AND IT HAPPENS!
WHAM
PLEASE.
YOU'RE LIKE A CHILD FUMBLING WITH A BOMB.
IT WILL BE A MERCY TO KILL YOU BEFORE YOU KILL YOURSELF.

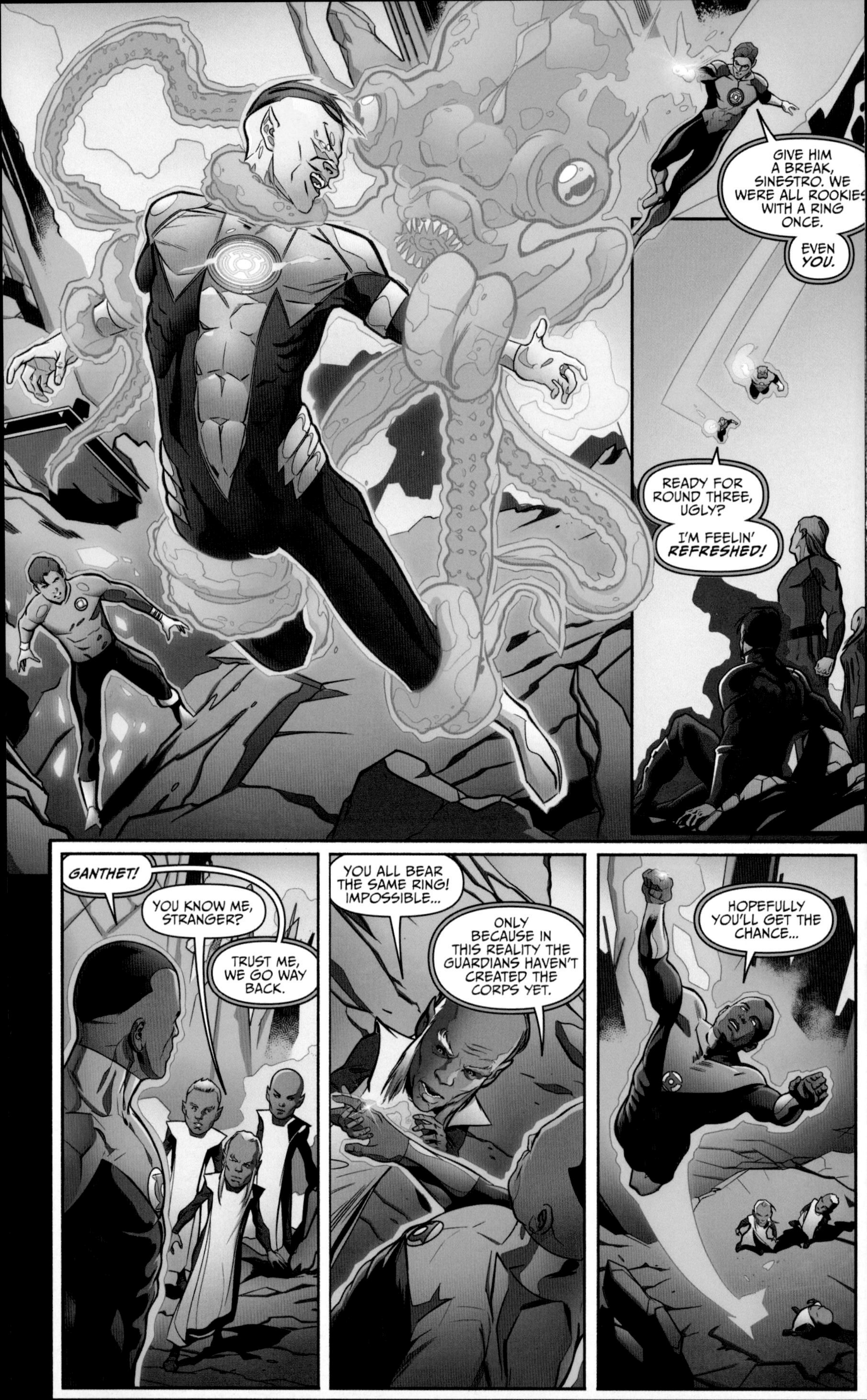
GIVE HIM A BREAK, SINESTRO. WE WERE ALL ROOKIES WITH A RING ONCE.
EVEN YOU.
READY FOR ROUND THREE, UGLY?
I'M FEELIN' REFRESHED!
GANTHET!
YOU KNOW ME, STRANGER?
TRUST ME, WE GO WAY BACK.
YOU ALL BEAR THE SAME RING! IMPOSSIBLE...
ONLY BECAUSE IN THIS REALITY THE GUARDIANS HAVEN'T CREATED THE CORPS YET.
HOPEFULLY YOU'LL GET THE CHANCE...

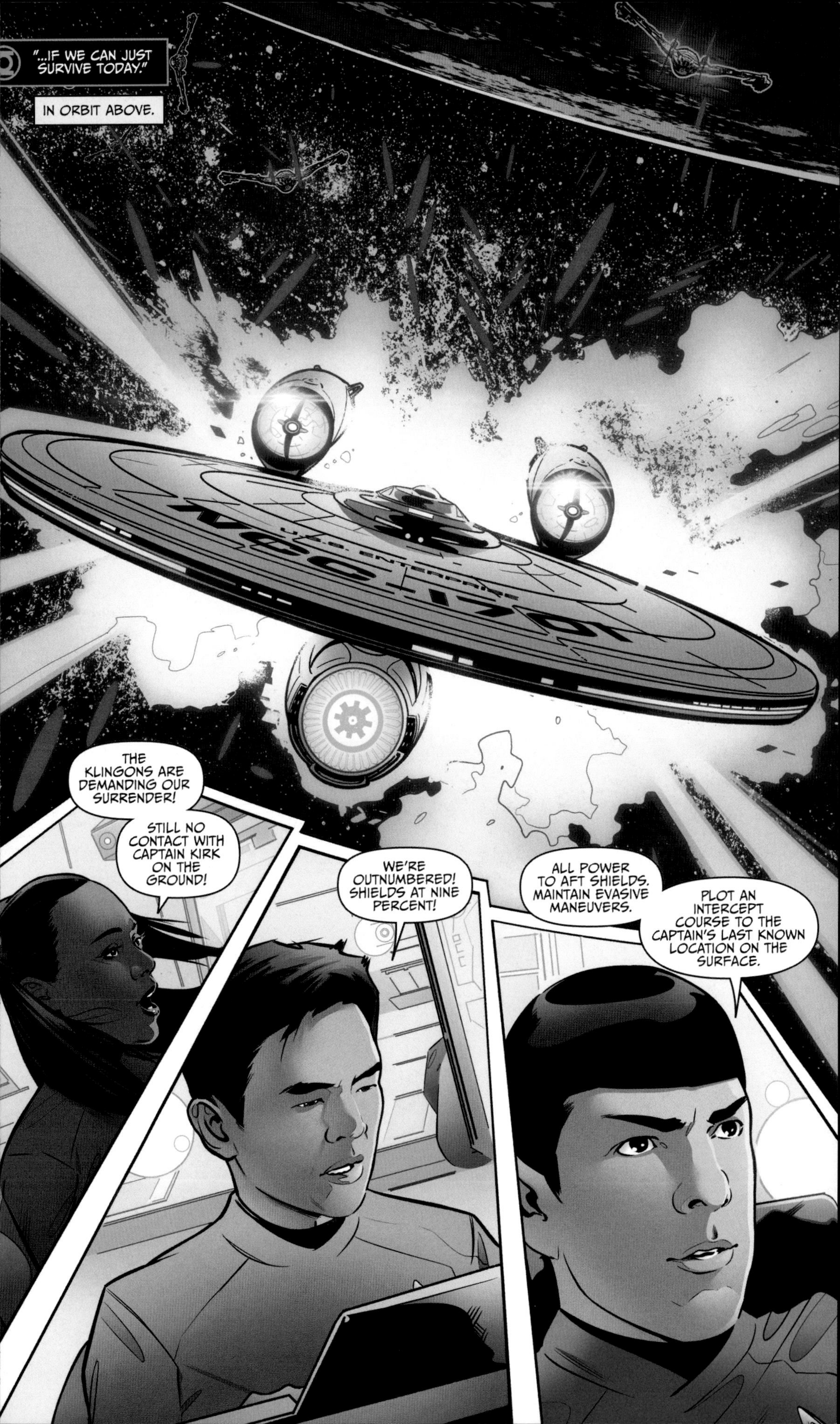
"...IF WE CAN JUST SURVIVE TODAY."
IN ORBIT ABOVE.
U.S.S. ENTERPRISE
NCC-1701
THE KLINGONS ARE DEMANDING OUR SURRENDER!
STILL NO CONTACT WITH CAPTAIN KIRK ON THE GROUND!
WE'RE OUTNUMBERED! SHIELDS AT NINE PERCENT!
ALL POWER TO AFT SHIELDS. MAINTAIN EVASIVE MANEUVERS.
PLOT AN INTERCEPT COURSE TO THE CAPTAIN'S LAST KNOWN LOCATION ON THE SURFACE.

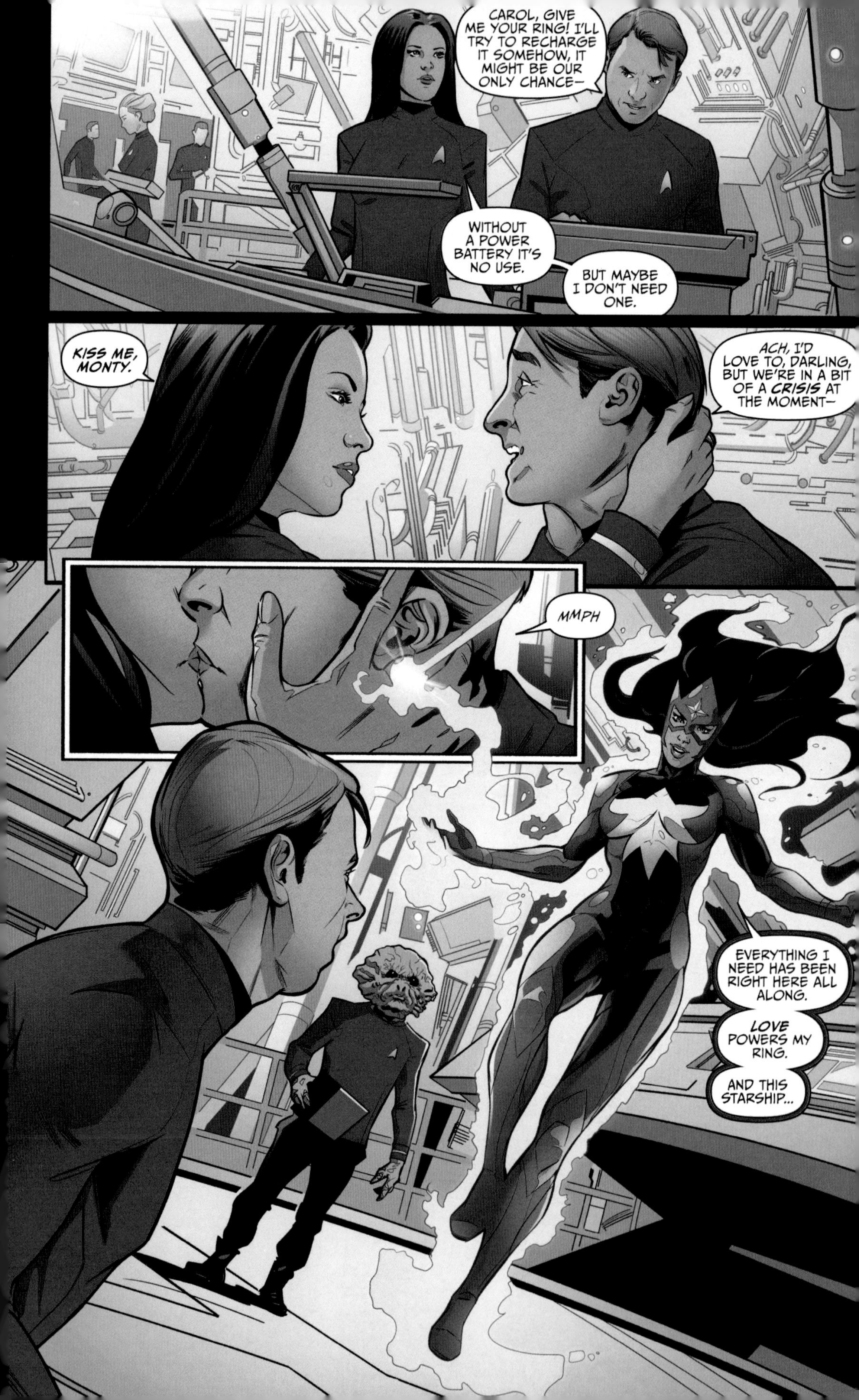
CAROL, GIVE ME YOUR RING! I'LL TRY TO RECHARGE IT SOMEHOW, IT MIGHT BE OUR ONLY CHANCE—
WITHOUT A POWER BATTERY IT'S NO USE.
BUT MAYBE I DON'T NEED ONE.
KISS ME, MONTY.
ACH, I'D LOVE TO, DARLING, BUT WE'RE IN A BIT OF A *CRISIS* AT THE MOMENT—
MMPH
EVERYTHING I NEED HAS BEEN RIGHT HERE ALL ALONG.
LOVE POWERS MY RING.
AND THIS STARSHIP...

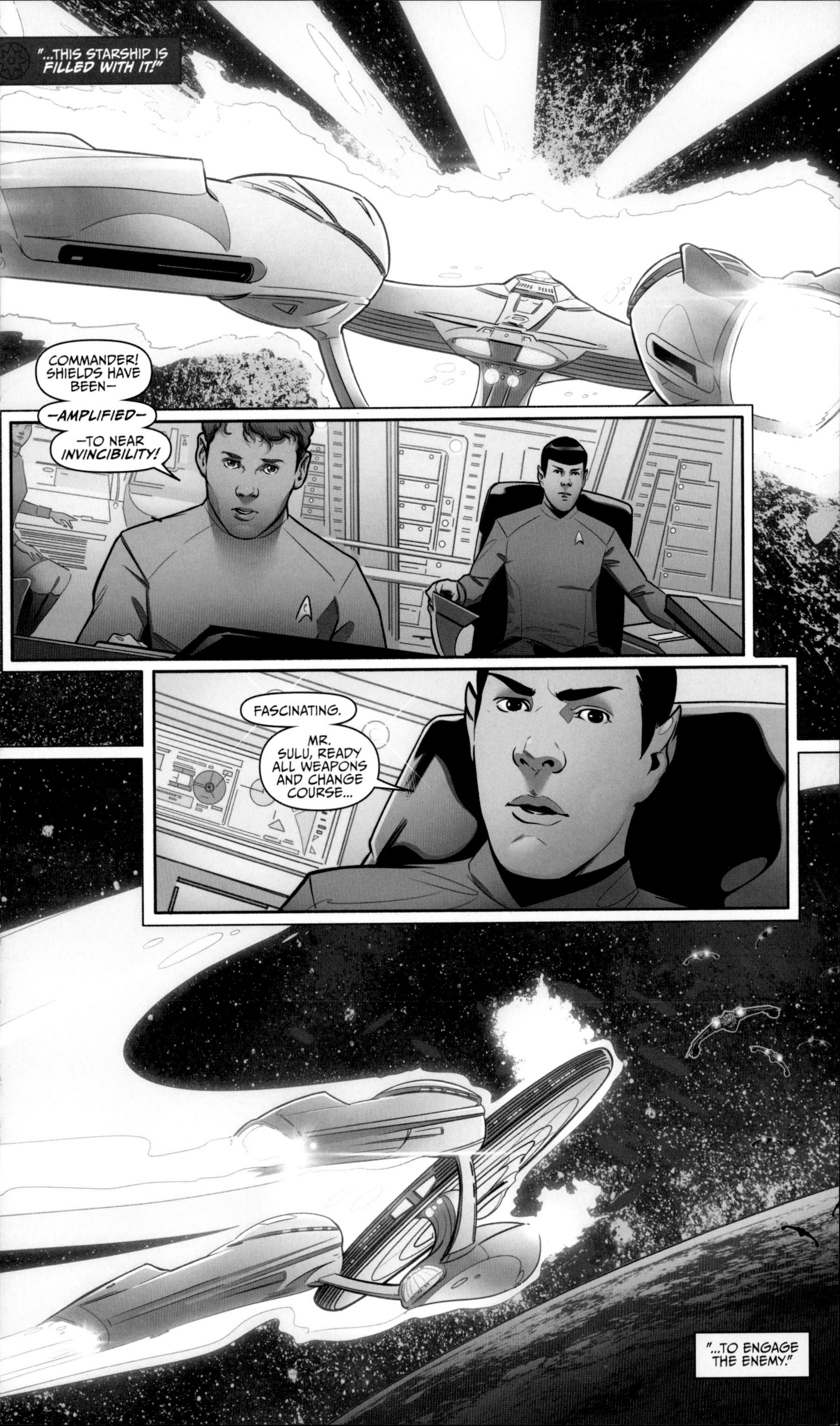
"...THIS STARSHIP IS FILLED WITH IT!"
COMMANDER! SHIELDS HAVE BEEN—
—AMPLIFIED—
—TO NEAR INVINCIBILITY!
FASCINATING.
MR. SULU, READY ALL WEAPONS AND CHANGE COURSE...
"...TO ENGAGE THE ENEMY."

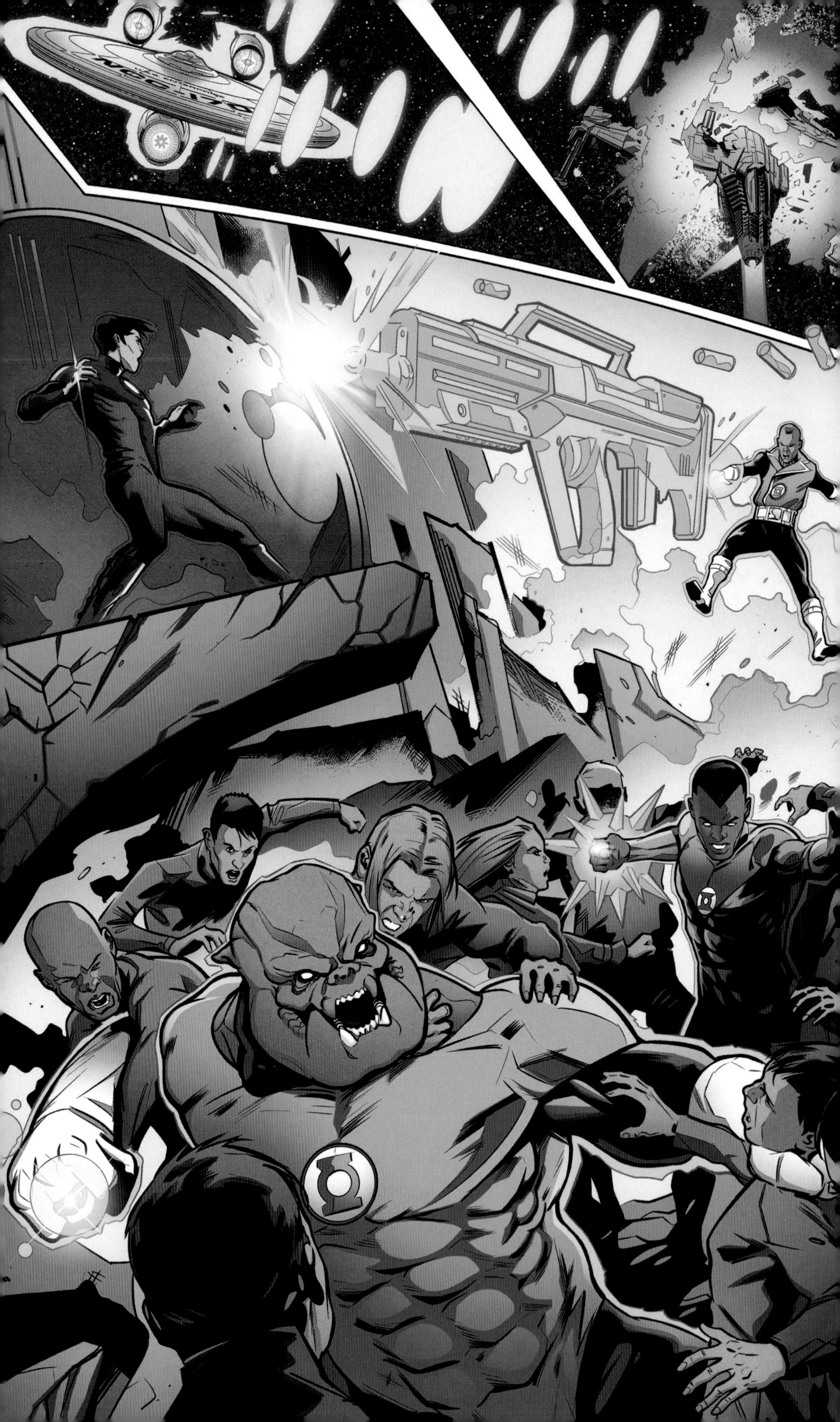

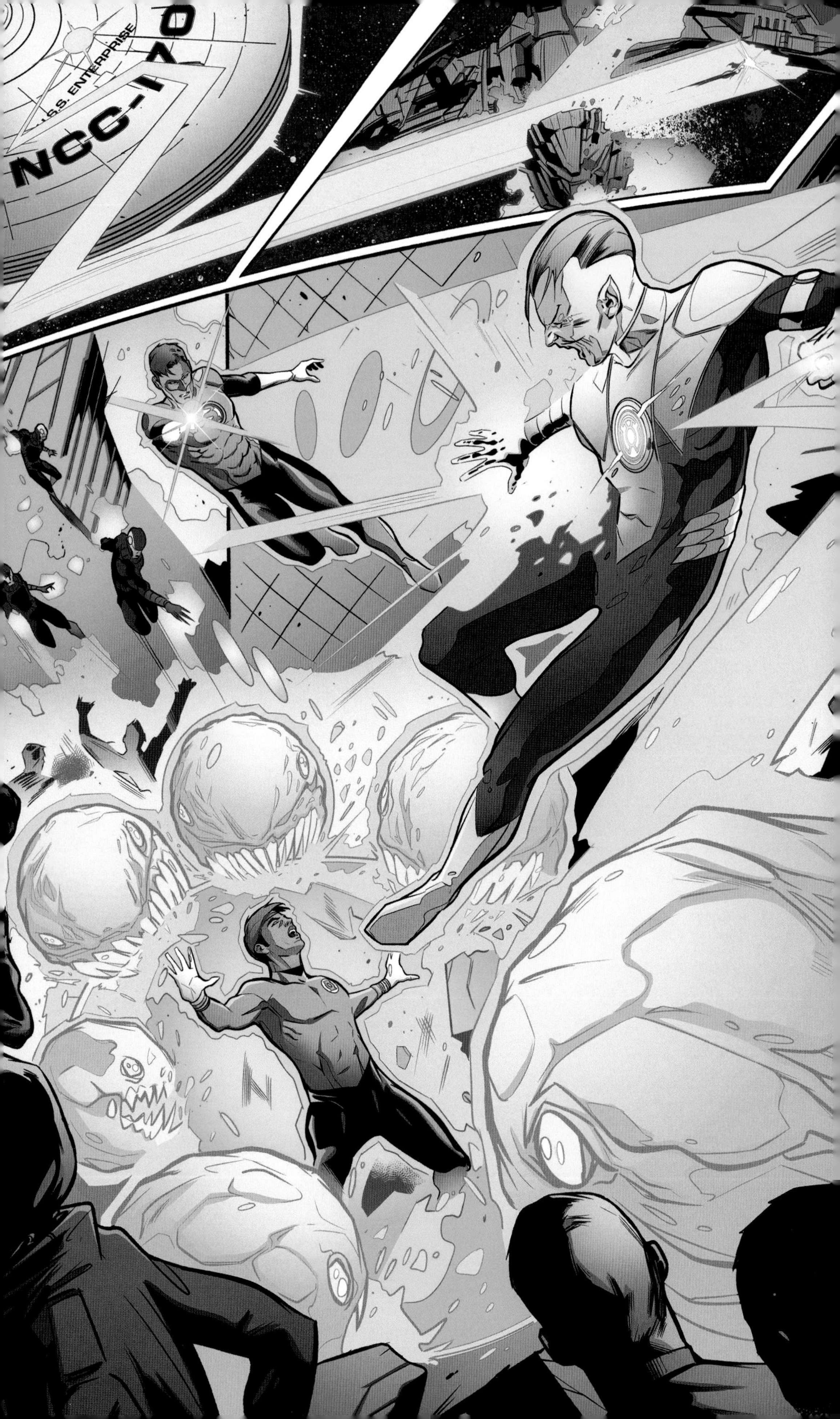
.S.S. ENTERPRISE
NCC-170

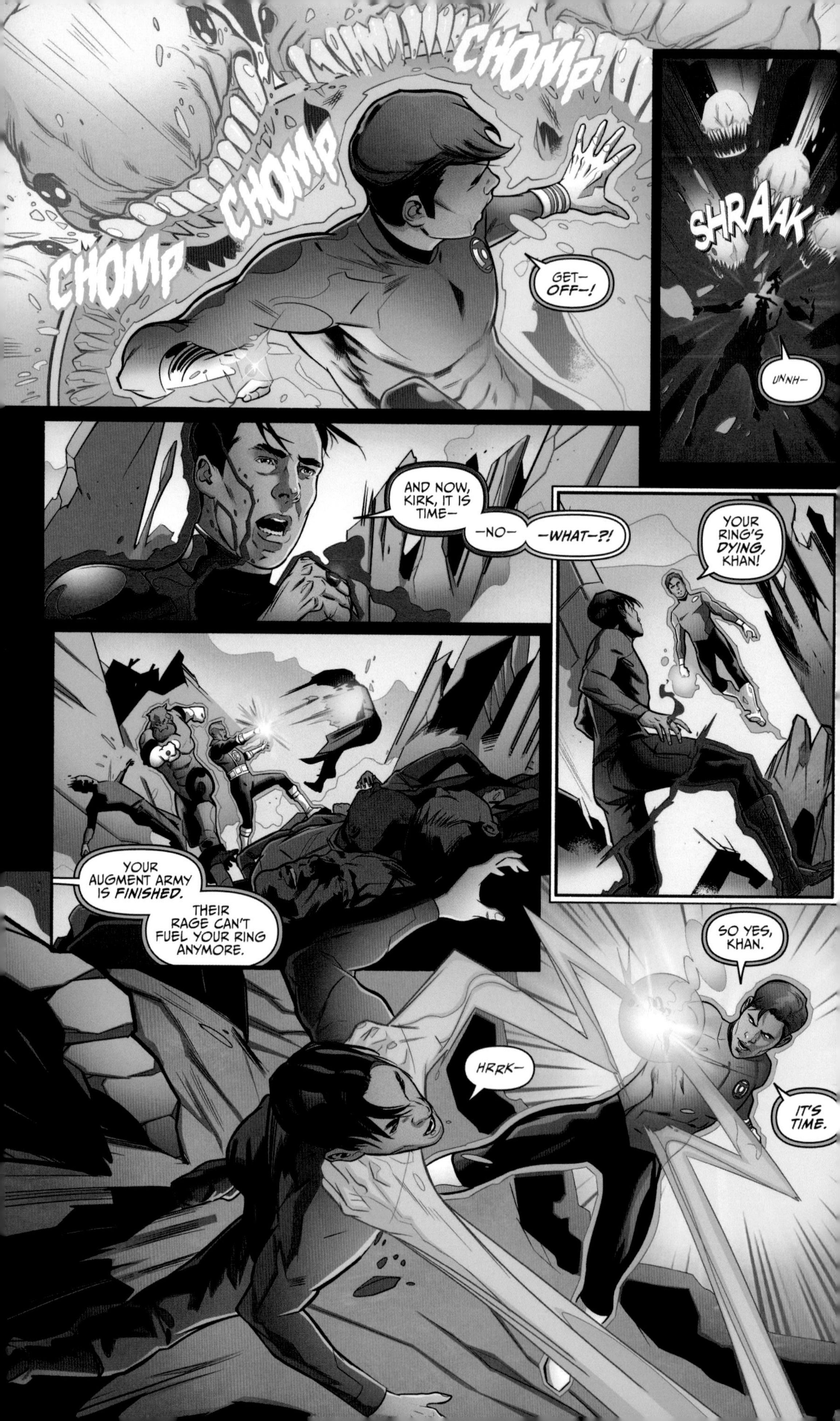
CHOMP
CHOMP
CHOMP
GET— OFF—!
SHRAAK
UNNH—
AND NOW, KIRK, IT IS TIME—
—NO—
—WHAT—?!
YOUR RING'S DYING, KHAN!
YOUR AUGMENT ARMY IS FINISHED.
THEIR RAGE CAN'T FUEL YOUR RING ANYMORE.
SO YES, KHAN.
HRRK—
IT'S TIME.

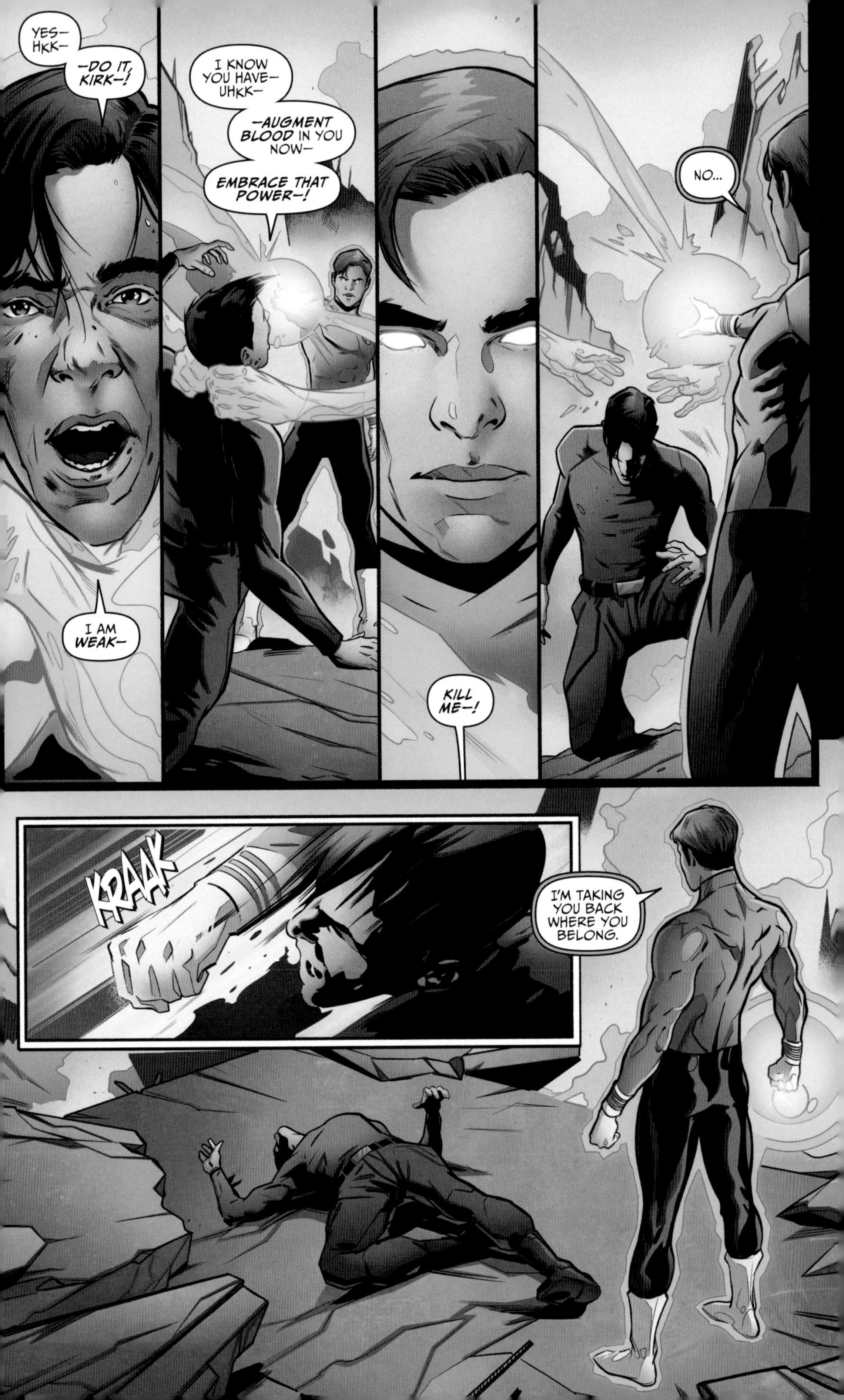
YES— HKK—
—DO IT, KIRK—!
I AM WEAK—
I KNOW YOU HAVE— UHKK—
—AUGMENT BLOOD IN YOU NOW—
EMBRACE THAT POWER—!
KILL ME—!
NO...
KRAAK
I'M TAKING YOU BACK WHERE YOU BELONG.

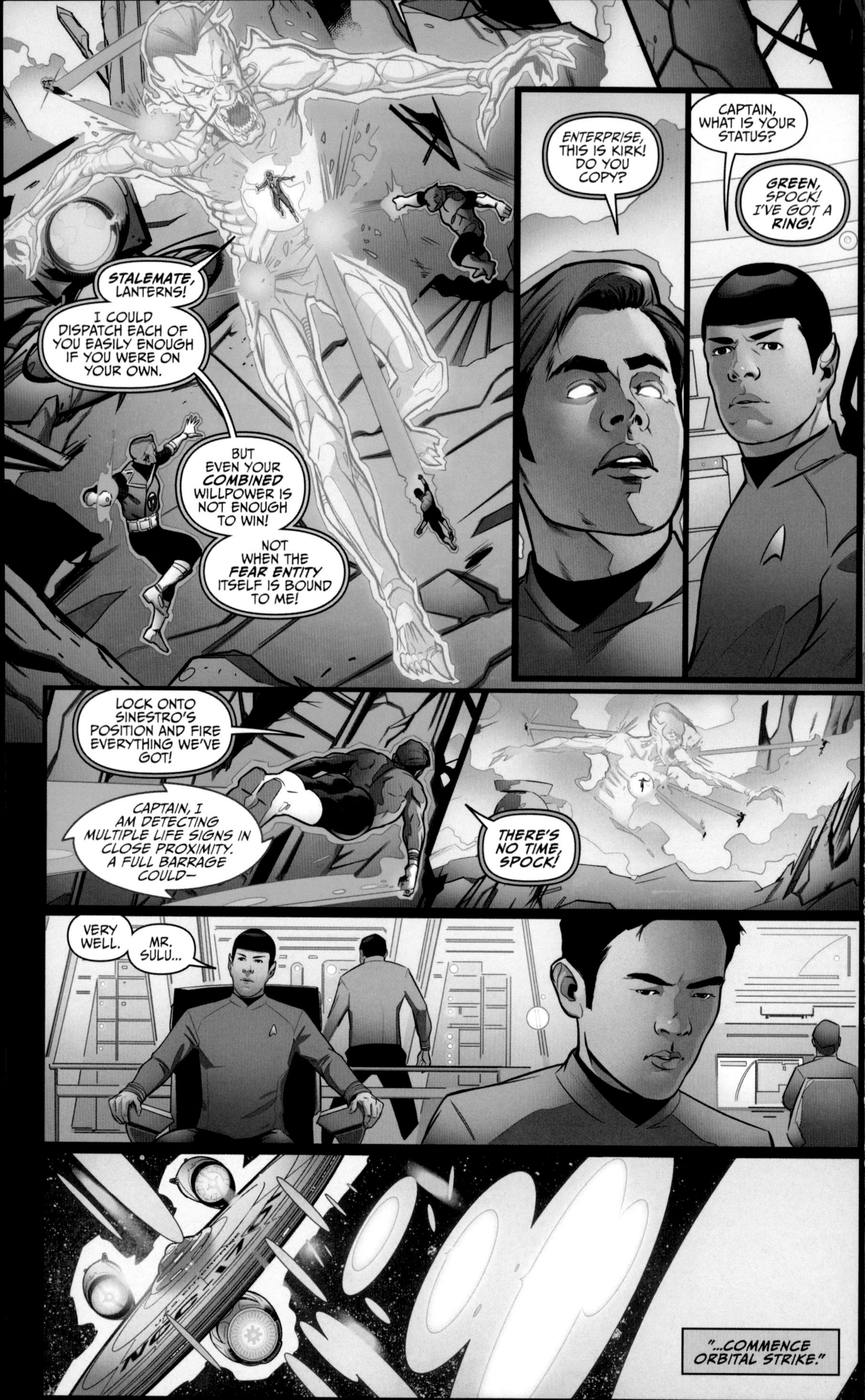
STALEMATE, LANTERNS!
I COULD DISPATCH EACH OF YOU EASILY ENOUGH IF YOU WERE ON YOUR OWN.
BUT EVEN YOUR COMBINED WILLPOWER IS NOT ENOUGH TO WIN!
NOT WHEN THE FEAR ENTITY ITSELF IS BOUND TO ME!
ENTERPRISE, THIS IS KIRK! DO YOU COPY?
CAPTAIN, WHAT IS YOUR STATUS?
GREEN, SPOCK! I'VE GOT A RING!
LOCK ONTO SINESTRO'S POSITION AND FIRE EVERYTHING WE'VE GOT!
CAPTAIN, I AM DETECTING MULTIPLE LIFE SIGNS IN CLOSE PROXIMITY. A FULL BARRAGE COULD–
THERE'S NO TIME, SPOCK!
VERY WELL.
MR. SULU...
"...COMMENCE ORBITAL STRIKE."

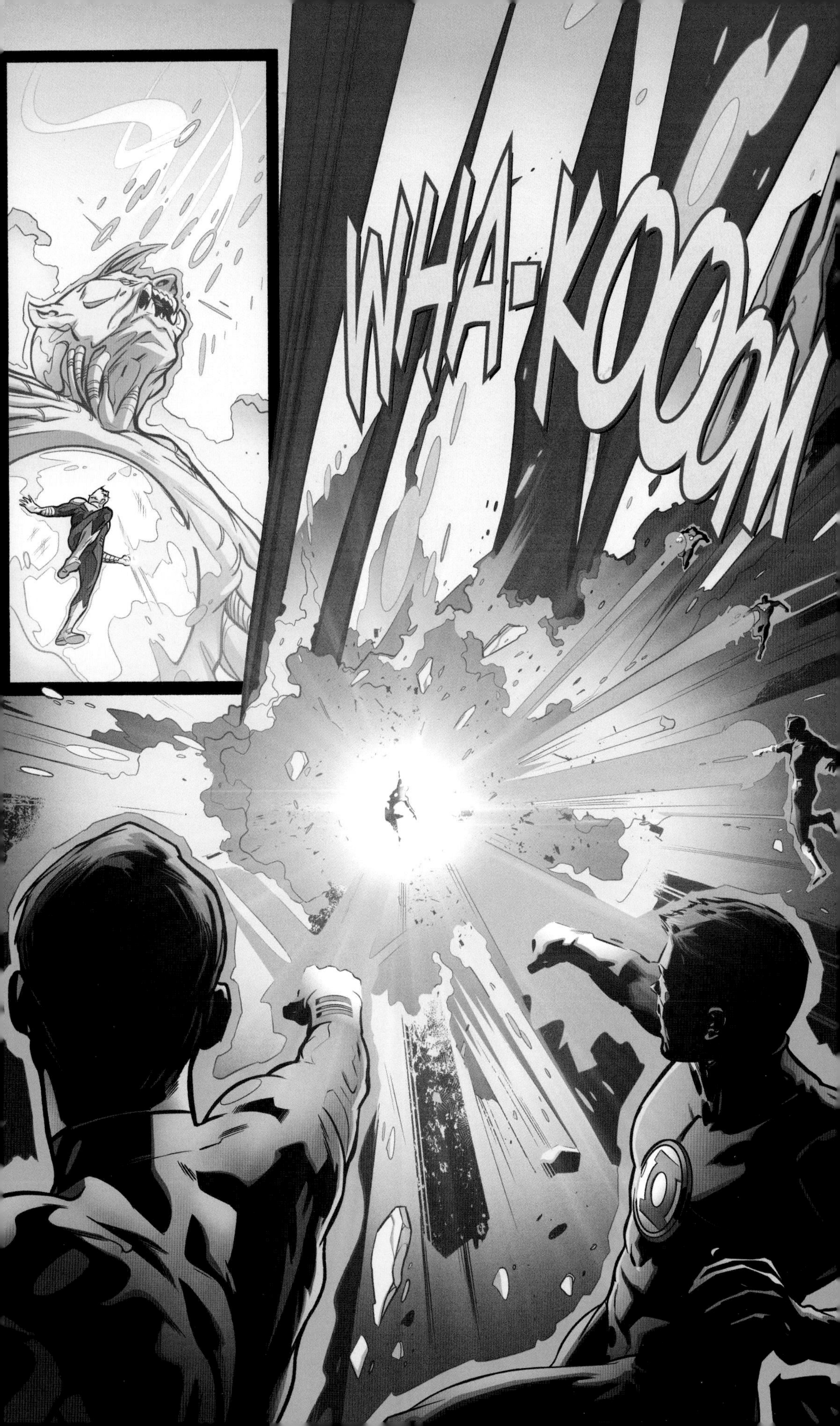
WHA-KOOOM

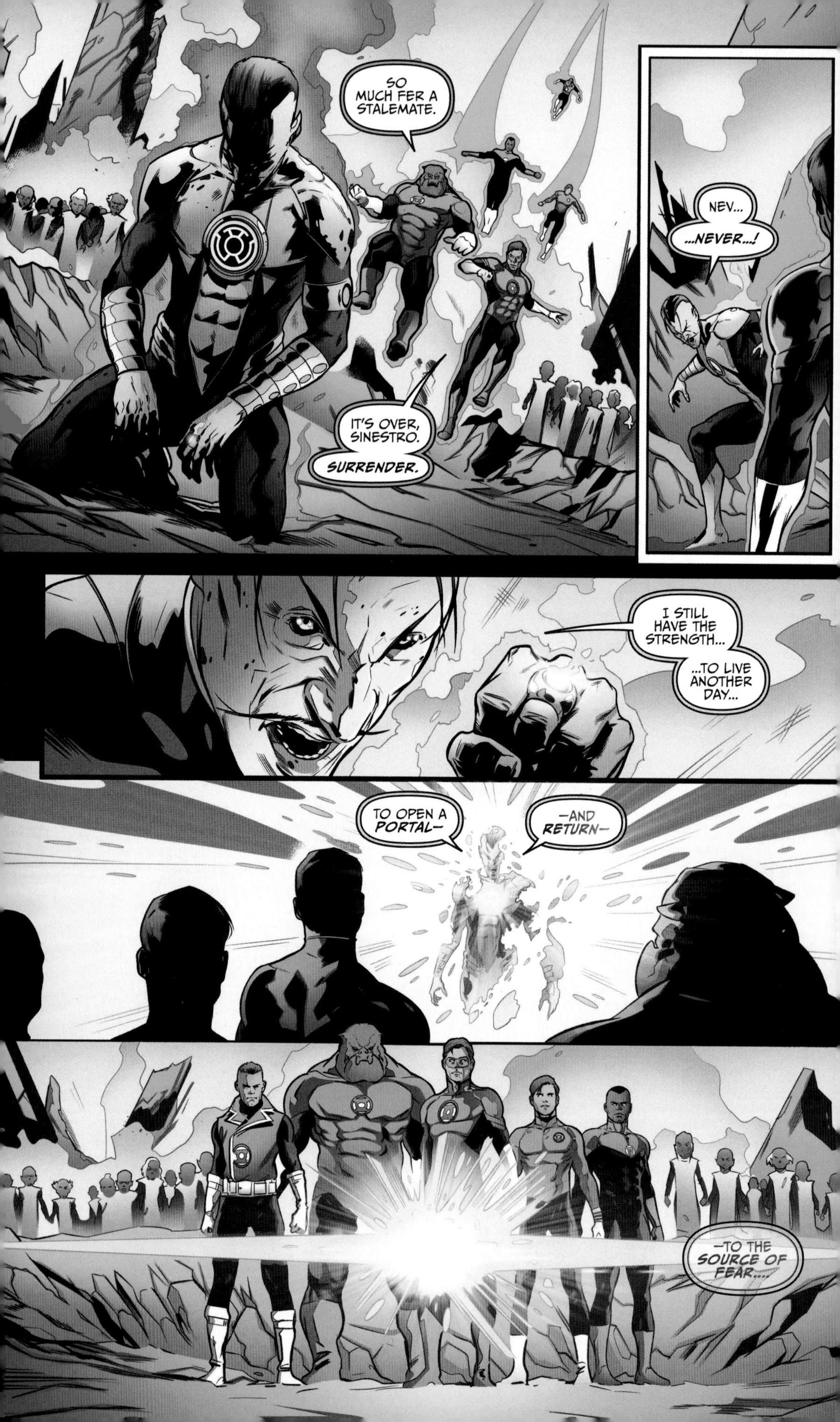
SO MUCH FER A STALEMATE.
IT'S OVER, SINESTRO.
SURRENDER.
NEV...
...NEVER...!
I STILL HAVE THE STRENGTH...
...TO LIVE ANOTHER DAY...
TO OPEN A PORTAL—
—AND RETURN—
—TO THE SOURCE OF FEAR....

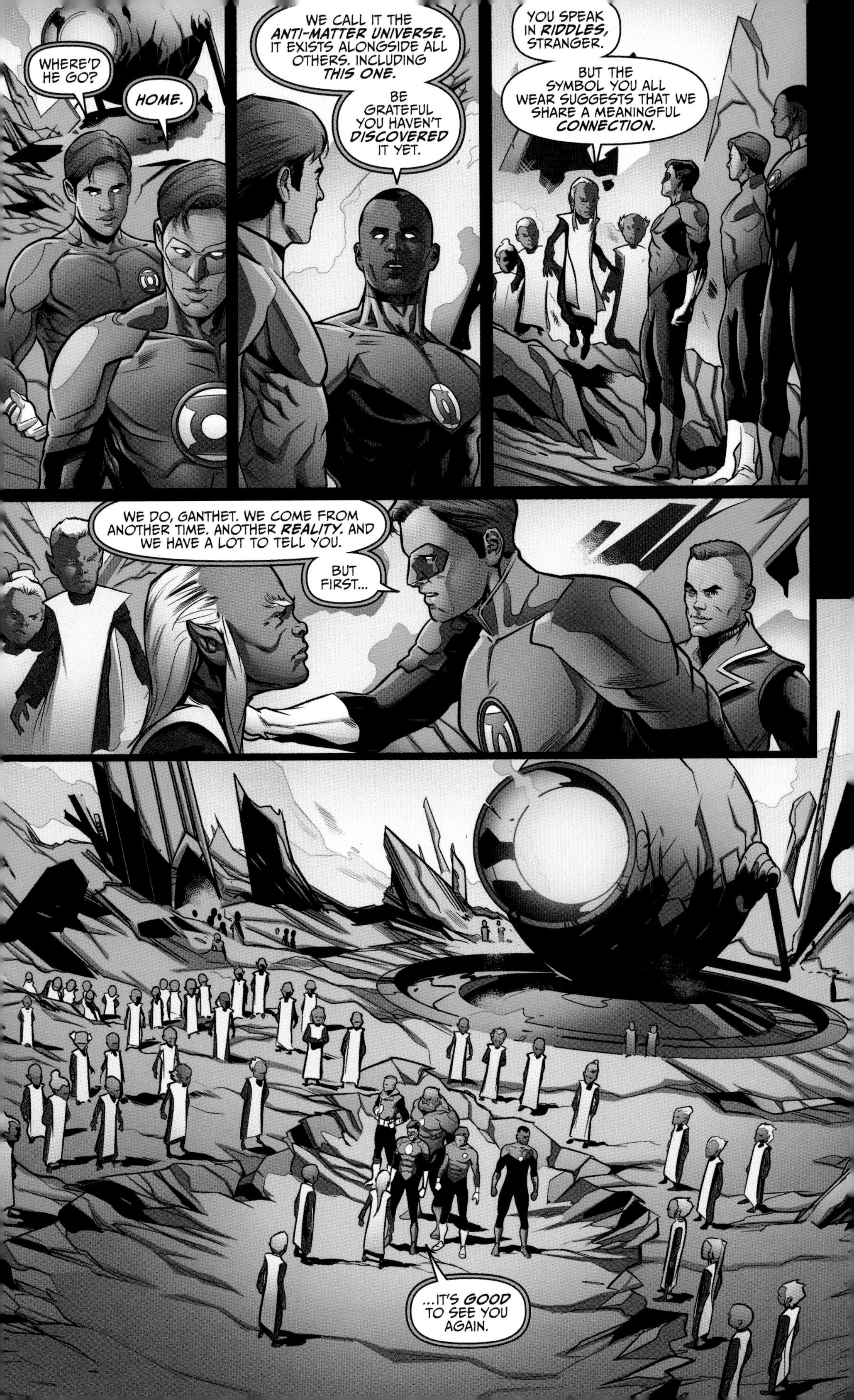
WHERE'D HE GO?
HOME.
WE CALL IT THE ANTI-MATTER UNIVERSE. IT EXISTS ALONGSIDE ALL OTHERS. INCLUDING THIS ONE.
BE GRATEFUL YOU HAVEN'T DISCOVERED IT YET.
YOU SPEAK IN RIDDLES, STRANGER.
BUT THE SYMBOL YOU ALL WEAR SUGGESTS THAT WE SHARE A MEANINGFUL CONNECTION.
WE DO, GANTHET. WE COME FROM ANOTHER TIME. ANOTHER REALITY. AND WE HAVE A LOT TO TELL YOU.
BUT FIRST...
...IT'S GOOD TO SEE YOU AGAIN.

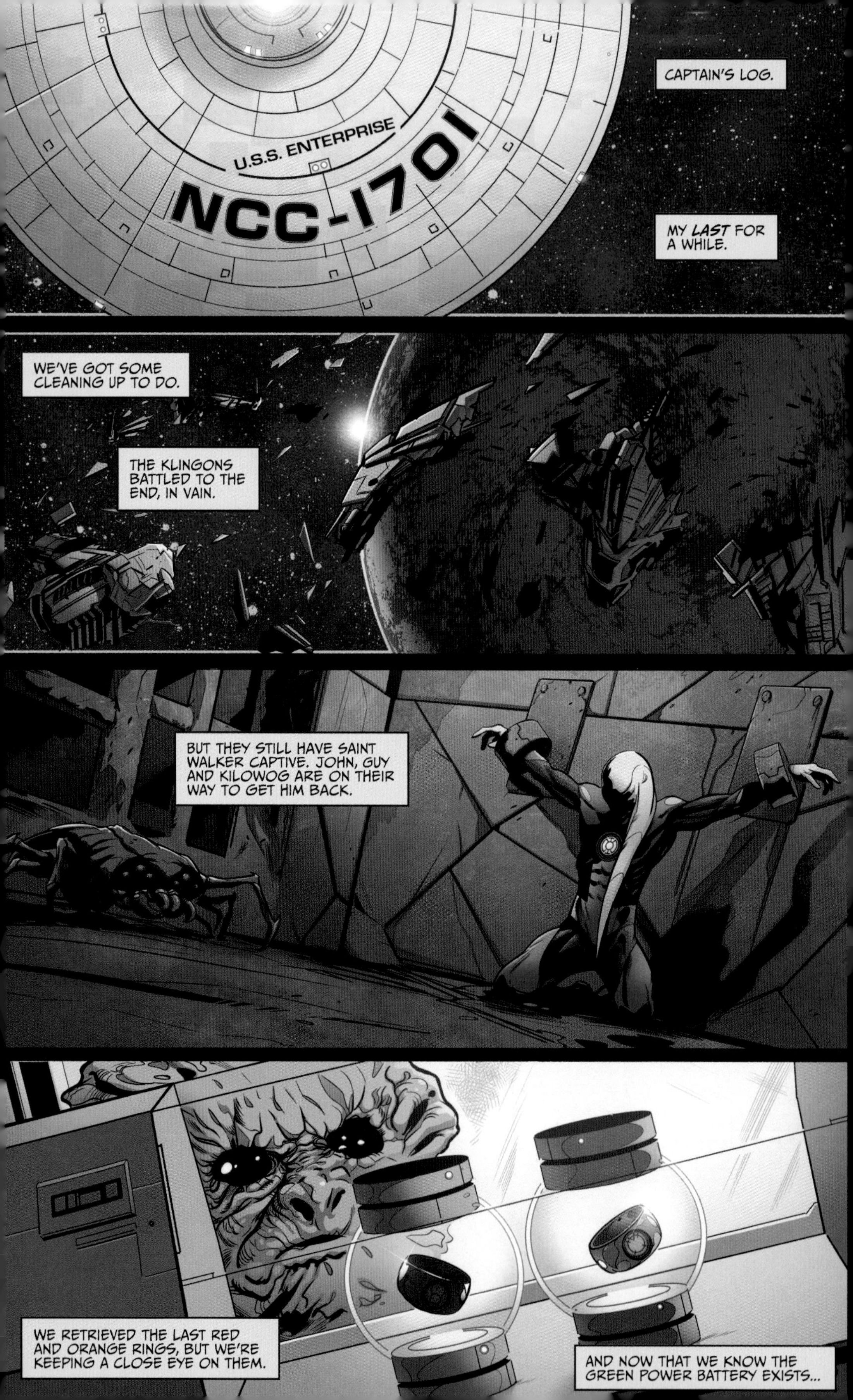
CAPTAIN'S LOG.
U.S.S. ENTERPRISE
NCC-1701
MY *LAST* FOR A WHILE.
WE'VE GOT SOME CLEANING UP TO DO.
THE KLINGONS BATTLED TO THE END, IN VAIN.
BUT THEY STILL HAVE SAINT WALKER CAPTIVE. JOHN, GUY AND KILOWOG ARE ON THEIR WAY TO GET HIM BACK.
WE RETRIEVED THE LAST RED AND ORANGE RINGS, BUT WE'RE KEEPING A CLOSE EYE ON THEM.
AND NOW THAT WE KNOW THE GREEN POWER BATTERY EXISTS...

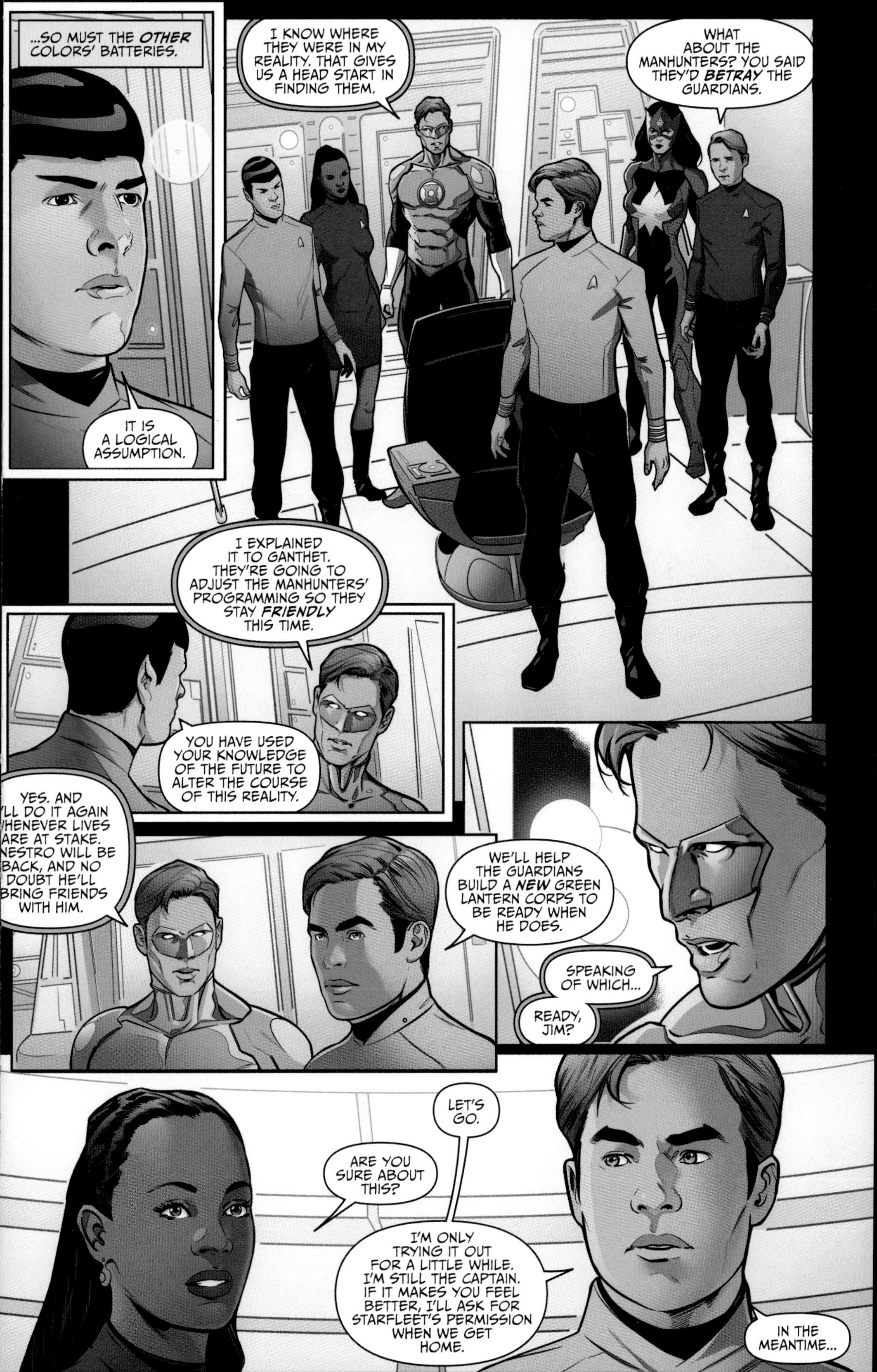
...SO MUST THE OTHER COLORS' BATTERIES.
IT IS A LOGICAL ASSUMPTION.
I KNOW WHERE THEY WERE IN MY REALITY. THAT GIVES US A HEAD START IN FINDING THEM.
WHAT ABOUT THE MANHUNTERS? YOU SAID THEY'D BETRAY THE GUARDIANS.
I EXPLAINED IT TO GANTHET. THEY'RE GOING TO ADJUST THE MANHUNTERS' PROGRAMMING SO THEY STAY FRIENDLY THIS TIME.
YOU HAVE USED YOUR KNOWLEDGE OF THE FUTURE TO ALTER THE COURSE OF THIS REALITY.
YES. AND 'LL DO IT AGAIN HENEVER LIVES ARE AT STAKE. NESTRO WILL BE BACK, AND NO DOUBT HE'LL BRING FRIENDS WITH HIM.
WE'LL HELP THE GUARDIANS BUILD A NEW GREEN LANTERN CORPS TO BE READY WHEN HE DOES.
SPEAKING OF WHICH...
READY, JIM?
LET'S GO.
ARE YOU SURE ABOUT THIS?
I'M ONLY TRYING IT OUT FOR A LITTLE WHILE. I'M STILL THE CAPTAIN. IF IT MAKES YOU FEEL BETTER, I'LL ASK FOR STARFLEET'S PERMISSION WHEN WE GET HOME.
IN THE MEANTIME...

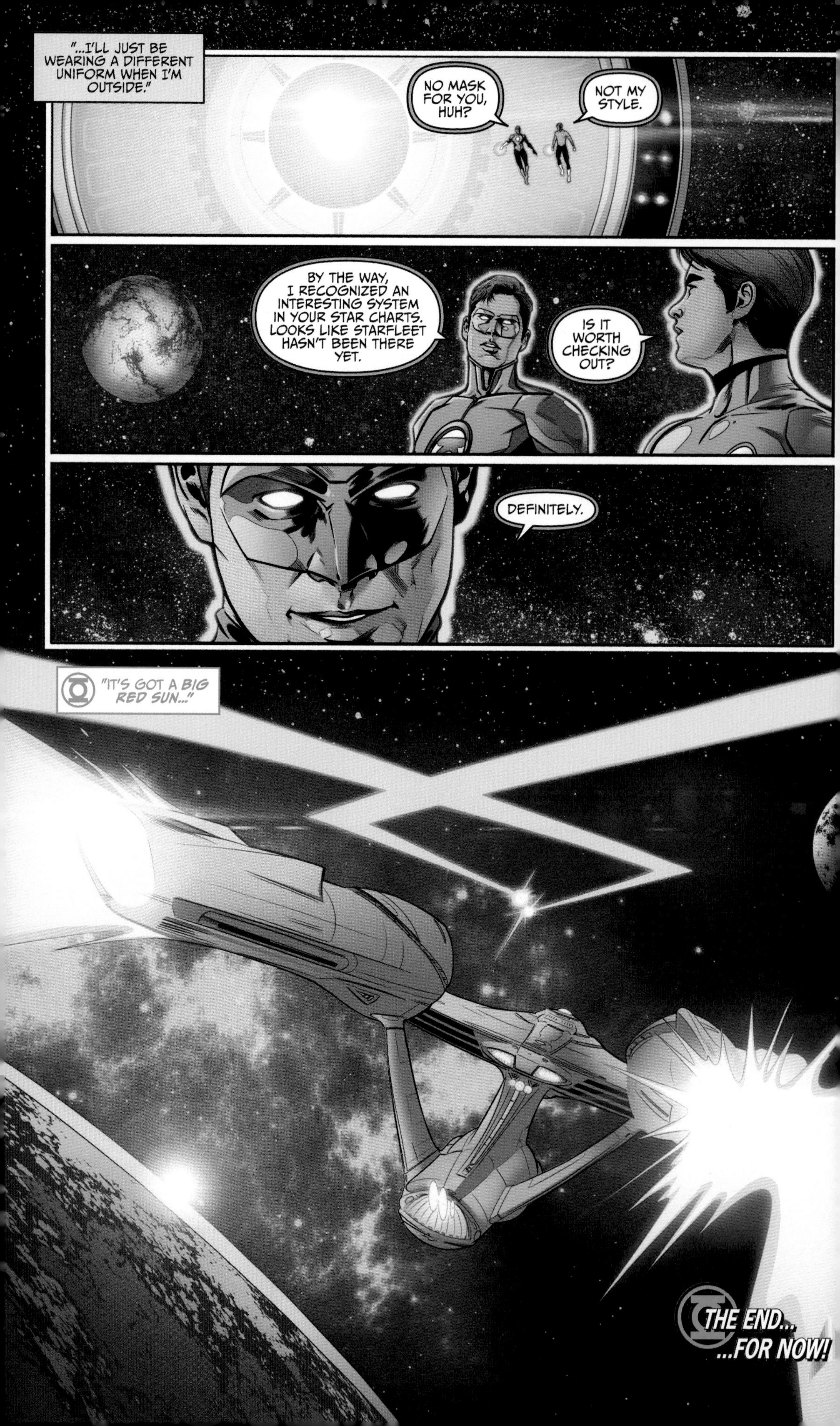
"...I'LL JUST BE WEARING A DIFFERENT UNIFORM WHEN I'M OUTSIDE."
NO MASK FOR YOU, HUH?
NOT MY STYLE.
BY THE WAY, I RECOGNIZED AN INTERESTING SYSTEM IN YOUR STAR CHARTS. LOOKS LIKE STARFLEET HASN'T BEEN THERE YET.
IS IT WORTH CHECKING OUT?
DEFINITELY.
"IT'S GOT A BIG RED SUN..."
THE END...
...FOR NOW!

ART GALLERY

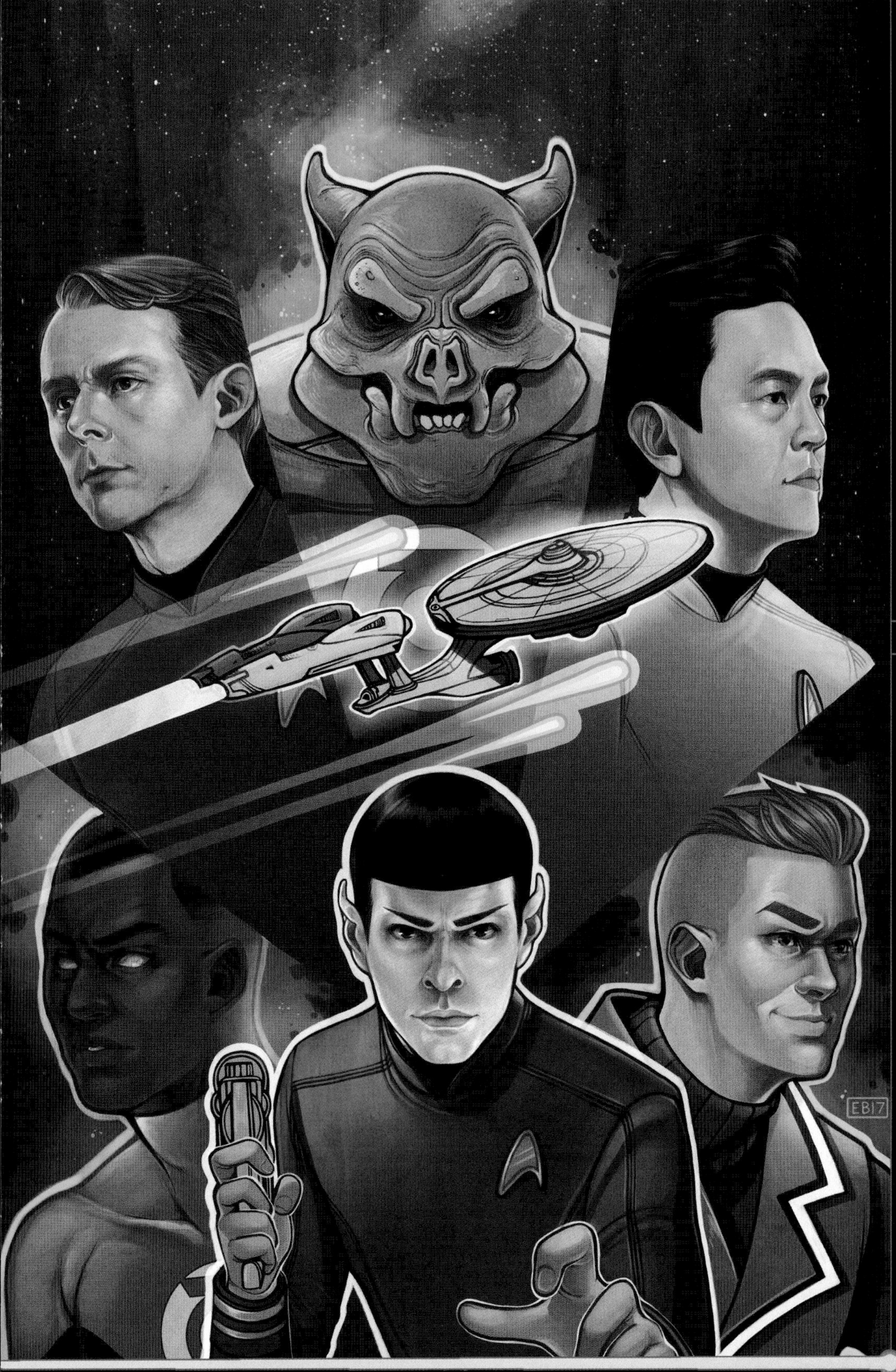
EB17

art by ELIZABETH BEALS

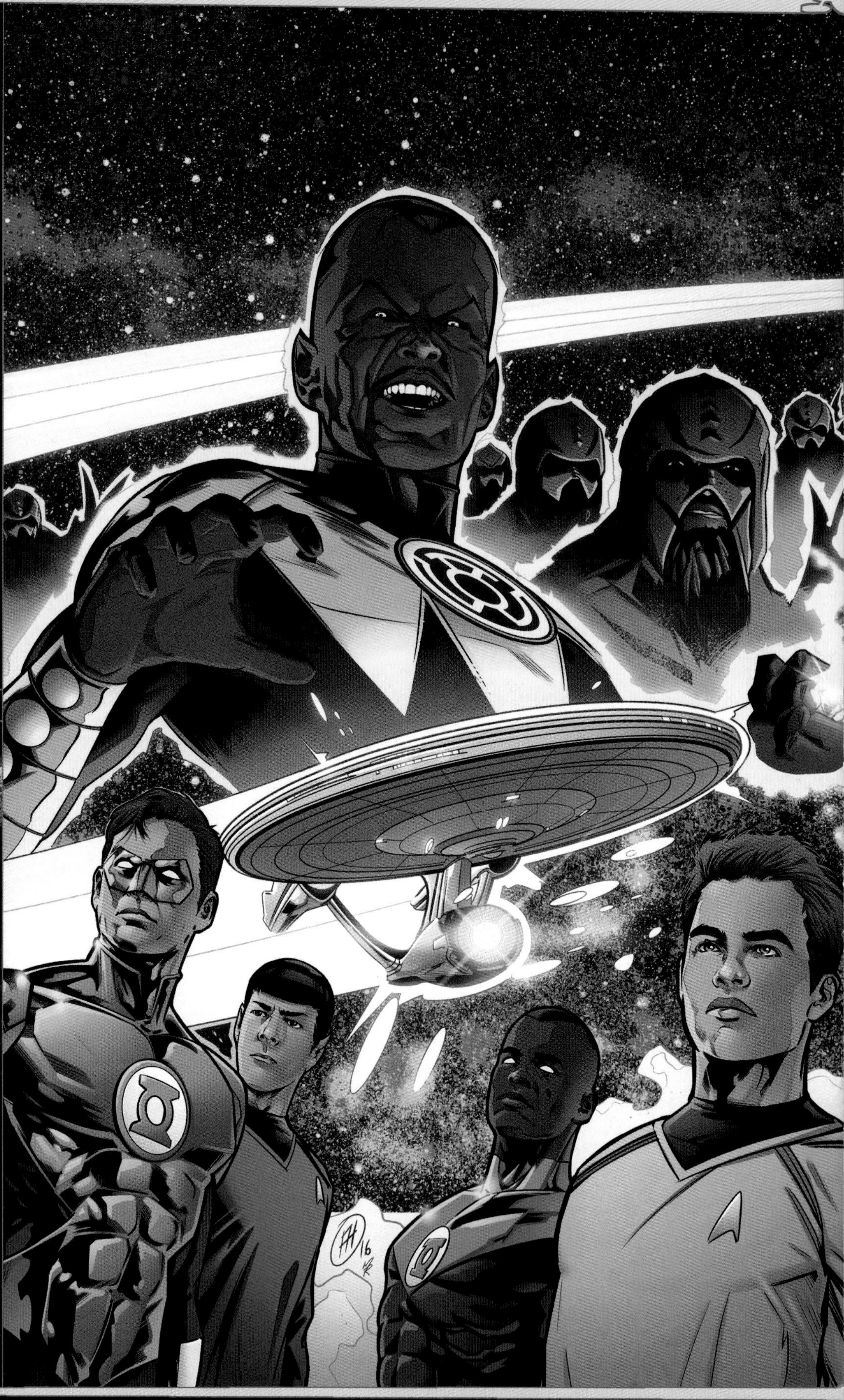

art by ANGEL HERNANDEZ • colors by MARK ROBERTS

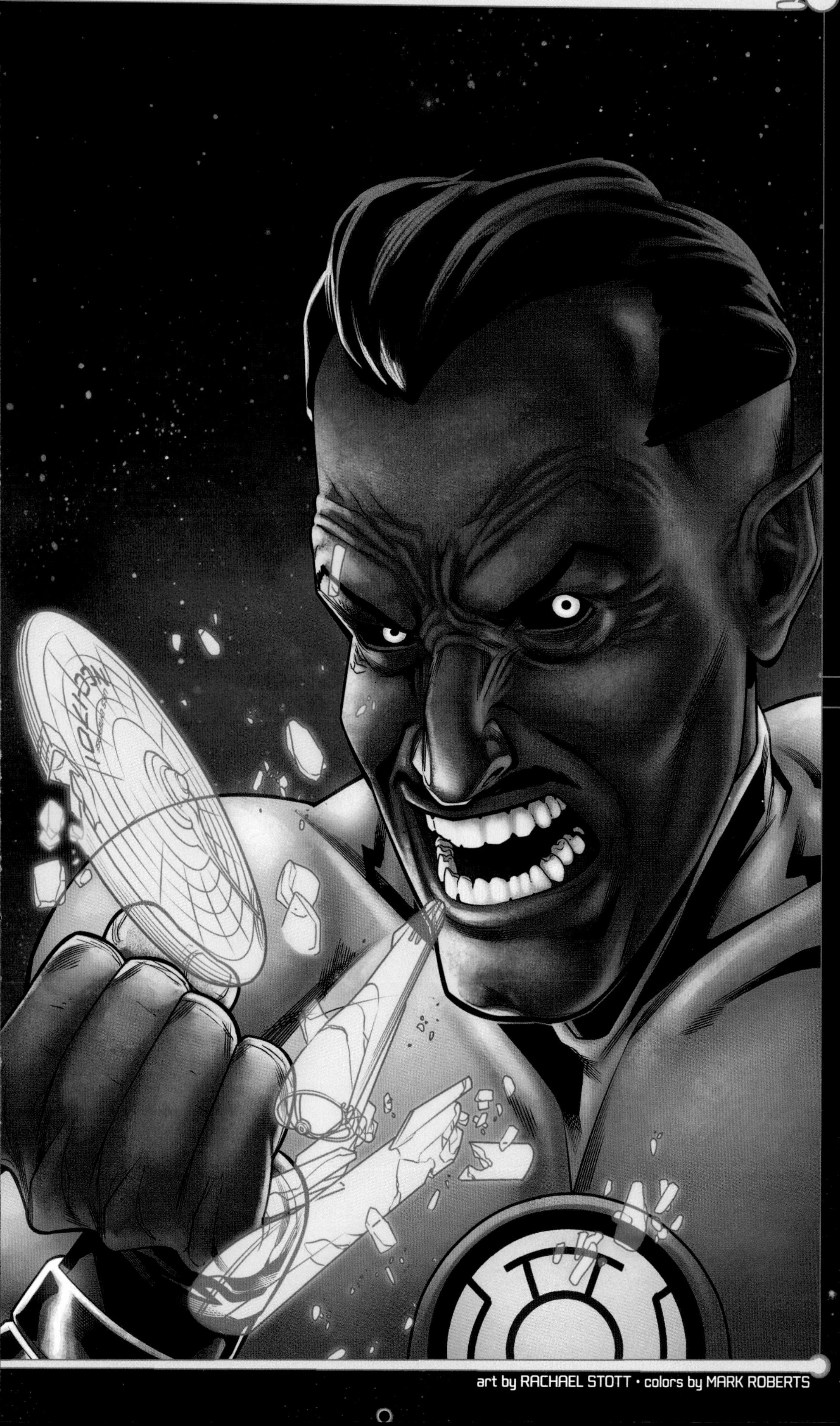

art by RACHAEL STOTT • colors by MARK ROBERTS

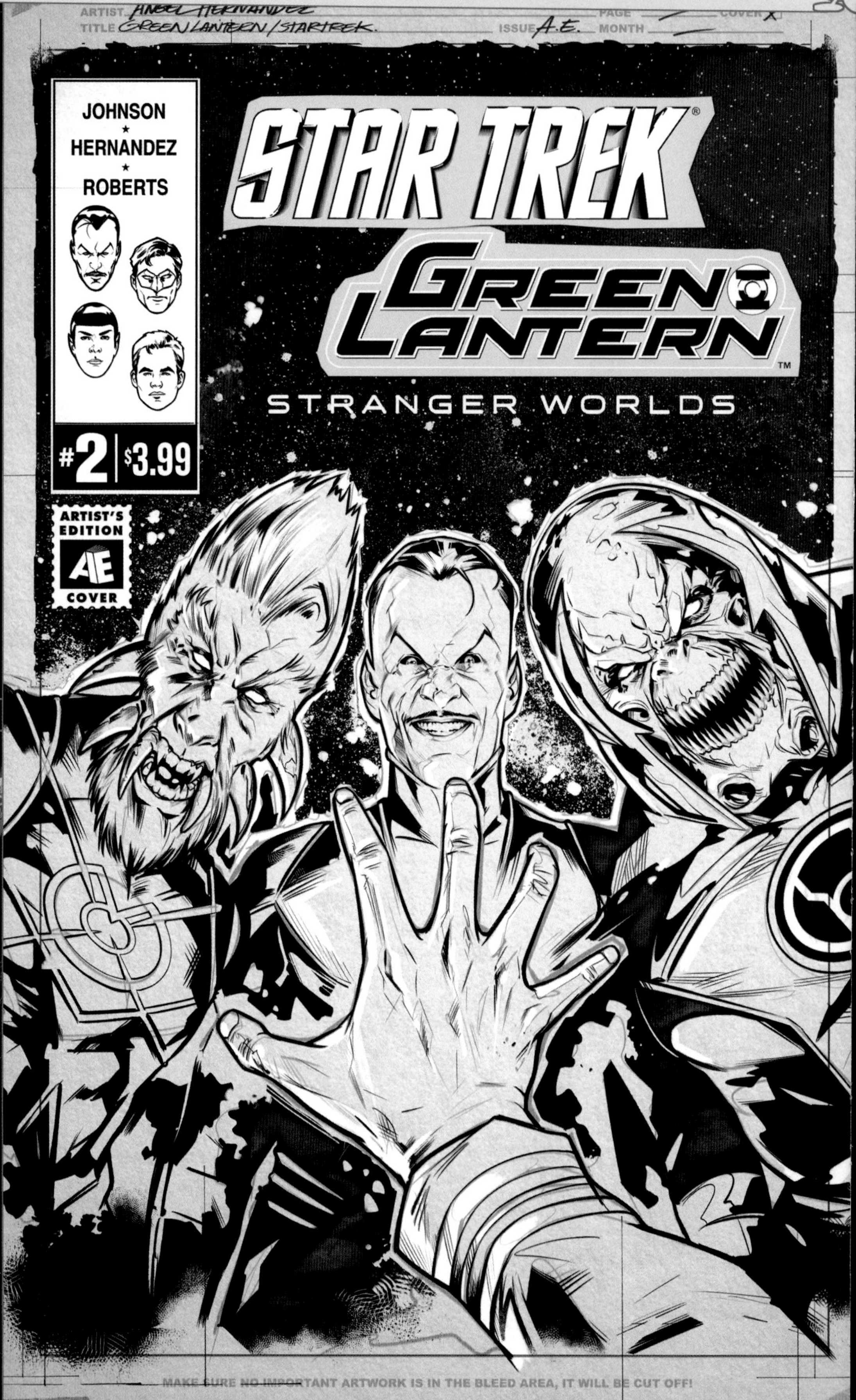

ARTIST ANGEL HERNANDEZ
PAGE
COVER X
TITLE GREEN LANTERN / STARTREK.
ISSUE A.E.
MONTH
JOHNSON
HERNANDEZ
ROBERTS
#2
$3.99
ARTIST'S EDITION
AE
COVER
STAR TREK®
GREEN LANTERN™
STRANGER WORLDS
MAKE SURE NO IMPORTANT ARTWORK IS IN THE BLEED AREA, IT WILL BE CUT OFF!

art by ANGEL HERNANDEZ

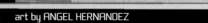

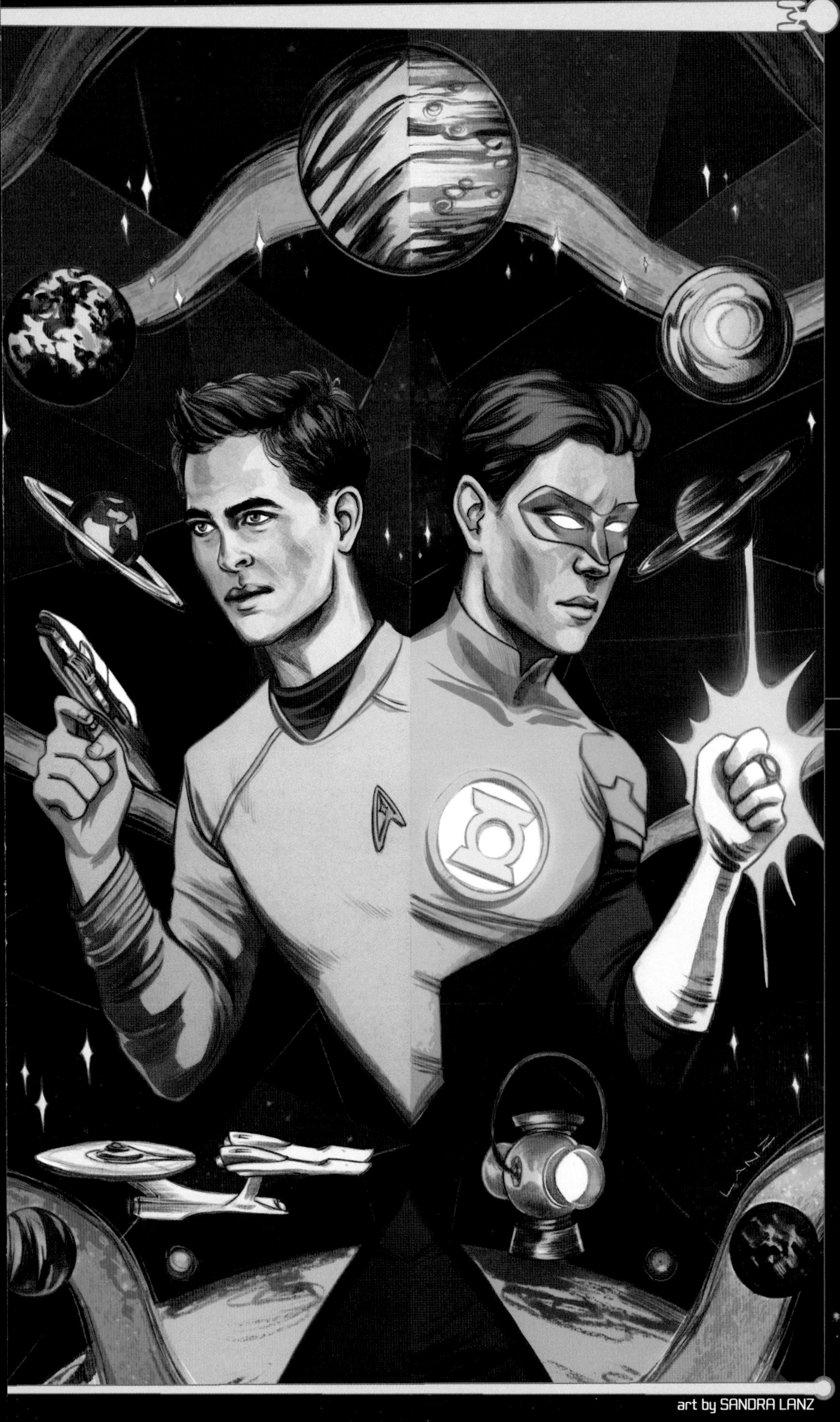
LANZ

art by SANDRA LANZ

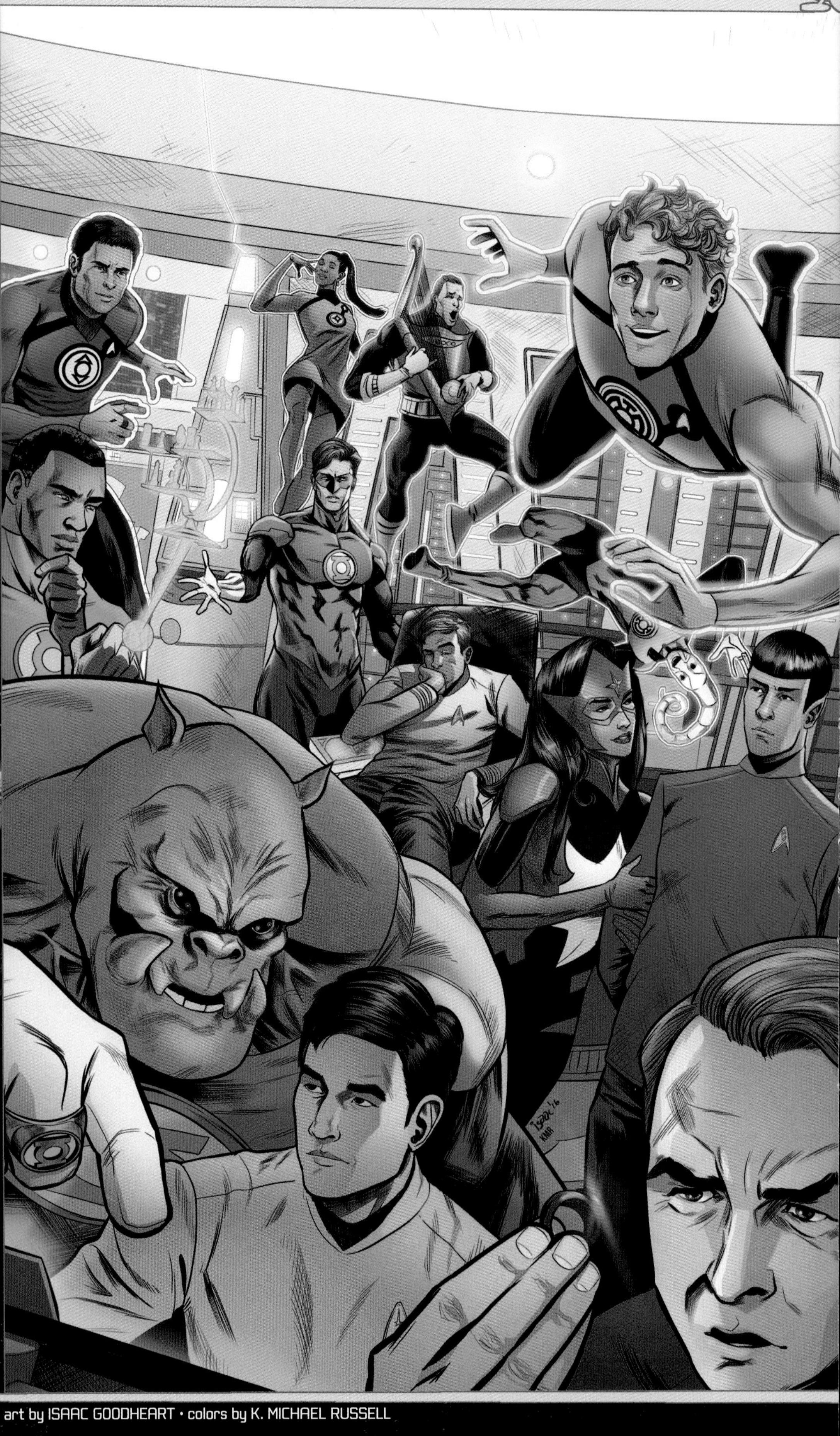

art by ISAAC GOODHEART • colors by K. MICHAEL RUSSELL

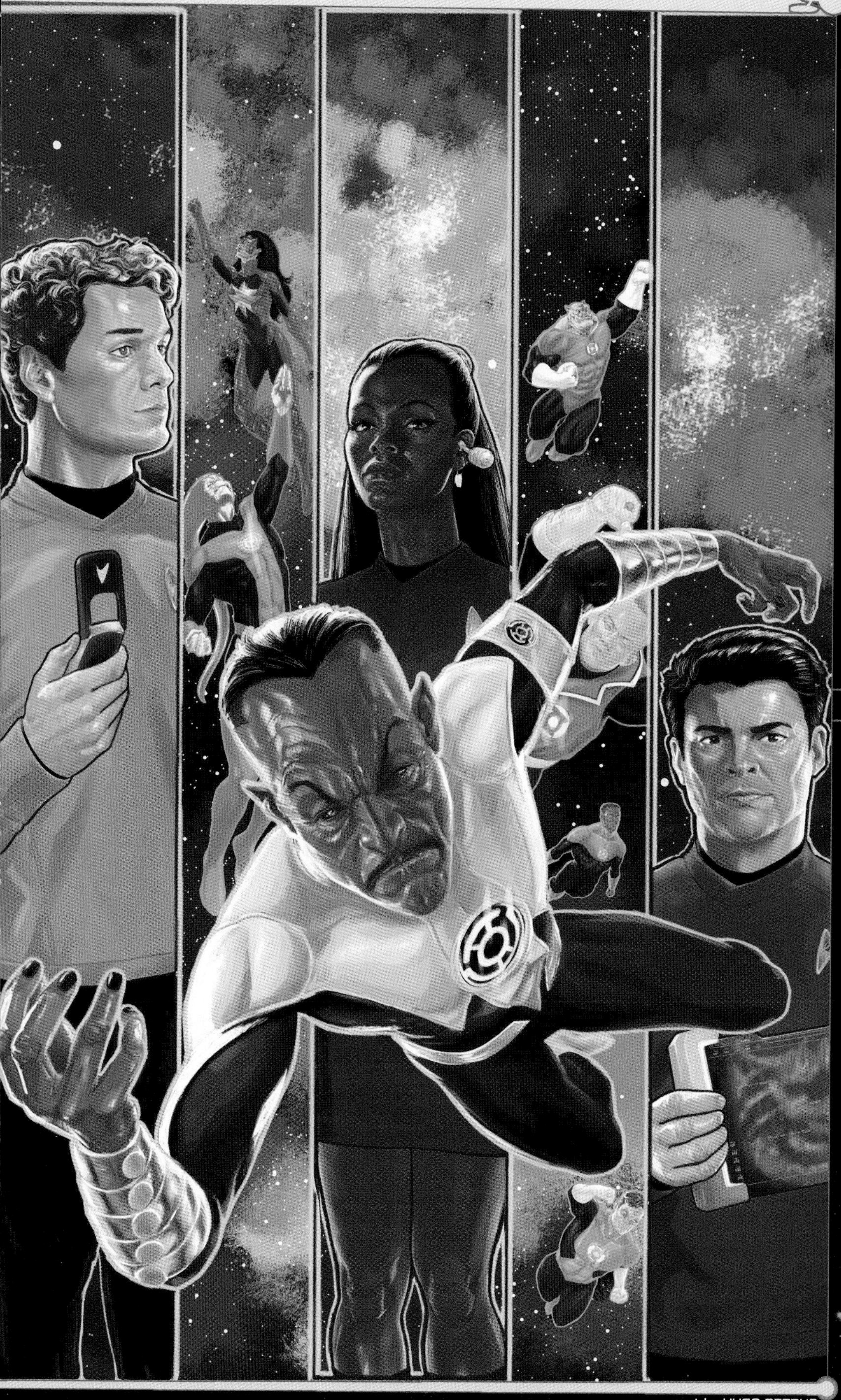

art by HUGO PETRUS

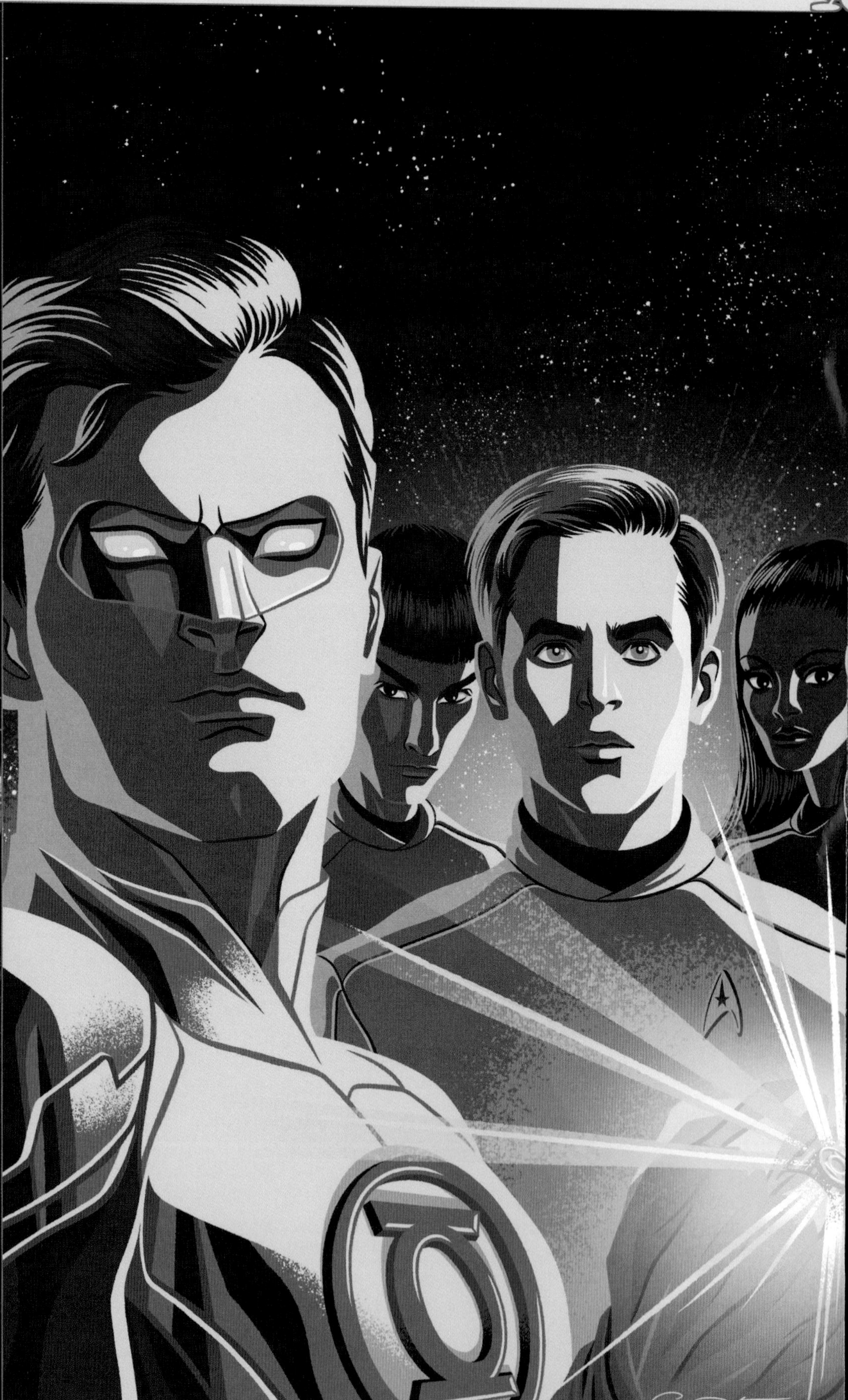

art by GEORGE CALTSOUDAS

Star Trek/Green Lantern, Vol. 1: The Spectrum War
ISBN: 978-1-63140-559-4

Star Trek: Manifest Destiny
ISBN: 978-1-63140-634-8

THE COLLECTED MISSIONS OF THE
STARSHIP ENTERPRISE!

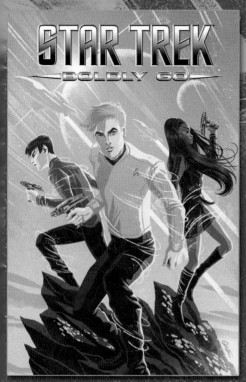

Star Trek: Boldly Go, Vol. 1
ISBN: 978-1-63140-923-3

Star Trek: New Adventures, Vol. 1
ISBN: 978-1-63140-177-0

IDW   www.idwpublishing.com

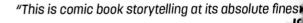

FROM THE WRITER OF
JUSTICE LEAGUE AND *THE FLASH*

GEOFF JOHNS
GREEN LANTERN: REBIRTH

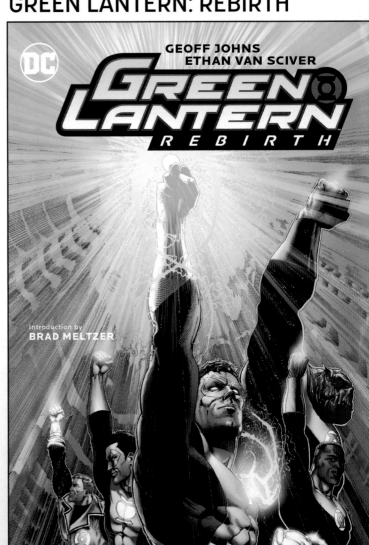

GEOFF JOHNS
ETHAN VAN SCIVER

GREEN LANTERN
REBIRTH

Introduction by
BRAD MELTZER